Hip-Hop Headphones

D1599211

Hip-Hop Headphones

A Scholar's Critical Playlist

James Braxton Peterson

Bloomsbury Academic
An imprint of Bloomsbury Publishing Inc

B L O O M S B U R Y
NEW YORK · LONDON · OXFORD · NEW DELHI · SYDNEY

Bloomsbury Academic
An imprint of Bloomsbury Publishing Inc

1385 Broadway	50 Bedford Square
New York	London
NY 10018	WC1B 3DP
USA	UK

www.bloomsbury.com

BLOOMSBURY and the Diana logo are trademarks of Bloomsbury Publishing Plc

First published 2016
Reprinted 2017 (twice)

© James Braxton Peterson, 2016

Library of Congress Cataloging-in-Publication Data
Names: Peterson, James Braxton, 1971- author.
Title: Hip hop headphones: a scholar's critical playlist / James Braxton
Peterson.
Description: New York: Bloomsbury Academic, 2016. | Includes index.
Identifiers: LCCN 2015043364| ISBN 9781501308253 (hardback: alk. paper) |
ISBN 9781501308246 (pbk.: alk. paper)
Subjects: LCSH: Rap (Music)–History and criticism.
Classification: LCC ML3531 .P48 2016 | DDC 782.421649–dc23
LC record available at http://lccn.loc.gov/2015043364

ISBN: HB: 978-1-5013-0825-3
PB: 978-1-5013-0824-6
ePUB: 978-1-5013-0827-7
ePDF: 978-1-5013-0826-0

Cover design: Louise Dugdale
Cover image and photography: Vincent Skyers and James Braxton Peterson

Typeset by Deanta Global Publishing Services, Chennai, India
Printed and bound in the United States of America

For Doreen V. Peterson, who always listened with love.

Contents

Part 5   Rapademics

Appendices

Acknowledgments

As always, there are too many folks to thank and acknowledge, given the time and space constraints of book publishing, but I will try once more. *Hip-Hop Headphones* was a crazy idea that coalesced over time and many many many conversations with students, friends, scholars, colleagues, artists, and family. Thank you all for always being so willing to engage me in the music and culture that we love—love to listen to and love to talk about.

So many of these critical conversations have taken place in the classroom with incredible students from across a variety of campuses and institutions. Again, too many to list here, but special thanks to Mahdi Woodard, Andrew Yaspan, Miles Davis, Rawle Sterling, Windsor Jordan, and my homie Wilfredo Gomez.

At this point, my friends are probably sick of me talking about Hip Hop, but I still cherish their time and their ears. Special thanks to Nick James, Malik Ford, Ogbonna Hagins, Sofiya Ballin, Michael Gaymon, Sheena Lester, Ted Chung, Aaron Jones, Adam Mansbach, and so many others.

There are many scholars who engage Hip-Hop culture, and many of them have been powerful influences on me and my work—especially Imani Perry, Mark Anthony Neal, Jelani Cobb, Joe Schloss, Jeff Chang, H. Samy Alim, Joan Morgan, Scott Heath, Marcyliena Morgan, Treva Lindsey, John Jennings, Regina Bradley, Marc Hill, and Michael Eric Dyson. "MAN" and "MED" are the two best mentors a brother could "ever" have. I love you both.

I have to acknowledge all of my colleagues who have been so patient with me and supportive of me through the processes of leading the Africana Studies program at Lehigh University and trying to maintain some semblance of a scholarly profile. Thank you, Kwame Essien, Monica R. Miller, Susan Kart, Darius O. Williams, Imaani El-Burki, Kashi Johnson, Lyndon Dominique, all of Africana Studies, and the entire English Department.

A special acknowledgement goes to all of the editors and readers involved with this project. Every single mishap, misstep, and mistake is all mine; but without these folks, this book could not exist in its current form. Thank you to "all" of the editorial staff at Bloomsbury, Bethany Grandy for the incredible manuscript preparation, Paul Farber, Emery Petchauer, Chiara Minestrelli, Justin McCarthy, Mark Anthony Neal (again), and so many others for edits, suggestions, and direction.

Many of you will have heard about or already listened to *Headphones: A Hip Hop Scholars Notebook,* the audio project produced by the amazing Taylor "Taylormade" Rivelli. The cover art for that project and the cover for this book were designed by Vincent Skyers. Thank you so much for your incredible work on all aspects of these projects.

Huge shout-outs to all of the artists who have spent their precious time with me over the years, including Snoop, 9th Wonder, Nas, Lupe Fiasco, Black Thought, Macklemore and Ryan Lewis, and (again) so many others. Thank you! Z's way up for the Black Jedi Chapter of the Universal Zulu Nation and please stay tuned for the guild-building work of The Society Of Spoken Art (SOSA).

Much love to all of my family, Erik Smith Chris Norwood, my proud and loving parents; my incredible siblings: Iva, Iver, Scott, Robert, Eunice, Elnora, and Barbara; my amazing nieces: Barbara, Gabrielle, and Kristian; my gigantic nephews: Davon, Robert, Aaron and Alex, and my extraordinary children: James and Breanna. I love you all. And to the love of my life, Belinda Peterson, here goes another one. Your love support, dedication, and attentive listening all mean the world to me. I love You.

Introduction: Critical Listening in Critical Times

Hip-Hop Headphones is a chaotic collection of definitions, essays, reviews, articles, round tables, and public talks mostly related to Hip-Hop culture, especially Hip-Hop music. The thematic core of these collected works summons the spirit of familial and communal listening that has been endemic to our experience with Hip-Hop culture. During Hip-Hop's early days, we circulated mixtapes—actual cassette tapes with mixes of music from recordings that we made from urban radio that only rarely played Hip Hop. When Kurtis Blow's "The Breaks" was becoming popular in 1980, New York "urban/black" radio played the song once a day. My brothers, sisters, and I would gather around the radio—when radios were large boxes with antennae and had cassette decks in them—at the same time every day. We would dance and rap the words to Blow's hit because these family rituals were our "breaks." Critical listening then was done mostly for the purpose of being able to recite popular rhymes from memory and to verbally ride all over break beats in our favorite Hip-Hop songs. But the process of memorizing rap lyrics by rote and the practice of reciting them over and over was one crucible through which we came to love the lyrics of Hip-Hop culture.

That love affair endures, but paying studious attention to the lyrics of Hip-Hop culture has taken on greater significance for me as a scholar of Africana studies and as a thinking/conscious person living in the critical conundrum that has become the twenty-first century. Kurtis Blow's "breaks" were about break beats, but it was also about brakes on vehicles, and the good and bad "breaks" that we get in life. Finding/discovering the multilayered meaning in words has always been a fascinating feature of sociolinguistic inquiry. In the land of the free and the home of the brave, the ability to discern the nuances of language has continued to be a critical skill in complicated—often Orwellian—times. Hip Hop's ongoing capacity to produce environments wherein we might engage in what Jay-Z refers to as "Lyrical Exercise" provides vital space for learning how to figure out (and figure in) the world in which we live. Hip-Hop generational folks have had to rip the sinister meanings from too many platitudes to list here but consider the real meanings behind and beneath the following political phrases: Mission Accomplished, The War on Drugs, The War on Terror, Stand Your Ground, No Child Left Behind, Race to the Top, Take Back Our Country, or my personal favorite—Citizens United.

Great lyrics of Hip-Hop culture produce opportunities for critical reflection in these complicated times. In "Daydreamin," maybe one of the best single Hip-Hop records of all time, Lupe Fiasco raps that he cannot sleep because he has the "hood" on him like "Abu Ghraib." Before I decode this complex simile, please note that this book is almost as much about the generation of critical lists as it is about the practice of critical listening. My assertion that "Daydreamin'" is one of the greatest Hip-Hop songs of all time is completely subjective—based only on my twenty-plus years of studying rap music and Hip-Hop culture, my upbringing in Newark, New Jersey, in the 1970s and 1980s in the shadows of the city where Hip Hop was born, and my research in the culture—interviews with artists; dialogues with journalists and scholars; reading, writing, and teaching about Hip Hop since about 1995; and so on and so on. Since before I became an "official" scholar of the culture, the discourses on who is the greatest and who/what you are listening to at any given point in Hip-Hop time have been the building blocks of critical listening and critical community—the substance of Hip-Hop culture itself—powerfully generated through what H. Samy Alim has defined as Hip-Hop Nation Language—the very way that we speak.

Back to Lupe's inability to sleep because he has the "hood" on him "like Abu Ghraib." Nas has a famous line from his 1994 debut, *Illmatic*'s "N. Y. State of Mind." In that lyric, he refuses to sleep because sleep is the "cousin of death." Both Nas and Lupe's notions of sleep figure on its perceived proximity to permanent dirt naps, but they are both also ruminating on notions of sleep being akin to an absence of consciousness—an inability to be aware of the critical goings-on in one's own surroundings and in the broader world in which we all live. Sleep in this sense has nothing to do with rest or restoration, dreams or nightmares, and has everything to do with consciousness and the awareness required to critically engage the world. This same lyrical phrase from Lupe features a morphemic figuration on the term "neighborhood" that has become common in Hip-Hop parlance. The 'hood is a contemporary catchall reference to the blocks, ghettos, and neighborhoods within which late-capitalist neoliberal outcomes are most pronounced in America. John Singleton's classic film *Boys N the Hood* lays bare some of the environmental pitfalls of modern urban life. But the 'hood here engenders both its locational meaning and its literal meaning—referring to the kind of hood (or hoodie) that Trayvon Martin wore on the evening of his tragic demise, as well as to those black hoods that were placed over the heads of those who were tortured in the nefarious Abu Ghraib prison. The lyric then intimates both a human and religious connection that Lupe establishes between his narrator and those who were subjected to torture, degradation, and humiliation at the hands of the United States in the Abu Ghraib prison in Iraq. Lupe is, after all, a practitioner of Islam, but the lyric challenges the denizens of America's 'hoods to make canny connections between the roles that law enforcement and military play in their lives as well as in those who are deemed to be foreign enemies of the state. A deeper interpretation of the lyric might work as a critique of both the US Army's practices of torture and dehumanization in the Abu Ghraib prison and the comparable practices carried out by the Saddam Hussein government on its own citizens prior to Iraq's second war with the United States (and its allies). A shorter, more compact iteration of the themes of this important Lupe lyric might be found in the popular Hip-Hop directive: *don't sleep.*

In order to follow the hashtag command to "stay woke" on issues of criminal justice, militarization, and incarceration, we need only reflect on the lyrical career of the inimitable Lauryn Hill. A recording on the Lauryn Hill *Unplugged* album, "The Mystery of Iniquity," is an incisive categorical dissection of our decrepit criminal justice system rendered in the modern era. Hill exclaims that it (i.e., the criminal justice system) will "all fall down," but not before her lyrical detailing of the atrocities have become one more compelling contribution to her artistic legacy. She indicts the system for its unchecked and racially imbalanced aggressiveness. At various points, she incriminates the judges, the prosecutors, the bailiffs, and the court reporters who are all too often more invested in headlines than in justice. Defense lawyers, expert witnesses, and jurors are not spared here either. Through Lauryn Hill's lyrics, the absurd depths of injustice in our criminal justice system are poetically exposed. The song stands (even now) as a diatribe that dismantles the myths of justice in our systems and deconstructs the "mystery" of the "iniquity" that plagues these systems. The album *Unplugged* was released in 2002, which is a decade prior to the publication of Michelle Alexander's *The New Jim Crow* and thirteen years before President Obama's widely praised "mass incarceration" speech delivered in the summer of 2015. Yeah, stay woke.

Lauryn Hill's lyrical body of work is relatively short in quantity, but it is qualitatively rich, speaking volumes of critical substance for potentially engaged listeners. In "Zealot," an overlooked track in 1996's immensely popular Fugees album, *The Score*, Hill quips the following: "Two MCs can't occupy the same space at the same time." In one verse, she explicates the physics of the Hip-Hop universe: that MCs cannot be exact copies of each other in the exact same time and space—at least not without attracting serious critique and ultimate erasure from/by the Hip-Hop community. Hill's lyric here alludes to the Pauli exclusion principle, named after Wolfgang Pauli, a scientist who configured the basis of the principle in quantum mechanics that governs how certain particles interact. The science is way beyond the orbit of my expertise, but the principle speaks to the physical behavior of everyday matter and as such is an apt metaphor/analogy for certain principles within Hip-Hop culture. That is, how MCs lyrically relate to each other, whether by overlapping cross-influenced styles or through intertextual themes and discourses, is an everyday matter for the critical listeners within the Hip-Hop nation. Although repetition, sampling, remixing, and appropriation are fundamental principles of Hip-Hop culture, biting or stealing without giving proper credit and the blatant absence of original style in MC-ing/rapping (in particular) are not only frowned upon but also ultimately impossible within the public spheres of Hip-Hop culture. Consider here the fact that the entire No Limit Records (second phase in the late 1990s) required that Tupac not be around (or alive) for constituents of Hip Hop to not reject the ways in which Master P, Sillk, and C-Murder borrowed aspects of Tupac's style and persona in order to launch their careers. Around the same time, Lil Kim and Foxy Brown lyrically fought to be the queen bee of Hip Hop; Lil Kim won. And after the murder of Biggie Smalls, a bevy of artists, including Sean "Puffy" Combs, DMX, and Jay-Z stepped into the gaping hole in Hip Hop left by his passing. Hip-Hop artists can be influenced by other artists; they can quote each other—and they do—but they cannot artistically occupy the same space at the same time. The culture rejects it and the aficionados of the culture protect the spaces in ways that prevent it. But Lauryn Hill said it, and in one lyrical speech act, she challenges listeners to critically engage the meanings of her assertion about the physics of/for MCs in Hip-Hop culture. By the way, there is only one Lauryn Hill, and despite numerous attempts by commentators to claim that some new(er) artist can stake a claim to her indelible imprint in Hip Hop, it will never happen and she spoke this theoretical fact into existence twenty years ago.

Some of what I am saying here can now be found in Hip-Hop discourses across various online platforms. The Original Hip-Hop Lyrics Archive (www. ohhla.com) was the platform of choice for those interested in seeing rap lyrics on the digital page, but Rap Genius, now just Genius (genius.com) pushed the transcription of rap lyrics idea to the next level—offering verified and (artist) verifiable transcripts of lyrics with annotations. The very existence of these web-based platforms signals an important (and paradigmatic) shift in the discourses on and about Hip-Hop culture. So many of the selections in *Hip-Hop Headphones* take an oversimplified historical framing of the culture into account in order to make certain claims about the critical listening that is endemic to the culture. The eras of Hip Hop help to shed some light on the various and interesting ways that the critical listening community engages in discourses about the music of the culture. For example, the oft-cited golden era of Hip Hop (from about the mid-1980s through the mid- to late-1990s) featured a shift in how we consume the music. The shift, a decidedly visual one that was characterized by the onset of music videos and music television, was a key development in Hip-Hop culture's ascension (or expansion) into American mainstream popular culture. If the visualization of Hip-Hop narratives in some ways obscured the central aspects of Hip Hop's lyrical wizardry, that obscuration was temporary. Made so by the simple fact that for critical listeners of Hip-Hop lyrics, words, rhymes, poetic technique, and linguistic mastery continue to matter even in our multimedia digital-based world. And this is why developments in the branding and innovation in the technologies that are used for listening to the music have taken on such seminal significance in Hip-Hop culture.

The cover art for *Hip-Hop Headphones* features a digitally and artistically enhanced image of my son, James Braxton Peterson, III, listening to Hip-Hop music (on an airplane), through a popular brand of headphones. One compelling feature in the historical developments of Hip-Hop culture is the fact that Hip Hop unfolds contemporaneously with a range of technological developments in how we produce and listen to music. For old-school-era Hip-Hop folks, the transitions from the boombox moment—a time when young Hip-Hop heads would carry portable (and I use this term lightly) radios around our neighborhoods with the latest rap tunes blasting from the radio's speakers—to the Sony Walkman and Discman moments of personalized listening, to the heyday of super-decibel car stereo systems (particularly on the West Coast), together reflect a whirlwind of distinct critical listening opportunities and situations. For all of that progress and distinction in the practices of how we listen to Hip Hop, few could have anticipated the birth of the iPod or of Hip-Hop branded "high-end" headphones.

The advent of the iPod (in 2001) signaled a rebirth of personalized critical listening opportunities. Now music aficionados could carry their entire music collections on a device that fits in a pants' pocket. iTunes software (released on Macintosh computers in 2000) allowed critical listeners to create (and now share) endless amounts and configurations of playlists. With this tremendous advancement in making entire music collections portable—in the true sense of the word sans the weight of the big boom boxes—it could not be long before the market place configured ways to further commoditize the listening experience. Headphones have always been part of Hip-Hop culture. DJs used headphones in innovative ways at the very onset of the culture. In the twenty-first century, we are now treated to a bevy of branded headphones that offer studio-quality listening capacity through headphones dripping with Hip-Hop cultural styles and the brand signatures of some of Hip Hop's most popular artists. I consider it a fortunate privilege to have been alive during the full range of these commercial and technological developments in how we listen to the music that I have loved and enjoyed for most of my life. But a critical question that *Hip-Hop Headphones* seeks to answer is what to do with these resources for listening to the vast repertoire of lyrical ingenuity that Hip-Hop music represents. One answer is to use all of the tools at our disposal to continue to listen to the music critically.

Soft drink giant, Sprite, has proven the fact that Hip-Hop lyrics are commodities across the eras and developments of the culture. In 2015, the company launched its "Obey Your Verse" ad campaign, signifying on the brand's popular "Obey Your Thirst" ads originally made popular by a 1995 commercial featuring the freestyle lyrics of Pete Rock, C. L. Smooth, and Grand Puba. Twenty years later, the "Obey Your Verse" ad campaign features a series of sixteen Sprite cans emblazoned with a set of classic verses from Nas: "The World is Yours"; Rakim: "Thinking of a Master Plan"; Biggie Smalls/ Notorius B.I.G.: "Lyrically I'm supposed to represent"; and Drake: "Know yourself/Know your worth." Any commercial intervention into the well-argued discourses on the greatest lyrics of Hip-Hop culture will undoubtedly invite ongoing debates about who is the greatest and what are the greatest lyrics of all time. Most will accept the assertion of Nas, Biggie, and Rakim as being a part of these ongoing debates. Drake's inclusion, however, poses certain challenges to these discussions, especially for old-school-era Hip-Hop heads. It is not just that he is too new or too popular to be considered among the greatest lyricists of all time, but that he comes into the culture from a different station in life and from a region (Toronto) that is not New York—that is, not from the birthplace of Hip-Hop culture.[1] Setting these authenticity and regional origin concerns aside, the lyrics of Rakim, Nas, and Biggie are established in their legendary status. Rakim's "Thinking of a master plan" from 1986's "Paid in Full" is a lyrical entrée into the mind of an MC who has often been referred to as "the God." "Paid in Full" is a deceptively simple narrative about the common plight of the poor and working-class constituents of Hip-Hop culture—having no money and thinking of all the ways to get some. Rakim's narrator in "Paid in Full" ultimately decides to forego any criminal means of acquiring capital and instead opts to focus on his music and artistry to get paid in full. Nas' lyric is actually the title of one of his most well-known tracks. In Peterson (2009), I contributed to a collection of writings about Nas' 1994 debut album, *Illmatic*, edited by Sohail Dulatzhai and Michael Eric Dyson. In it, I focus in on the lyrics and samples of "The World Is Yours" and argue that

Nas' interpretation of the phrase—derived from classic imagery from the 1983 version of *Scarface*, starring Al Pacino—relies heavily on racial romanticism and certain aspirational narratives related to underground economies that appeal to Hip-Hop artists across the eras of the culture. "The World Is Yours" takes into account the imperative to get "Paid in Full" and pushes past the idea that Hip-Hop artistry is in and of itself the only means by which Hip-Hop constituents might claim this world as their own. These lines are and have been classic staples in the lyrical tapestry of Hip-Hop culture. Adding Biggie's "lyrically I'm supposed to represent" to this mix makes sense because debates about Biggie's greatness in comparison to Nas and Rakim (and to others, including Jay-Z and Tupac) in many ways resolve on who represents the culture the best through his/her lyrics. This classic quip from Biggie speaks poetic volumes to the value of Hip-Hop music and culture in the lives of these artists and in the lives of millions of their fans. Biggie asserts that there is an inherent imperative to lyrically represent himself, his neighborhood, his city, his Hip-Hop nation. That impulse to represent is one of the driving value systems within the culture itself.

All of the featured lyrics in the "Obey Your Verse" ad campaign wrestle with material and other value systems within the culture. Material and monetary gain, whether through the artistry or through underground economies, factors into the imperatives to represent where we are from and the socioeconomic circumstances within which much of Hip-Hop culture was produced. It is in this way that Drake's "Know yourself/Know your worth" begins to make some critical sense in the ad campaign. Again, to the extent that constituents of the culture can set aside the aforementioned resistance to including Drake among this established pantheon of lyrical masters—Rakim, Nas, and Biggie—we might consider an interpretation of Drake's words within the Hip-Hop value system frame. "Know yourself/Know your worth" can function on the level of the individual—that is, in order to claim the world, get paid in full, and represent where you are from, you have to first know yourself and thereby know your value. But Drake has been known to speak on behalf of (i.e., represent) Hip Hop more broadly—listening to Drake's popular 2013 single "Started from the Bottom" and its many remakes and remixes proves this point. If the lyric "Know yourself/Know your worth" can be applied to the culture itself—and in fact it should be applied to the lyrics of the culture, given the commercial contexts of the "Obey Your Verse" ad campaign—then the lyric points to how and why we can and should value the lyrics of Hip-Hop culture.

Sprite and many other consumer product corporations have monetized the lyrics of Hip Hop in order to sell any and everything. One assumption in *Hip-Hop Headphones* is that these same lyrics have discursive and *educational* value for the listening communities associated with the culture. Critical listening is one practice through which we have (and will continue) to harvest the educational value in the lyrics of Hip-Hop culture. In this sense, knowing what the culture is, how it has developed, and how it has been historically framed are all important parts of the process of fully understanding the culture's educational "worth," so to speak. My hope is that *Hip-Hop Headphones* will become a staple resource for all educators who are interested in and committed to teaching the history, artistry, and culture of Hip Hop at all levels of education. If we can come to embrace critical listening as a practice akin to critical thinking, to be used as a tool to develop critical media literacy, then the educational value of Hip-Hop culture might be fully realized.

Chapter 1, "RE: Definitions," culls together a set of definitions of Hip-Hop culture that were designed/conceived from various vantage points and/or frames. In order to develop a framework for the cultural and historical contexts from which critical listening emerges, this chapter defines Hip Hop through various frames. Some of these frames or vantage points include the categorical or elemental frames for defining Hip Hop—Graf art, Breaking, DJ-ing, and Rapping. Other approaches settle in on the historical eras of Hip Hop—the old school, golden, and platinum eras or ages formulate one of the critical bedrocks upon which Hip-Hop discourses continue to be cultivated by critical listening communities. Still other approaches feature analyses through race or racial lenses and/or sub genres of the music. This multifaceted approach to defining Hip-Hop culture sets in motion the machinery of discursive practices that substantiate the communities of Hip Hop and help to harness the educational potential that might be derived from a critical interface with Hip-Hop music.

Chapter 2, "Becoming and Being a Hip Hop Scholar," takes a slight autobiographical turn in order to chart my academic development, in part, to reveal the unfolding of certain lived experiences in Newark, New

Jersey, at the onset of Hip Hop's old school era. This chapter focuses less on defining what a Hip-Hop scholar is and tends more toward operationalizing the pedagogical approaches to teaching (as well as writing and research) that underwrite the value of critical listening as a scholar and would-be aficionado of the culture. Being a scholar of Hip Hop challenges academics to engage in discourses emanating from within popular culture on topics and subject matter that might not always produce neat or comfortable course outcomes and safe class discussions. But learning how to listen to students in the twenty-first century might be the most significant aspect of the critical listening directives of and within this work. Chapters 1 and 2 constitute the "Definitions" section of the book, a longer form of introduction of sorts where I attempt to define the culture and an academic subjectivity that emerges out of that culture.

Chapters 3 ("Ashy to Classy"), 4 ("Best Never Heard") make up Part 2 of *Hip-Hop Headphones*. Each of these short essays attempts to re-present concepts and insights from public academic talks given at Georgetown University, University of Pennsylvania, and Northeastern University and at various points over the course of my academic development. "Ashy to Classy" signifies on a well-known line/lyric from Biggie Smalls/Notorius B.I.G. and contemplates the lyrical "phrases of poverty" that have populated Hip-Hop discourses over the last several decades of the culture's existence and development. Defining Hip Hop in or through certain socioeconomic contexts requires critical listening, an educational intervention into class-related themes in the lyrics of Hip-Hop music. "Best Never Heard" briefly highlights the pedagogical potential of playlists in the classroom and beyond the walls of educational institutions. Through the discourses available in Hip-Hop culture, the culture's constituents take full advantage of the Black public sphere in certain contexts/ situations presenting important learning environments and opportunities for education within the culture.

Part 3, "Scholarly Reviews," consists mostly of republished and slightly refurbished reviews of books and films. "Angry Black White Boyz" is less of a review and more of a revisiting of my experiences listening to a range of white male artists within Hip-Hop culture. Given the ongoing critical and popular discourses related to cultural appropriation, artistic authenticity, and whiteness in Hip Hop, this selection serves as an overview (and review) of the white male rappers who have captured the imaginations of Hip Hop's (largely white) consumer audience. The other reviews—of two films and two books—are for the most part self-explanatory, but the process of writing reviews—a process that most scholars of all disciplines engage in at some point—usually early—in their careers—is a process that requires critical listening and the subsequent distillation of the listening (and viewing) experience into an assessment of the text under review. I see the writing involved in review processes as important and substantive outcomes of the critical listening project.

Part 4, "Rap Around the Table," transcribes an academic roundtable at Ohio State University's outstanding perennial "Hip Hop Literacies" conference hosted by Dr. Elaine Richardson. Roundtables are loosely organized discussion sessions—skull sessions if you will—that mirror and model the discursive practices that work in tandem with the critical listening practices that I am arguing are an important educational aspect of Hip-Hop culture. This roundtable features Treva Lindsay, Scott Heath, and Regina Bradley. The conversation ranges in reach and in scope to cover some of the important themes in contemporary Hip-Hop scholarship. The (academic) roundtable is an exercise that relies heavily on the everyday practices of critical listening. Each participant/speaker and/or moderator on these roundtables has spent hundreds if not thousands of hours listening to Hip-Hop music. Some of those hours have been critical listening hours and that shows in the erudite insights found in this section.

The final section of *Headphones*, "Rapademics," collects three academic essays that critically engage Hip-Hop scholarship from various topics and perspectives. Chapter 11 "These Three Words," revisits various censorship efforts directed at the use of profanity and controversial language in Hip Hop and considers whether or not the censorship project operating within and in response to Hip-Hop music can ultimately have merit and impact in the ways that its supporters imagine. Chapter 12, "Corner Boy Masculinity," revisits the story world of HBO's *The Wire* in order to read Common's "The Corner" over and against the corner boys featured in Season 4 of the critically acclaimed socioeconomic drama set in Baltimore, Maryland. And finally, Chapter 13 showcases the value of Hip-Hop cultural approaches to the college composition classroom.

In addition to critical listening, this chapter considers other Hip-Hop pedagogies and strategies that inform and innovate the traditional rhetoric and composition courses. A brief conclusion and an appendix that includes course syllabi, course descriptions, and several of the pedagogical playlists referenced in Chapter 4 round out this chaotic collection on the critical, educational potential inherent in Hip-Hop culture. The best way to "read" *Hip-Hop Headphones* is with your music collection on deck. Happy listening!

Part One

Definitions

Re: Definition

I Defining rap

In his 1976 book *Roots*, Alex Haley wrote about his extraordinary journey to excavate the narratives of his African ancestry, including his encounter with a griot (an African oral historian) in a West African village.[1] This seventy-three-year-old griot recited a protracted history of the tribe—recounting its origins and establishing direct connections between Alex Haley and his mythological ancestor, Kunta Kinte. The scene, as detailed by Haley, is as enigmatic and unforgettable as any of the episodes of the 1977 *Roots* television miniseries.[2] Haley was overcome with gratitude as the tribal community worked together to bring his long-lost African relatives to him, so that this momentous occasion could be captured through photography. Flash forward thirty-eight years to 2015 and Kendrick Lamar's "King Kunte," a deceptively simple-sounding track on his critically acclaimed second studio album—*To Pimp A Butterfly*—and Haley's ancestor inhabits the world of Hip Hop as a king of lyrical/verbal artistry and invention. King Kunte boasts of his success in the rap game, challenges other rappers who may not be writing their own lyrics, and celebrates his roots (via "the yams") and the potential that Hip-Hop artists have to wrestle an ancestral history from obscurity, a history too often inaccessible to the Hip-Hop generation as an ongoing consequence of chattel slavery and various systematic attempts to erase the humanity and the history of Black folks in America.

Amid the powerful energy of ancestral reconnection and historical continuity in Haley's roots-based recovery narrative, one might gloss over a key element in the retelling: How is it possible that the griot is able to retain centuries of genealogical information and perform it on demand? One part of the answer to this query is that griots perform history in verse. The griot is, in this instance, the ancestral progenitor of the modern-day rapper—hence Kendrick Lamar's allusion to Haley's Kunta Kinte. Griots preserve tremendous amounts of cultural information for spontaneous performances in verse for tribal communities. Of course, years of repetition help to instantiate these tribal histories in the collective memories of the griot as well as his audience, but Alex Haley's experiences and the powerful narrative that emerged from these experiences suggest enduring connections between ancient African griots and prominent rappers of the twentieth and twenty-first centuries.

In no small way, the history and political economy of rap music is reflected in this *Roots* moment. First, the power and political potential of rhymed verse is readily apparent in Haley's interaction with the West African griot. Second, rap music, notwithstanding its modern-day origins as entertainment, has always been challenged to shoulder the social responsibilities of the communities from which it emerged. In 1979, rap music exploded onto the popular landscape with the enormous success of a single by the Sugarhill Gang entitled "Rapper's Delight."[3] Following its release in October 1979, "Rapper's Delight," with its complete sample of the group Chic's disco hit "Good Times," was a mainstay on the Billboard Pop charts for twelve weeks.[4] Although it was not the first rap record to garner popular acclaim (i.e., Fatback Band's "King Tim III (Personality Jock)," which was released earlier in 1979), "Rappers Delight" is still considered the popular point of departure for contemporary rap music.[5]

The griot is only one of several African or African American progenitors of the rapper. In fact, there is a continuous trajectory from griot to rapper that underscores the ever-present relationship between the oral poet and the community within the African and African American traditions. Other oratorical precedents to rappers and rap music that emerged after the griot but before "Rapper's Delight," include: Jamaican-style toasts (a form of poetic narrative performed to instrumental music); various blues songs (especially where conversational talking styles are dominant); prison toasts; playing the dozens (an endless repertoire of verbal insults); disc jockey announcer styles, such as that of Douglas "Jocko" Henderson; the Black Power poetry of Amiri Baraka; the street-inflected sermons of Malcolm X; and the rhetorical prowess of nearly all of the prominent Black poets of the early 1970s, including Gil Scott Heron, Nikki Giovanni, Sonia Sanchez, the Watts Poets, and the Last Poets.

Rap music might not exist (at least in the way it does today) without the precedential, iconic influence of James Brown. The "Godfather of Soul" was also the preeminent forefather of rap music. James Brown's celebrated call-and-response technique—coupled with his conversational vocal style, his incredible interaction with his band and audience, and his ear for the most contagious break-down arrangements in the history of Black music—positions him at the genesis of Hip-Hop culture from which rap music was derived. Listening to a James Brown classic, such as "Funky Drummer"[6] or "Funky President,"[7] will immediately render his impact on rap music apparent. Indeed, Brown was rapping before rap music became reified as a popular phenomenon. It is no mistake that James Brown's music is still one of the most sampled and copied sounds in rap music.

When all of the historical and influential touchstones for rap music are considered, the fact that rap has become the premier element of Hip-Hop culture, a culture that has spread all over the world, should be fairly unremarkable. Since 1979, thousands of known and unknown rappers have produced records, and some of them have achieved commercial success. In order to develop a definitive sense of rap music, especially concerning its connections to race and African American culture, as well as its relationship to inner-city populations and American popular culture, various subcategories of the genre warrant some further explanation/definition. The following taxonomy divides rap music into four somewhat simplistic categories: mainstream, underground, conscious, and gangsta.

Mainstream rap music is the category most widely listened to by the majority population. It is a fairly fluid category. At one point (during the old school and golden age eras of Hip Hop, from about 1975 to 1990), mainstream rap was conscious and consistently political. For example, during their heyday (c. 1988 to 1989), Public Enemy—whose music was motivated by a sustained critique of white supremacy and their deep dislike/distrust of governmental politics and policies—was the most popular rap group on the most popular recording label, Def Jam Recordings. By the mid-1990s, mainstream rap's content had completed a dramatic, paradigmatic shift toward more violent and misogynistic narratives allegedly designed to denounce the horrific conditions of American inner cities. By the late 1990s and through the first half of the first decade of 2000, the content of mainstream rap shifted yet again, this time toward the celebration of conspicuous consumption. Some scholars and fans refer to this current mainstream moment of rap as the "bling bling era" (the term "bling bling" was coined by the New Orleans rapper B.G., short for "Baby Gangsta," in onomatopoeic allusion to the glistening radiance of his diamond-encrusted platinum jewelry).[8]

Underground rap music is even more difficult to define because it generally takes its cues from mainstream rap and often does not (and by some definitions cannot) enjoy the popular distribution, exposure, and financial attention and rewards of mainstream music. Underground rap tends to be predicated on regional or local development and support, although with the advent of the internet and the imminently transferable mp3 music files, underground networks have expanded across local, regional, and even international barriers. Underground rap must also, in both content and form, distinguish itself from popular mainstream rap. Thus, when mainstream rap is about being a gangster, underground rap tends to be more politically conscious, and vice versa. When mainstream rap production is sample-heavy with an explicit emphasis on beats per minute (BPM) hovering in the mid-1990s, underground rap will dispense with samples and sport BPMs well into the 100s. This symbiotic relationship between the mainstream and the underground is far too complex to fully explicate here, but inevitably, one defines itself against the other, sometime through reverse reciprocity. Most mainstream styles of rap were at one time or another considered underground. Some of the most talented underground rappers and rap groups are: Rebel Diaz, Invincible, The Living Legends, MF Doom, Immortal Technique, The VI-Kings, The Last Emperor, Medusa, Chillin Villain Empire (CVE), Aceyalone, and Murs.

Conscious rap music came into prominence in 1982 with the release of Grandmaster Flash and the Furious Five's "The Message."[9] The term "conscious," as it is being employed here, refers to an artist's lyrical realization of the various social forces at play in the poor and working-class environments from which many rappers hail and from where the music and culture of Hip Hop originated. "The Message" was a powerful response to/commentary on postindustrial inner-city conditions in America. Since then, the subgenre of conscious rap music has continued to produce some of the most inspired songs for the enlightenment and uplift of Black and brown people. Run–D.M.C's "Proud to Be Black"[10]; KRS-One's "Self-Destruction,"[11] "Why Is That?,"[12] and "Black Cop"[13]; and Public Enemy's "Can't Truss It,"[14] "Shut 'Em Down,"[15] and "911 Is a Joke,"[16] all come to mind. Conscious rap thrives in the shadows of both underground rap and mainstream rap, even as it innovates and informs a genre that most people associate with violence and consumerism.

Gangsta rap is a subgenre that stems from a complex set of cultural and sociological circumstances. Gangsta rap is a media term partially borrowed from the African American vernacular form of the word *gangster*. African American Vernacular English [AAVE] employs many systemic rules and features. One of these features is "r-lessness," meaning that speakers drop or significantly reduce the "r" in certain linguistic situations. When the popularity of rap music shifted from New York City and the East Coast to Los Angeles and the West Coast (between 1988 and 1992), this geographic reorientation was accompanied by distinct stylistic shifts and striking differences in the contents and sounds of the music. This paradigmatic shift took place in the late 1980s through the early 1990s and is most readily represented in the career peak of the late 1980s conscious group Public Enemy (PE), as well as the subsequent, meteoric rise of N.W.A. (Niggaz With Attitude), a group from Compton, California. Just as the marketing and retail potential of rap music was gaining prominence (both PE and N.W.A. were early beneficiaries of rap music's now legendary platinum-selling potential), the music industry media clamored to find acceptable terminology with which to report on this new, powerful, and vulgar phenomenon. Since the challenges of gang warfare in Los Angeles were already journalistic and cinematic in legend (consider gangster narratives such as *The Godfather Saga, Goodfellas, and Scarface*), the term "gangsta rap" was aptly coined in response.

Yet even at its inception, gangsta rap compelled scholars, journalists, and critics to confront the cruel realities of inner-city living (initially in the South Bronx and Philadelphia with KRS-One and Schoolly D, and almost simultaneously with Ice-T and N.W.A. on the West Coast). Still, only the rudimentary realities of poverty, police brutality, gang violence, and severely truncated opportunity have been subject to any real investigation or comprehension. The whole point of a rapper rapping is to exaggerate, through oratorical narration and hyperbole, in order to represent one's community and culture in the face of violent social invisibility (e.g., consider the collective shock at the rampant poverty in New Orleans revealed only after the media reported on the devastation caused by Hurricane Katrina). It is not surprising, then, that gangsta rap was a radical wake-up call illuminating the aforementioned social ills. Its popularity, however, is more an indication of mainstream audience's insatiable appetite for violent narratives than it is a reflection of any one individual's particular reality. That is to say, in all genres of rap music, the relationships between author and narrative are not necessarily autobiographical. However, these narratives, in their most authentic forms, tend to be representative of certain postindustrial, inner-city African American realities.

II The elements and eras of Hip-Hop culture

Although rap music, especially the lyrical content of the music, will be foregrounded throughout *Hip-Hop Headphones*, it is important to rehearse the fact that rap is but one element of what scholars, artisans, cultural critics, and journalists refer to as Hip-Hop culture. Over the last forty years, Hip-Hop culture has progressed from a relatively unknown and largely ignored inner-city culture into a global phenomenon. Throughout these pages, you will find that I use the term "Hip-Hop music" more often than rap music. This choice in terminology signals an attempt to foreground the elemental nature of Hip-Hop culture in contexts where the music is the central subject. The foundational elements of Hip-Hop culture (DJ-ing, MC-ing, Breakdancing, and Graffiti/Graf) are manifest in youth culture around the globe, including Ghana, India, Japan, France, Germany, South Africa, Cuba, and the UK. Considering its humble beginnings in the South and West Bronx, the global expansion and recognition of Hip Hop is an amazing cultural feat. Its global popularity suggests and reflects its culturally diverse origins. Moreover, the presence of rap music and other elements of the culture in marketing and advertising signals mainstream acceptance. In fact, its dominance in popular culture almost completely obscures the negative, and at times malicious, treatment of Hip Hop in the public sphere. With all of its attendant complexities and apparent contradictions, Hip Hop is one of the most difficult cultural phenomena to define.[17]

By the mid-1970s DJ Kool Herc's parties were becoming well-known in New York City. In fact, Hip-Hop jams were the affordable alternatives to overpriced disco clubs. As early Hip-Hop DJs began to hone the various techniques of premature DJ-ing, the potential of the culture emerged in anxious excitement among young b-boys and b-girls. The early Hip-Hop DJs invented the concept of scratching, or skillfully manipulating vinyl records to sonically rupture recorded music and play fragments of it back at will. Even before the concept of scratching was developed, DJs isolated and looped break beats from popular records. Early b-boys would battle with one another, and through battling, the various technical aspects of breakdancing were honed and developed. There were several crews of young folk who participated in the development of break dancing. One of the earliest and now most legendary breaking crews is the Rock Steady Crew. Bronx b-boys Jimmy D. and Jojo established the legendary Rock Steady Crew and were later joined by Crazy Legs and Lenny Len in 1979.

In addition to DJs and break-dancers, there were also MCs present during these early Hip-Hop jams. As a point of clarification, all MCs rap, but not all rappers are MCs. The crucial distinction is as follows: a rapper is an entertainer, while an MC is an artist who is committed to perfecting the crafts of lyrical mastery and call-response audience interaction. MCs were not initially (as they are now) the front men and women of Hip-Hop culture. KRS-One, a well-known MC, once remarked that as an MC he was happy to just carry his DJs crates. These days, Hip-Hop culture and rap music especially tend to marginalize most of the foundational elements of the culture and overemphasize the role of the MC. According to Rakim, an MC who is widely referred to as "the god": MC means "move the crowd" or "Mic Control." MCs improve their skills through freestyling and battling as well. Freestyle rhyming is when an MC raps without aid of previous rhymes committed to paper or memory. Much like their jazz-improvising counterparts, a freestyling MC performs lyrical rifts and cadences from an ever-evolving repertoire in order to deliver extemporaneous rhymes that reflect their immediate environment and/or address the present opponent. Conversely, battling is when MCs engage in lyrical combat in a series of discursive, alternating turns. In fact, verbal battles between MCs have become legendary, and at times, notoriously violent on and off record.

The final foundational element of Hip-Hop culture is graffiti art. For many people, this designation is an oxymoron. After all, graffiti, in its most rudimentary form, is an act of vandalism. It is against the law to spray paint names and/or images onto public property. Somewhat unlike the other elements of Hip-Hop culture, graffiti completely predates the developments of DJ-ing, MC-ing, and breaking. However, there are some distinct qualities to how and why graffiti has developed in Hip-Hop culture. This moment is distinct for several reasons: (1) Considering Hip Hop's global prominence in the new millennium, the multicultural origins of Hip Hop certainly explain some of its universal appeal. A Greek graf writer fit in perfectly with the diverse array of cultural constituents, including African Americans, Jamaicans, West Indians, Puerto Ricans, Asians, Dominicans, and Cubans (2) Several scholars[18] have referred to some of the activity of early adopters of Hip-Hop culture as a process of reclaiming public spaces.[19] Sometimes this reclamation is signified through sound (i.e., consider the boom boxes of yesteryear or the current boom-box-like sound systems in cars) but sometimes it is illustrated through the writing of names and images on/in public spaces. (3) The appropriation of the subway, as a means to quickly and effectively circulate the tag, "Taki 183" throughout the five boroughs was a masterstroke. It underscored the urge to manipulate public property and services for the benefit of youth culture and in particular here, the processes of self-identification among inner-city youth.

In addition to the four foundational elements of Hip-Hop culture, there are several secondary elements framing the culture as well. These elements include fashion/modes of dress, entrepreneurship, and complex systems of knowledge (particularly elaborate language and other linguistic phenomenon). Fashion has always been an integral component of Hip-Hop culture. The DJs, b-boys, b-girls, and MCs had serious dress codes. Some of the earliest (and most notable) brands of choice were Adidas, Puma, Lee Jeans, Cazal (eyeglasses), and Kangol (hats). True to their artistry, some of the early graf artists would spray paint names and designs onto sweatshirts, jackets, sneakers, and hats. So a distinct sense of fashion was established early on in Hip Hop's cultural development. As the culture grew in popularity, fashion became an overt sign of Hip Hop's entrepreneurial sensibility. Hip-Hop clothing brands such as Karl Kani, Cross Colours, and eventually Phat Farm, FUBU, and Rocawear all signified the fact that youth influenced by, and living through, Hip-Hop culture were deeply invested in economic empowerment most readily manifest in owning one's own business.

Entrepreneurship should not be confused with the kind of conspicuous consumption often associated with the (now dated) term, "bling." The ideophone "bling bling" came into vogue during the platinum era of Hip Hop and reflects earlier descriptions of African American culture—what Zora Neale Hurston referred to as "the will to adorn."[20] Wearing ornamented jewelry and sporting gold teeth can be viewed as a cultural strategy by young people to symbolically flash their financial success and to thereby challenge social invisibility in a materialistic society. It is a means of self-identification and self-promotion that harkens back to early African American and American traditions, and more importantly, underscores the knowledge element of Hip-Hop culture. Knowledge Reigns Supreme Over Nearly Everyone—KRS-One—this simple acronym, the MC moniker of Kris Parker (formally of Boogie Down Productions), gestures toward the value of knowledge especially for the initiates of Hip Hop. Younger folks (and certainly people outside of Hip-Hop cultural discourses) may not have heard of KRS-One. They may not know that he started his recording career with the group BDP. In fact, they may not even know what BDP stands for or that the "Boogie Down" is a nickname for the Bronx—the birthplace of Hip Hop. This is just one example (albeit a very simplistic one) of thousands of linguistic cues, local references, acronyms, and code names that require constituents of Hip-Hop culture to be "in the know." A popular rhetorical statement that derives from Hip-Hop culture sums it up best: "If you don't know—you better ask somebody."

All of this culturally diverse energy tends to disguise some of the socioeconomic factors that set the stage for Hip Hop's early developments. In *Prophets of the Hood*, Imani Perry, warns against using deficiency models to define and/or describe the sociocultural contexts for Hip Hop.[21] That is to say, the following discussion about the socioeconomic contexts for Hip-Hop culture is not an attempt to account for the developments of Hip Hop in total. The significance of various socioeconomic factors in the developments of the culture will be readily apparent. The outsourcing of high-tech jobs has become an issue of public discourse in the new millennium, but outsourcing has been a challenge among the working class and impoverished since the early 1970s. In the 1960s, many urban centers in the United States relied economically on the manufacturing industries. As these industries outsourced labor and developed advanced technological means to manufacture their products, unemployment increased exponentially. In New York City, this deindustrialization was complemented by the erasure of public school support for the arts and musical training. In the Bronx, the construction of a beltway for commuters displaced thousands of residences.[22] The combination of these economic factors created a stifling environment for young people in inner cities in the mid-1970s. With escalating residential depression and limited outlets for artistic expression, young people were relegated to an economically and artistically stagnant environment. For ready reference, view the 1982 film, *Wild Style*. Not only does the film chronicle the early days of Hip-Hop culture, but it is also filmed in the Bronx; and aside from living in or visiting the South Bronx circa 1979, these are some of the most authentic images of the setting for the early developments of Hip-Hop culture.[23]

From these origins, Hip Hop's development can be categorized into three loosely organized eras:

1. The Old School Era: From 1979 to 1987, Hip-Hop culture cultivated itself by and through all of its elements usually remaining authentic to the countercultural roots in the postindustrial challenges manifested in the urban landscape of the late twentieth century. Artists associated with this era include DJ Kool Herc, Grandmaster Flash and the Furious Five, Grandmaster Caz, Grand Wizard Theodore, Busy Bee, Crazy Legs, Lady Pink, The Sugarhill Gang, Lady B, Big Daddy Kane, Run–D.M.C., and Kurtis Blow, among others.
2. The Golden Age Era: From 1987 to 1993, rap and rappers began to take center stage as Hip Hop exploded onto the mainstream platform of

American popular culture. The extraordinary musical production and lyrical content of rap songs artistically eclipsed most of the other primary elements of the culture. Eventually, the recording industry contemplated rap music as a potential billion dollar opportunity. Mass mediated rap music and Hip-Hop videos displaced the intimate, insulated urban development of the culture. Significant artists associated with this era include: Run–D.M.C., Boogie Down Productions, Eric B and Rakim, Salt-N-Pepa, Queen Latifah, De La Soul, A Tribe Called Quest (ATCQ), Public Enemy, N.W.A, and many others.

3. The Platinum Era: (From 1994 to approximately 2004), In the twenty-first century, Hip-Hop culture has enjoyed the best and worst of what mass mediated popularity and cultural commodification has to offer. The meteoric rise to popular fame of gangsta rap in the early 1990s set the stage for a marked content shift in the lyrical discourse of rap music toward increasingly violent depictions of inner-city realities. Millions of magazines and records were sold, but two of Hip Hop's most promising artists, Biggie Smalls and Tupac Shakur, were literally gunned down in the crossfire of a media-fueled frenzy between the so-called East and West Coast constituents of Hip-Hop culture. With the blueprint of popular success for rappers stripped bare, several exceptional artists stepped into the gaping space left in the wake of Biggie and Tupac. This influx of talent included: Nas, Jay-Z, Master P, DMX, Big Pun, Snoop Dogg, Eminem, and Outkast. In the new millennium, gangsta rap has been displaced (and in some ways erased) by the kind of affective rap popularized by artists like J. Cole, Drake, Macklemore, and Kendrick Lamar. And the most popular figure from Compton, California is not Ice Cube, Dr. Dre, Suge Knight, or even The Game; it's Kendrick Lamar.

The current era of Hip Hop is still unfolding, but since the demise of Tupac Shakur and The Notorious B.I.G., the rise and resultant malaise of the platinum era, and the more contemporary turn toward affect and emotional intelligence in popular forms of the music, social justice issues and movements (e.g., the Prison Industrial Complex or anti-brutality efforts and the #BlackLivesMatter movement) have impacted the content of the music and the political subjectivity of most Hip-Hop generation artists. I will return later to the emergence of scholars who critically engage the culture, but it is worth noting here that by the early 1990s, Hip-Hop culture was emerging as an area of serious study on the university level. Courses about Hip-Hop culture, history, and aesthetics were instituted on college campuses across America. The field of Hip-Hop studies, which features a wide variety of college-level Hip-Hop courses across a number of disciplines—including English/literary studies, history, sociology, religion studies, theater, anthropology, education, and linguistics—has developed via the dual pressures of Hip-Hop generational scholars entering the academy as graduate students and more recently as professors and the steady pressure, interest, and inclinations of younger Hip-Hop generational students who continue to find Hip Hop–related courses of vital interest in their undergraduate studies.

III Hip Hop's holy trinity

Three figures are regularly referenced as the founders and/or forefathers of the culture. In fact, Afrika Bambaataa, DJ Kool Herc, and Grandmaster Flash are collectively referred to as the "holy trinity" of Hip-Hop culture.[24] Kool Herc (Clive Campbell), who immigrated to the United States from Kingston/Trenchtown, Jamaica, in 1967, is the consensus founder of Hip-Hop culture. He was one of the first DJs to isolate and loop break beats at parties, and he borrowed various elements from Jamaican culture and implemented them in the earliest outdoor parties that constituted Hip-Hop culture in the late 1970s. Grandmaster Flash (Joseph Sadler), who was born in Barbados in 1958, but raised in the South Bronx, is the earliest and most important innovator of the turntable, the cross-fader, and other techniques and technologies associated with the process of transforming the turntable into an indelible instrument of sound production. Afrika Bambaataa (Bambaataa Kahim Aasim) is the most enigmatic of these three founding fathers of the culture.[25] His most significant artistic contribution to the development of the culture was his aesthetic commitment to mining rare sounds and interpolating them into the artistic fabric of Hip-Hop music. Bambaataa was born in America, but his parents were from Jamaica and Barbados.

For all of the praise that is lavished on these three figures, few scholars have seriously considered the significance of their particular cultural origins and the confluent impact of these origins on the creation of Hip-Hop culture. Moreover (and maybe more importantly), little scholarly attention has been directed at the antiviolent nature of their respective contributions. DJ Kool Herc, Afrika Bambaataa, and Grandmaster Flash came of age artistically amid the gang violence of New York City in the 1970s; through a brief look at their engagement with early Hip-Hop culture, an ideological portrait of nonviolence emerges. Each member of Hip Hop's holy trinity made deliberate efforts to confront, navigate, and/or manage violence in their communities through the culture of Hip Hop. Their promotion of nonviolent resistance challenged young people to wrestle with, and ultimately redress, the everyday violence in their communities.

It is worth reiterating here that my reference to these three figures as the holy trinity of Hip-Hop music is not original nor does it rest with one (or even two/three) scholars, writers, or journalists. Scholars, journalists, and artists concur that Herc, Bam, and Flash produced and represented the early sound of Hip-Hop culture. In a nearly comparable consensus, journalists and scholars also agree upon, and pay homage to the fact that, especially in the artistic and real-life work of Herc and Bam, nonviolence and antiviolence themes were central to their collective ethos, the communities in which they lived, and the ideologies-in-practice exercised by the entire trinity of Hip-Hop culture. One irony present in the discourses on Hip-Hop culture is that what many regard today as the machinery that produces popular images of misogyny, consumerism, and inner-city violence was, in its origins, deliberately and successfully antiviolent. Although I will rehearse some of the more interesting narratives that point to these origins and ironies, I am actually more concerned with how the trinity of Hip Hop was able to achieve such a feat. The "why" and/or the factual nature of the stories that explicate the nonviolent mission of Hip Hop's holy trinity are ultimately not as significant as the "how." This is especially important if we are invested in considering the current and future potential of Hip-Hop culture to engage violence and other social justice issues in the communities that birthed it (as well as the communities that birthed the trinity of the culture's forefathers).

Although the means by which Herc, Bam, and Flash sounded a nonviolent ethos in early Hip-Hop culture are wide-ranging and multifaceted, for the purposes of this chapter, I have limited the discussion to the following four categorical examples: (1) The trinity of Hip Hop individually and collectively projected a fluid sense of masculinity in the face of rigid strictures for Black masculinity that were prevalent in the early 1970s in inner-city New York. (2) At least two of the three directly mediated and/or intervened in violent confrontations. That is, the trinity of Hip Hop vigilantly addressed and confronted violence in their communities. They not only did rap about it or throw parties to address issues of violence, but rather, chose to be direct actors in their own nonviolent campaigns. (3) Each member of the trinity invented artistic techniques that inspired technological advancements in the creation, production, and representation of music. (4) Each member of the trinity generated a mythological narrative (particularly via their monikers or nomenclature), that was based upon their abilities to mediate violence and to speak (or produce art) from an authentic subject position that very few of their peers or constituents could or would ever challenge.

At a 2002 Hip-Hop conference held at Princeton University, Selwyn Hinds, author of *Gunshots in My Cook-Up*, and one of the legendary editors of the *Source* magazine, stated that Hip-Hop culture exists almost exclusively within the purview of masculinity.[26] For Hinds, Hip Hop was synonymous with masculinist culture. Arguing with Hinds on this assertion did not make sense at that moment. Rap music and other elements of Hip-Hop culture tend to center male voices, narratives, and perspectives. In *Beyond Beats and Rhymes*, one of the most compelling documentaries of or about Hip-Hop culture, Byron Hurt suggests that for the constituents of Hip-Hop culture (around the globe), "manhood is in a box."[27] For Hurt, traditional American notions of manhood and the inextricable nature of the relationship between masculinity and violence have atrophied in the music and culture of Hip Hop. Hurt directs his camera toward the Dionysian exploits of the culture on display at large festival-like gatherings, in music videos such as Nelly's infamous "Tip Drill," and in the classic imagery of an American film.[28] Through his lens, the entrapped condition of Black masculinity becomes self-evident; and the dimensions, shapes, and angles of the box are almost exclusively drawn by violent acts.

The kind of masculinity projected by and through Hip Hop's trinity warrants some discussion of how masculinity might be defined. Timothy J. Brown's essay "Welcome to the Terrordome: Exploring the Contradictions of a Hip Hop Black Masculinity" employs Todd Boyd's models for Black masculinity in order to read NBA All-Star Allen Iverson in the context of the media attention directed at him during his domestic dispute with his now former wife/partner Tawanna during the summer of 2002.[29] Brown borrows Boyd's model that divvies Black masculinity into three discriminating categories: the race man, the new Black aesthetics, and the nigga.[30] According to Brown:

> The race man ... represents the ideology of cultural advancement by presenting images of the race that are acceptable to both the dominant white culture and African American culture. ... New black aesthetics is based on the nationalist politics of Malcolm X ... and the nigga, having no political agenda or any identifiable leader, is primarily concerned with giving voice to and representing the truly disadvantaged.[31]

Brown concludes that the nigga version of Boyd's model of Black masculinity is, especially as it is signified through Allen Iverson's public persona, Hip-Hop Black masculinity. Accordingly, he asserts, "A Hip Hop black masculinity is countercultural and resists conforming to many of the dominant culture's precepts."[32] For Brown, Hip-Hop Black masculinity gives voice to the voiceless, counters culture, and resists mainstream domination.

The texts of Brown and Boyd are useful to the extent that Hip Hop's trinity reflects Hip-Hop Black masculinity in its simplest sense. Yet, the various nuances of their lives and the narratives available to us in order to better understand those lives, paint a more complex picture. For example, in the following exchange between journalist extraordinaire, James Spady and Afrika Bambaataa, Bam explains some of the reasoning behind his work during the earliest/formative days of Hip-Hop culture to transform the Black Spades, one of New York City's largest and most violent gangs, into the Universal Zulu Nation, one of Hip Hop's largest and oldest community arts organizations. Spady poses the following question: "What was the key factor in moving from the Black Spades to the Zulu Nation?"[33] To this, Bam replies:

> There were a lot of killings, a lot of people fighting over negative shit such as, "You stepped on my sneakers," or "You looked at the sister wrong," or the

drugs. I couldn't stand the drugs in our community. There is one thing I have to say about the Black Spades, we kept a lot of that drug shit out of our area. I brought the same element into the Universal Zulu Nation. Then to have the teachings of the Honorable Elijah Muhammad made me realize that I could go out and use these teachings.[34]

Bambaataa's reply captures some complexity that is not readily apparent through the provisional definitions of Boyd and/or Brown. Bam embodies both the new Black aesthetic through the teachings of Elijah Muhammad, as well as the nigga and/or Hip-Hop Black masculinity through his participation in gang warfare as a leader of the Black Spades. However, he also presents himself as a model for others to emulate. Bambaataa was the first figure in Hip-Hop culture to instantiate knowledge as the fifth element. He thus challenged all constituents of Hip Hop to have knowledge of themselves, their histories, and of the structural forces framing their existence. In the immediacy of now, Bam is most likely considered by younger constituents of Hip Hop (provided they know who he is) to be an elder statesman of sorts.

If Brown and Boyd's definitions are somewhat limiting, Linden Lewis' explication of masculinity generates more space for the projections of masculine identity promulgated by Bam, Herc, and Flash. According to Lewis, "Masculinity is a set of social practices of men in society that revolves around ideas of appropriate gender roles, ways of behaving, ways of experiencing and navigating one's way through a world that demands conformity of individuals through rewards and punishes expressions of difference."[35] Lewis' opening salvo on masculinity reflects the parameters of socialization that were present in the world into which the trinity of Hip Hop entered. Herc was no stranger to structural or communal violence. As a boy growing up in Trenchtown, Jamaica during the 1960s, he recalls the following: "I remember police riding around in big old trucks, tanks. And some people who were brothers or friends would turn on each other. It was like a civil war"[36] [referring to the conflict between the JLP (Jamaica Labour Party) and the PNP (People's National Party)]. The "conformity" demanded of Herc was that he was forced to witness, and ultimately participate in this violence. Unfortunately, even after migrating to Bronx, New York in 1967, this particular demand—and the requisite punishment for those who tried to resist the conventions of this senseless violence—remained consistently brutal. In fact, the Bronx in 1970 was itself, a war zone. According to Alex Ogg and David Upshal,

> The Bronx of the (late) 1970s was an area synonymous with poverty and hardship, a breeding ground for internecine warfare in which the American Dream was subservient to codes of survival. Though a uniquely vibrant environment, it was also a dangerous place to live. ... The Bronx was declared one of the most destructive places in America. It was infested by a lot of drugs and a lot of street gang activity.[37]

Each member of Hip Hop's trinity confronted the demands that an American city besieged by violence placed upon young people at that time. Each member also exploited all of the tools at their disposal, including physical size and presence, crews/gangs, street connections, and the amazing magnetism of the Hip-Hop DJ—an identity that the trinity forged in the cauldron of gang violence that New York City had become. Here again, Lewis' discussion of masculinity is instructive:

> Masculinity is the practice of an awakening consciousness of one's self as a man. It is a consciousness of an identity that is forged in relation, and in opposition, to that of femininity. It means therefore that masculinity has much to do with men seeking the approval of women but more importantly, seeking the honor, respect, and recognition of other men. ... Masculinity ... tells us more about aspects of culture as constraint rather than the freedom we imagine it to be.[38]

Each member of Hip Hop's trinity had specific experiences that expanded their capacity for self-awareness. For Herc, it derived from his experiences growing up in Trenchtown and his critical perspective on the New York City gangs that "terrorized the whole neighborhood."[39] For Bam, it was being born to, and raised by, "parents of Jamaican and Barbadian descent."[40] His was a family "immersed in international Black cultural and liberation movements."[41] For Flash, born in Barbados but raised in the Bronx, it was his father's record collection. A collection he was forbidden to even touch: "Flash was fascinated not just by the music but by the records themselves. For him, they were things to be looked at, touched and handled, not just played."[42] These awakenings constituted the very origins of Hip-Hop culture's collective consciousness.

Hip Hop's trinity pitted the magnetism of technological mastery against the violent tendencies that had become so commonplace among Black and brown youth in New York City during the 1970s. In Lewis' terms, they renegotiated the boundaries of "constraint" and "freedom" with respect to notions of Black manhood in inner-city New York. It was not all technique and technological mastery though since Bam has been referred to as "barrel-chested" and "stoic."[43] Nelson George referred to Bambaataa as "a large man with a brooding, authoritative presence; [who] rarely smiled."[44] His imposing physicality was exacerbated by the fact that Bambaataa had, by 1974/1975, collected as much street credibility as any single figure could amass. When Bam threw a party, he had an army with him, and even though his sound system could quite literally blow away the competition, his commitment to a nonviolent ethos could rarely be questioned. One anecdote is particularly revealing here. We know that Bambaataa regularly DJ-ed parties at a Bronx community center. On one such occasion, a fight broke out just outside the event:

> Bambaataa paused and then addressed the whole audience. "No Violence ... no violence ... no violence," he said evenly and calmly, his voice having a pronounced effect on the more skittish ones in the group. He set the needle on a James Brown record and let it play a few seconds before abruptly lifting it. A few members of the audience—the hard-core dancers—moaned. "You like that?" taunted Bambaataa. "Music. That's what I'm talkin' about." He put the needle back on the record and let it play. The lights went out and the crowd began to dance. Apparently no one was hurt and the dispute was moved out of the area.[45]

Herc and Flash did not have nearly as much street credibility or as many gang affiliations as Bam. Kool Herc enjoyed the protection afforded by members of the 5 Percent Nation (an offshoot of the Nation of Islam founded by Clarence 13X). Herc himself was not a member, but their cloak of protection provided him the mobility and credibility to host Hip-Hop jams throughout the Bronx and other boroughs of New York. It helped that Herc was, himself, a formidable figure. Old school legend, MC Melle Mel claims that Herc was "this huge character, and he had a beard. He really was like fuckin' Hercules; he was built and shit. He was, just from my images of right now, just this really mythical character."[46]

Herc and Bam established the DJ as an authority figure within Hip-Hop culture, and each member of the trinity contributed specific forms of mastery to further substantiate the DJ as the arbiter of cool. This extraordinary intersection of technique and technological mastery cannot be overstated since it essentially buttressed the nonviolent ethos sounded by Hip Hop's trinity. Kool Herc provided the foundation upon which Hip-Hop musical aesthetics rest. Taking his cues from women (especially his sister who organized and promoted his first party, the first documented Hip-Hop jam/party), Herc isolated the break beats and began to develop techniques for looping and extending them. One such technique, appropriately termed the "merry-go-round," featured an endless string of break beats from a wide variety of records. Herc manipulated two turntables, so that he could seamlessly move from one break to the next. The merry-go-round technique—which is still employed by DJs today—created a kinesthetic frenzy on the dance floor. It generated the musical space and time for breakers (b-boys and b-girls) to demonstrate the full range of their skills and it also served as a platform for the very first MCs to give shout-outs and make announcements over the microphone. Consequently, Bam became known as the "Master of Records" as a direct result of his verbal and physical dexterity, as well as his unmatched ability to introduce unique sounds into the Hip-Hop cultural space.

If Grandmaster Flash was somehow lacking in the street credibility department with respect to the other members of Hip Hop's holy trinity, then he may have compensated for it in terms of his contributions to the (intersections of) technological mastery and technique in the DJ element of Hip-Hop culture. According to George:

> Grandmaster Flash is now best known as a recording artist, but there are several purely technical DJ breakthroughs that owe their existence to his hand-and-eye coordination. ... "Punch phrasing"—playing a quick burst from a record on one turntable while it continues on the other—and "break spinning"—alternately spinning both records backward to the repeat the same phrase over and over are credited to Flash.[47]

Flash, much more than Bambaataa or DJ Kool Herc, was a showman. Trained to be an electrician, Flash manipulated the available technology in order to perfect the skills of mixing, cross-fading, clock theory—or the ability to "read records by using the spinning logo to find the break,"—and of course, scratching (which Flash may not have invented, but certainly revolutionized). Flash, more than any other member of Hip Hop's trinity, made technological mastery aspirational in the minds of young folk who became the first artisans of Hip-Hop culture.

Each member of Hip Hop's trinity sports a moniker that engenders specific mythological narratives that are integral to, and in service of, the mythological Hip-Hop narratives generated through their lives as the founders of one of the most popular youth cultural forms to emerge out of the Black diaspora. DJ Kool Herc, was given the name "Hercules" by his basketball teammates. He was at first reluctant to accept this nickname, but his size and athletic ability made it stick. Once he gained traction as a DJ, Herc's muscular build and ability to throw a party/jam "from the muscle," an expression used colloquially to connote street prowess and mastery, became the legendary narratives of Hip-Hop culture. Afrika Bambaataa is "the name of a famous nineteenth-century Zulu Chief—and is translated to mean 'Affectionate Leader'." Bam first encountered imagery of the Zulus in the 1964 film starring Michael Caine, but his own sojourn to Africa in 1975, coupled with his revolutionary upbringing, helped to solidify him as a definitive sociological influence on the emergence of Hip-Hop culture. Grandmaster Flash takes his name from the character of Flash Gordon, a time-traveling, alternate-dimension-traversing hero, who uses his athletic ability (i.e., his hand-eye coordination and other skills) to conquer his adversaries. To suggest that Flash took his moniker to heart is to patently suggest the obvious. Whatever the origins of these monikers, they each reflect the ways in which Hip-Hop culture heaps myth upon these three figures: Clive Campbell, Kahim Aasim, and Joseph Sadler. Although myth in nomenclature or cultural narrative has its limitations, the contributions of Hip Hop's holy trinity require some revisiting as their mark on the culture unveils the ability for youth movements to redress shifting and limited conceptualizations of masculinity and the challenges of communal violence throughout the Black diaspora.

IV Defining Hip Hop in a racial context

Based upon its origins in inner-city America, the influences derived from African American oral and folk culture, and its interface with concepts of masculinity, Hip-Hop culture has always shared a complex relationship with race. From its inception, the relationship between Hip Hop and race has been fragmented, decentralized, and, in many ways, volatile. The cultural and economic environment that catalyzed Hip Hop's development directly reflected the negative effects of a postindustrial society and a rapidly changing economy. Inner-city communities were devastated by the emergent service economy and the shift from domestic manufacturing to overseas outsourcing. At the same time, the social and racial environments in which Hip Hop developed were multifaceted and incredibly multicultural. The youth involved in Hip Hop's genesis were from a diverse array of African, Latino, and European origins. In fact, Hip Hop would not exist as we know it without the varied contributions of pioneers and artists from the Caribbean and Latin America, as well as their African American neighbors and counterparts in the boroughs of New York City.

While each of the constitutive elements of Hip Hop (DJ-ing/turntablism, B-boying/breaking, MC-ing/rapping, and Visual/graffiti art) can stand on its own, with its own artisans, audiences, and commercial products, the intersection of these components in the West and South Bronx facilitated the cultural revolution of Hip Hop that we know today. The following explanation of these elements underscores their original emergence and sets the stage for the corresponding racial connections. These tentative racial connections are postmodern in the sense that they reflect a crisis of representation that runs through the discourses of Hip-Hop culture, but ultimately certain racial and cultural heritages inform the complex elements of Hip Hop and certain elements attract artisans from experiences and/or cultural backgrounds that predispose them to affinities for the practices within each particular element.

DJ-ing is the deliberate and technical manipulation of the turntable— ultimately transforming it, through sound engineering and science, into an articulate instrument with its own arsenal of sounds such as scratches, temporally manipulated tones, sonic cuts, and samples. B-boying refers to the kinesthetic responses to the DJs isolation of break beats on vinyl records. B-boys and b-girls would break during the isolation and looping of break beats at the original Hip-Hop jams. To reiterate, the break is that part of a song where the track is stripped down to its most fundamentally percussive elements. The connection between the highly percussive or beat-oriented segments in Hip-Hop music and the power of the drum in African and African American cultures should not be overlooked or underestimated. Hip-Hop music captures and reflects the commanding power of the drum in its dance and music.

The MC is the verbal arbiter of Hip-Hop culture. Originally cast as a tangential hype man for the earliest well-known DJs in Hip Hop, the MC has since graduated to the foreground of the culture. The poets, MCs, and rappers of Hip Hop have become the primary purveyors of rap music's dominance on the pop culture landscape.

Graffiti art is the element of the culture that most clearly and singularly predates the creation of Hip Hop. Indeed, graffiti is a relatively primordial art form that can be traced back to ancient times. However, its development in conjunction with the other foundational elements of Hip-Hop is particularly striking. Graffiti provided a viable artistic platform for poverty-stricken inner-city youth whose artistic outlets were diminished in most public institutions. In the 1970s, there was a drastic reduction of music and arts programs in public schools, and of the funds that supported recreational centers and other public channels for creative expression. Many scholars have referred to Hip Hop's graffiti art as one of the most salient signals of young people's reclamation of public spaces, which had been utterly privatized in this postmodern era. Consider how one generation's rampant vandalism is indeed another generation's revolutionary movement.

At the risk of promoting racial essentialism in Hip Hop culture, the following outline of several of the seminal figures in the origins, development, and growth of Hip Hop underscores the postmodernity of the racial dynamics within the culture. As previously mentioned, the consensus founder of Hip-Hop culture is DJ Kool Herc. Born in Kingston, Jamaica, not too far from Bob Marley's neighborhood of origin, Herc moved with his family to the West Bronx in the late 1960s. Before long, he borrowed elements of Jamaican dub and yard cultures and infused these public performance techniques with African American soul music, the verbal styles radio disc jockeys, and the aforementioned developing elements of Hip Hop (especially graffiti art).

Herc's sensibility for these forms, and his understanding of their potential to entertain inner-city youth in postindustrial New York culminated suddenly in the summer of 1973 when he took over for a DJ at his sister's birthday party. From that moment forward, the Hip-Hop jam became the fastest-growing and most engaging form of youth entertainment. In interviews and in public appearances, Kool Herc readily concedes the importance of his relationships with African American and Latino youth, as well as his Jamaican heritage and love of African American soul music. In particular, James Brown's soulful stylings and magnetic musical performances kindled Kool Herc's desire to isolate the break beats of records in order to extend the most danceable aspects of the original Hip-Hop jams. Although youth from all backgrounds have experience with breaking (sometimes referred to as break dancing), the earliest pioneers are of Latin American origins. One of the first breaking crews was the Rock Steady Crew. One of this group's leaders and most endearing television personalities is Crazy Legs, who starred in a number of Hip Hop–related films, including *Flashdance* (1983).[48] Though he witnessed a decline in the mainstream popularity of breaking, he continues to be an ambassador for Hip-Hop dance forms over the world. One of the first MCs, Busy Bee, starred in the groundbreaking docudrama, *Wild Style* (1982).[49] Of African American origin, MCs and rappers like Busy Bee, Coke La Rock, Grandmaster Caz, and Melle Mel extended the African American oral tradition (including field hollers, ring shouts, spirituals, the blues, sermons, toasts, and playing the dozens) into the twenty-first century with their rap lyrics. Generally speaking, the strongest, most critically acclaimed rappers and MCs (both past and present) have been of African American origin with Rakim, Jay-Z, Nas, Lupe Fiasco, Lauryn Hill, Black Thought, Tupac Shakur, and more recently, Kendrick Lamar topping the list. This is not to exclude their West Indian counterparts, chief among them—The Notorious B.I.G.—whose Jamaican American heritage informed his milky and melodic delivery. One of the most noted pioneers of graffiti art in Hip-Hop culture was a young Greek-American named Demetrius. His graf tag, "Taki 183," is credited as one of the first monikers to go "all city" (i.e., to be recognized in all five boroughs of New York City) via its ubiquitous presence on subway trains of various neighborhoods. Many graffiti pioneers were of Latin American descent, such as the extraordinary Lady Pink, who braved the same dangers and pitfalls of graffiti writing as her male counterparts. Clearly, graf art is another element of Hip-Hop culture in which African American ethnicity is not an essential prerequisite to artistic or commercial success.

It is a racially essentialist conclusion to assert that any of the aforementioned elements of Hip Hop are dominated by any particular ethnic group. Yet each element, through its pioneers and most significant contributors, often suggests a particular ethnicity's penchant for a given artistic expression. Therefore, it may be more appropriate to conclude that young people of European descent have (at least in America and Europe) been more prominent in graffiti artistry than in MC-ing or rapping. Likewise, Latin American acrobats have been more prominent in breaking and b-boying than in MC-ing or rapping. DJs tend to run the ethnic gamut, though various DJs of Asian ethnicity dominated international competitions during the early twenty-first century. Ultimately, these racial assignments and categorizations deconstruct and undermine the inclusive spirit of Hip-Hop culture. The cultural affinities for one element of Hip Hop or another are byproducts of artistic socialization more than any one group's inherent capacity to excel in a particular element of the culture.

In each attempt that I have made or that I continue to make to define Hip-Hop culture—either through the eras/moments of the culture or through the elements, or through its historical connections, or through any number of lenses: founding figures, race, class, etc.—I continue to discover new ways of conceptualizing what all Hip-Hop culture has become over the course of its relatively brief history. This process of discovery—what I define as one of the educational elements of the culture itself—continues to inspire the artistic production within the culture and I believe it will also continue to inspire scholars, teachers, and educators to return to Hip-Hop culture as both an important subject matter for academic inquiry and a critical lens through which we can challenge ourselves and our students to wrestle with the world in which we live.

Becoming and Being a Hip-Hop Scholar

I

I grew up in Newark, New Jersey, and I was born in 1971. I can remember sitting on the steps in my house and hearing "Rapper's Delight" for the first time on the radio in 1979.[1] If you listen to "Rapper's Delight" now, it may sound dated and parochial compared to contemporary rap music, but sitting on my steps in 1979 and hearing "Rapper's Delight" on the radio for the first time was probably my earliest watershed moment with Hip-Hop culture. I was, for the first time, hearing the voice of my generation, what Bakari Kitwana has dubbed the Hip-Hop Generation—those folks born between 1964 and 1985 who consider themselves cultural constituents of Hip Hop; those folks who mark their watershed cultural moments in life vis-à-vis a series of postcivil rights (or what Mark Anthony Neal refers to as Post-Soul) moments, including the rise of neoliberalism, deindustrialization, globalization, and the privatization of the prison system. In the context of my life, the vocals of "Rappers Delight" were instantly compelling to me—in form more than in content. These were young Black men from inner-city America speaking on a record. And that fact was almost enough to pull me fully into the culture. Looking back, I cannot fully convey all of the ways that "Rapper's Delight" resonated with me. It was not the content that captivated me. In fact, the content itself was not groundbreaking; it was the kind of materialistic fair so often associated with the braggadocio at the heart of most rap music. What moved me was *how* they were speaking and, more importantly, *how* it transformed my consciousness in that particular moment. In hindsight, I believe that I had an early affinity for verbal virtuosity and (socio)linguistic wordplay, an affinity that ultimately made for a compelling intellectual relationship with rap music and Hip-Hop culture. In the extended version of the song, Wonder Mike narrates a story of having to eat at a friend's house where the food "just ain't no good." Just before he begins this story—of having to try multiple ways of politely not eating his friend's food, ultimately feeling nauseous and having to take some medicine for an upset stomach—he raps a series of (almost) oxymoronic similes. Paraphrased examples of these lines—like beer that is sweet, or like a millionaire who has no money or *like* a rainy day that is not wet—reveal that they follow no logical narrative structure and in some ways confounded my young mind about the cohesiveness of rap lyrical content. I would imagine it was a listless list of similes like this one in "Rapper's Delight" that made many of the older generation of the time think of rap music as lyrically illiterate gibberish. But the series of (almost) oxymoronic similes in the extended version of "Rapper's Delight" said something else to me. It spoke to the Sugar Hill Gang's willingness to deconstruct the formal properties of popular music. Like a live or recorded James Brown session—the rappers in "Rapper's Delight" were willing to include warm-ups and recognizably improvisational moments on the record itself. The string of similes was a rap warm-up, it presaged the more formal narrative voice that detailed the story about trying not to eat the terrible food at a friend's house. Maybe referring to these simile-laden lines as a "warm-up" is not the most accurate way to assess them, but they communicated the improvisational feel that we more commonly associated with the aesthetics of freestyle ciphers in Hip Hop. Like many other lines in "Rapper's Delight" these lines dissolve into onomatopoeic allusions to banging beats and boogie-ing bodies. Ironically, these are the more timeless aspects of "Rapper's Delight." So many lyrics of the song are encapsulated in the materialism of that moment—a common penchant for bragging about cars, jewelry, clothes, etc., that the "hip hop, bang-bang, boogie, and rhythm of the beat" lyrics are both the most memorable and the most meaningful aspects of the song mostly because they invite listeners—even now—to think/experience beyond the material conditions of that historic moment and the song itself.

Growing up in Newark meant that I was predisposed to the kind of globalized postindustrial environments that Hip-Hop culture continues to represent through music, lyrics, and videos. Well before I ever drank my first beer, the Pabst Blue Ribbon factory (which was located on South Orange

Avenue in the heart of Newark, NJ) was both a historical landmark of pride and a symbol of Newark's bygone industrial urban history. I carried a burgeoning understanding of the relationship between rap music and the socio/economic/ cultural contexts of those early moments of the old school era with me throughout my youth. From fifth through eighth grade and through my Mom's sheer determination, I was admitted to Newark Boys Chorus School in the early 1980s. From my perspective, my entire education was priceless: one because my family could not afford it, but also because it efficiently traveled me up and down the East Coast and around the world—even before I went to college. Coming to terms with the ways in which (as Chuck D has oft been quoted as stating) rap music reports on the environments in which rappers/rap poets (emerge as points of consciousness), I realized early on that through the forms of rap music we might all see the underside of (at that time) postindustrial urban communities critically wrestling with the consequences of unchecked neoliberal policies. Fast forward through fifteen years of both my development and Hip-Hop culture's to when/where I found myself at Duke University as Hip Hop was on the cusp of becoming the most popular music in the world. When I was preparing to graduate from college, I was in deep contemplation about my career; I wanted to be a professor. I was still fascinated by language, and more specifically, I have always been intrigued by how Black people speak. Eventually, and for me—remarkably, I was able to develop this abiding interest in Black speech and Hip-Hop culture into a professional career. I have been teaching Hip-Hop courses at the collegiate level since 1997. That makes me one of the earlier professors to teach about Hip-Hop culture at the collegiate level, and I certainly wear that badge honorably.

The very first Hip-Hop course that I taught was at the University of Pennsylvania in the spring of 1997. The course was called "Writing in and about Hip Hop Culture." Imagine a first-year writing course, themed around Hip Hop, with all of a traditional composition course's attention to rhetoric, argument, concision, and accuracy. That was my first Hip-Hop course. Interestingly the academic year of 1996–1997 spring's semester fell about four months after Pac was murdered, about two months before Biggie was murdered, and in the midst of the Ebonics controversy. There was a firestorm of criticism and debate in response to the controversy, plagued by the public's sense that teachers were teaching Black kids how to speak Ebonics in the classroom. This misunderstanding was exacerbated by the media's coverage of the Oakland School Board's decision to allow teachers to pedagogically account for students who spoke African American English (AAE), especially vernacular variants of AAE. The decision itself is part of a long history of the tensions between Black speech and Black literacy in a public education system that aggressively polices adherence to Standard American English (SAE) in all of its curricula. Members of the Oakland School Board were less interested in teaching students how to speak Ebonics and more invested in creating opportunities for teachers to assess and educate AAE speakers without tracking them in remedial courses. Despite how the media depicted it to us, what was really happening is that they were trying to raise awareness among teachers to not track students of color based specifically on speaking a certain dialect.[2]

Those three events: the murder of Pac, the impending murder of B.I.G., and the Ebonics controversy framed the earliest developments of my own experiences with Hip-Hop pedagogy. From that course forward, I insisted that my classes always find connections to current events and social justice issues sometimes just beyond the confines of the classroom. I eventually taught Hip-Hop lessons, units and courses at the high school level, and in a variety of institutions within the Prison Industrial Complex. So, although I have been fortunate to teach at elite institutions of higher education I also try to make sure that the work that I am doing with Hip-Hop culture resonates in and with the community. This particular academic journey may not be a followable model, considering that I came into this field from the inner city, and I have had the privilege of teaching in the midst of certain transformational moments. For these reasons I am compelled to insure that my work reaches as many different places and people as possible.

In my course work and in much of the related work that I conduct within the community, I chronicle the history of Hip Hop as a way of challenging the constituents of the culture, to consciously and comprehensively connect to its historical origins. Hip-Hop culture can inspire and empower the youth in many different communities to find their voices and to develop an engaging stake in their own education. It is worth noting here that I am not convinced in this particular moment that Hip-Hop culture is synonymous with youth culture. What I am convinced of, however, is that if we understand Hip-Hop culture, we can intellectually and culturally connect to the ways in which youth culture operates in the present moment.

Hip Hop is probably the most dominant form of youth culture that we have witnessed in the late twentieth century. In "The Evolution of Popular Music: 1960-2010," a brilliant 2015 study conducted by Matthias Mauch et al., all of the anecdotes about the popularity and the pervasiveness of rap music have been realized as scientific data. What was once (or what has been) an anecdote has been transformed from an anecdotal hypothesis into a quantified theorem: rap music is the most dominant, popular form of music in America over the last fifty years. In employing "dominant" here, I do not mean colonial dominance, although there is definitely some of that present. I also do not mean gender dominance or capitalist dominance—although aspects of both are manifested by and through the culture of Hip Hop. The most accurate way to articulate the findings in the "Evolution of Pop Music" study is to realize that Hip Hop is ubiquitous. Most folks who "hear" rap music or only "see" Hip-Hop culture via mainstream media outlets probably define Hip-Hop culture by what is promoted on popular television networks like MTV or BET or radio stations owned by Clear Channel or Radio One. In educational settings—whether those are in classrooms or in prison "rec rooms"—the task for Hip-Hop scholars/educators is to work with students to develop their knowledge of the culture, especially their sense of the historical narratives that might reframe their experiences with rap music. Hip Hop has a story.

The story of Hip Hop begins in the late 1960s, when Clive Campbell and his family moved to the South Bronx from Kingston, Jamaica. One thing that we should know about Clive Campbell—particularly for those unfamiliar with the history detailed in Chapter 1—is that his musical tastes were shaped by both Bob Marley (who lived very close to where he lived in Kingston) and James Brown (who was one of his favorite artists). A certain degree of critical listening is required to comprehend the percussive genius of James Brown's production or the lyrical wizardry of your favorite Bob Marley tune and the same goes for Hip-Hop music. Soul and Reggae music are among the various cultural and musical inputs for Hip Hop and these musical and cultural influences were present at the beginning of the story. Not only are most young folks disconnected from the *narrative* of origins that pertain to Hip Hop, but young people are also disconnected from the *history* of Hip Hop. Clive Campbell, also known as DJ Kool Herc, moved to the South Bronx at a moment when New York was becoming a much more diverse community, but it was (and in some areas continues to be) a community suffering from poor urban planning and structural erosion. As Professor Imani Perry (2004) has astutely pointed out, we cannot, however, define Hip Hop solely through the prism of any deficiency model. We need to instead define Hip Hop more by the ingenuity of young people like Kool Herc.

DJ Kool Herc hosted the first Hip-Hop jam in 1973 in a recreation room of the Sedgwick Housing Projects. He threw this party for his sister, Cindy Campbell. And as noted previously, the first Hip-Hop jam was a back-to-school party. This initial jam marked a starting point for Hip-Hop culture's interface with the world of knowledge and education. Moreover, the tangible immediacy of the old school era established a sense of community among Hip Hop's most loyal constituents. Of course, you had to be part of the community to partake in these communal celebrations. But the immediacy of the only way to experience Hip-Hop culture fostered an integrated, antiviolent community that was focused on knowledge—primarily with respect to the arts. Knowledge was a central theme for Hip-Hop culture, especially in the old school moment. To not understand these origins of Hip-Hop culture and teach them to young people who consider themselves constituents of the culture is detrimental for young people who think that Hip Hop is one of the defining forms of their own cultural moment. Likewise, for educators and community members not to (know and) teach this history is equally disadvantageous, because we are not harnessing the potential of one of our greatest resources in terms of interacting with young people.

There are other eras of Hip-Hop culture often added to the discourses on the history. Following the old school era of Hip Hop is the golden age (the soundtrack of my formative years). The golden age references a particular moment in Hip-Hop culture—specifically the late 1980s and early 1990s—just as the culture began to shift, a shift signaled by the juxtaposition of two of the most popular groups in Hip Hop: Public Enemy and N.W.A. Listening to the first N.W.A. record, *Straight Outta Compton*, one can distinctly hear Public Enemy's influence. In fact, you can actually see some facets of PE's political themes reflected in some of their most popular music videos. In the second N.W.A. record (*Niggaz4Life*), it becomes apparent that popular Hip Hop is shifting into gangster rap. For better or worse, this transition reflected a change in the aesthetics of the music—especially in terms of the content. The substance of that content changed radically and ushered in Hip Hop's most popular moment—the platinum era. In the late 1990s, rap music becomes the most pervasive and popular form of music—selling at unprecedented and unparalleled rates. This is after the Biggie and Tupac/East-Coast-West-Coast era that garnered global media attention. Emphasis on the old school era is essential because that knowledge challenges students to overcome some of the discontinuity between Hip Hop and young people with respect to youth culture.

As a corollary to this, Hip Hop comes of age during a time when globalization and the information age are aggressively appropriating the culture. For this reason, I am always hesitant to be dismissive of emergent technologies, social media platforms, and popular styles of rap music—take trap music, for example. Many professors encourage students to use social media in conjunction with course assignments and class discussions. Initially, educators were skeptical of social media, but my students have produced critical discourses on these platforms, at least in part because these are the modes of communication with which they are most familiar and most frequently interacting with each other. At the time of this writing, Snapchat is an immensely popular social media platform for University students. It's icon, "Ghostface Chillah" aptly nicknamed after Wu-Tang Clan's enigmatic rhyme wizard, Ghostface Killah. Hip-Hop culture continues to be intimately connected to technology and technological advances. Hip Hop–based courses can harness that energy. Globalization, technology, and Hip Hop converge in very compelling and sophisticated ways, and it would benefit scholars and educators to be receptive to that intersecting relationship.

II

Over the course of many years teaching, serving and volunteering in the community, through churches, prisons, and high schools, I have not been experiencing, learning, and writing about Hip-Hop culture in isolation.

Many of the scholars mentioned, quoted, cited, and otherwise referenced throughout *Hip-Hop Headphones* have powerfully shaped and informed my journey as a scholar. For example, in *Book of Rhymes*, Adam Bradley crafted multiple approaches for how to evaluate the poetics of the lyrics of rap music. The debates about the poetics of rap music shape the discourses that constituents of the culture consider to be among the most important parts of the conversation within Hip-Hop scholarship, journalism, and culture. The following rubric is a combination of aspects of the rubrics authored by several scholars, including Tricia Rose and Adam Bradley, as well as many of my own students, encountered along the way, who continue to shape and inform my sense of how we do this—this being how we talk about what we listen to. This is how we posit ourselves as critical listeners in Hip-Hop culture; we figure out the assessment tools that will best afford us those critical opportunities to wrestle greatness from the convoluted conversations about who is your favorite rapper. Fundamentally, what follows is a rubric for appreciating, evaluating, and understanding the impact and importance of rappers and/or MCs. A rapper is someone who spits rhymes (at least sometimes), writes rhymes, and releases records. If a rapper finds or is seeking mainstream access and success, then usually he/she is more invested in the industry and in the music business than they are in the craft. Conversely, an MC is an artist who possesses the same qualifications as a rapper, but is invested in both the industry and the craft of rapping itself. That is to say, they are invested in the development of the artistic and aesthetic aspects of rhyming over beats. This is an implicit distinction that many journalists, scholars, and students make when engaging the common discourse around "who's you're favorite rapper". At the same time, the ritualistic nature of these discourses challenges all constituents of Hip-Hop culture to formulate categorical rubrics for assessing the listening experiences with individual artists and albums. The rubric below is at least one approach toward establishing the critical listening ethos that informs Hip-Hop scholarship as well as the broader, more general Hip-Hop discourses related to lyrical/verbal skills in rap.

- **Category 1**—Lyrical Flow and Content. The category of lyrical flow and content concerns itself with aesthetics related to tone, articulation, word choice, and vocabulary. Lyrical flow also involves the manipulation of the poetics of language. It encompasses all of the formal poetics of language, including metaphors and similes. It also considers how complex the formal aspects of Hip-Hop music might be—taking into account not simply the meaning of a particular song, but rather, what linguistic properties are present in that song. Lyrical content focuses on what rappers/MCs are saying. Content is an important aspect of this category because its receptivity is contingent upon so many factors—age, space, and place, just to name a few. Content that is compelling and relevant to someone born in 1971 in Newark, New Jersey, is probably not the same content that may be compelling or relevant to someone born in 1991 in rural Pennsylvania.

- **Category 2**—The Dual Rhythmic Relationship (DRR). The second category is what Bradley refers to as the DRR. It is, in the simplest sense, how an MC interacts with a particular beat. The beat can assume many forms, but DRR is always present. It also concerns how the vocalists use their voices as instruments and how they use their voices percussively. Consider unusually strong staccato rappers like Busta Rhymes, as exhibiting sophisticated examples of the DRR. There is the rhythm of the beat itself and then there is the complementary rhythm of the vocalist. Essentially, the DRR is trying to capture how those varying aspects/components coalesce to create a spectacular sound.

- **Category 3**—Artistic Persona. In short, this is the artist's name, presentation, and how they represent themselves in public. Other tangentially related factors—such as fashion sense or appearances in related media like film or television—might also be included here, but for the sake of conciseness, name and presentation can suffice.

- **Category 4**—Historical Knowledge and Respect. For many old-school Hip-Hop heads and older Hip-Hop scholars, a premium is placed on this category. To what extent do Hip-Hop artists explicitly respect the artists that have preceded them both within Hip-Hop culture and beyond? And to what extent does a Hip-Hop artist's respect for Black musical forms manifest itself in the music that they make (or the ways in which they make it)? We are talking about rappers and MCs here; however, in general, if we are having a comprehensive conversation about Hip Hop, the full culture can be under consideration. I am always interested in the ways that new artists pay homage to history and their musical predecessors or how they acknowledge them artistically.

- **Category 5**—Space and Place. This concerns where a particular artist is from and how successfully they represent that place (and those roots). It also relates to where they are presently and how they dominate any particular moment of their career in the rap music industry.

This rubric is the product of years of teaching and interacting with young people about these artistic virtues, in addition to directly talking to artists as well as reading and incorporating relevant scholarship on Hip Hop. It is a fairly clear-cut, comprehensive rubric through which we can discuss any MC. We can plug any MC into this rubric, and using scales of 1–10 begin to crunch the numbers, and figure out who is a strong artist according to the aforementioned attributes. I teach a course called "Critical Approaches to Hip Hop Culture" (syllabus available in the appendix). It is usually a seminar that meets once a week and tends to be a popular course among students, largely because some of our class discussions center on current events, contemporary sociocultural contexts and emerging rap artists. Both high school students and college undergraduates seldom exude more excitement in classroom discussion than when they feel it is their duty to educate their classmates (and often the professor/instructor) about an artist that they feel is either unknown or underappreciated. It is in this pedagogical context that the rubric for determining certain aspects of a rappers/MC's artistry becomes most useful. It transforms arbitrary flat discussions about "favorites" and "bests" into more comprehensive conversations about aesthetics, location, and mastery of/in performance.[3]

III

For a variety of reasons, rapper, Nicki Minaj has been one of the artists that students tend to want to discuss in Hip Hop–related courses over the last several years. Some of this attention is due to her general popularity, but some of the attention derives from students' sense that Nikki Minaj is talented lyrically but as a popular artist, she has attained her success through projections of an over-sexualized Black female subjectivity. Critically engaging students on popular culture often requires teachers to discuss artists (and issues) that may not be of personal/professional interest to them but can likely be used as portals to topics/issues of contemporary significance. I do not consider myself to be a fan of Nicki Minaj but the paucity of women in the rap music industry warrants discussions (and courses) of its own.[4] Hip-Hop scholars should feel compelled to pay close attention to women rappers who emerge in such a male-dominated industry—if only for the sake of some semblance of gender balance in artists covered in Hip-Hop curricula. At the behest (mostly students) of those who solicited my opinion on Nicki Minaj, I have followed her career and listened to some of her music. For lyrical flow and content, I rate Nicki Minaj at about an eight. Be mindful that this rating is much more for flow than it is for content. For me, her content is not necessarily that substantive, although many students can and have debated this point—questioning the extent to which her content is socially relevant or not. Her flow, that is, her tone, delivery, and the formal aspects of what she does poetically, is exceptional. List a short series of poetic terms (like metaphor, simile, assonance, consonance, and rhyme scheme), listen to her music, and check off each time she deploys a specific poetic feature. Check off every time she uses an internal rhyme scheme. Her manipulation of these poetic devices is impressive. If you do the same exercise for other popular rappers—Nicki's male counterparts—you will find that many of them are not engaging those poetic forms to the same extent.

Regarding the content of Nicki Minaj's lyrics, many people (students included) comment that "it is sexually explicit." In *Pimps Up, Ho's Down: Hip Hop's Hold on Young Black Women*, Tracey Sharpley-Whiting explores the complicated interface between Black women, Hip-Hop music, and sexuality.[5] Sharpley-Whiting's analysis provides some context to better understand how Nicki Minaj positions her artistic persona in terms of her content and delivery. For Whiting, there are a few defining criterion for the ways in which Hip Hop has a hold on Black women. The most pervasive and prevailing are the twin myths that have dominated the representation of Black women in the American public sphere since the institution of slavery. The twin myths to which Sharpley-Whiting refers are hypersexuality and accessibility. Since the institution of slavery, Black women have been stereotyped as hypersexual and accessible. Together these twin mythologies form a debilitating combination in terms of the imagery of women in the public sphere and the abject objectification to which Black women are all too often subjected in reality.

Sharpley-Whiting argues that Hip Hop continues in, and consciously perpetuates, that tradition. Most listeners of popular rap music believe that Nicki Minaj fits that stereotype well. Through her lyrics, she seemingly promotes the twin myths that Black women are hypersexual and accessible. Yet, if you listen critically, one could debate the accessibility claim, because although she may be hypersexual, through the lyrics of her music, Nicki Minaj does not overtly position herself as someone that is easily accessible. The term "hypersexual" might also be relative here depending on social conventions and the extent to which we allow for artistic personas created by rappers to stand in for the actual sexual behaviors of the artists themselves. While it may seem like her lyrical content echoes the familiar, negative discourses that we see and hear in reference to Black women, Nicki Minaj suggests in interviews and through her music that she is deploying sexuality as a tool for power and sometimes for control over her own body and her sexuality. Even if you consider her early career alter ego, Nicki Lewinsky—which is a specific reference to Monica Lewinksy and her sexual interaction with former President Bill Clinton—she is signifying on sexual politics and power in a somewhat nuanced way. The fact that Nicki Minaj chooses to reference the Lewinsky-Clinton event does not simply mean that she is endorsing Monica Lewinksy as much as she is highlighting the very fact that sexual acts or transgressions and political power often intersect. This is why those twin myths are important for students to understand and contextualize in both the historical and contemporary moment. There is a marked difference, for example, between Nelly's "Tip Drill"[6] video and what Nicki Minaj is doing in a song like "Cuchi Shop."[7]

The considerable difference between "Tip Drill" (which is the deliberate fragmentation, exploitation, and display of Black women's bodies for the male gaze) and "Cuchi Shop," where Nicki Minaj personifies a madam and posits the sex trade as a metaphor for her offering as a rapper in the music industry, pushes discussions of sexuality in Hip Hop through deeply contested, problematic terrain. Both songs celebrate sexual exploitation, but they operate from oppositional perspectives. This might just be a choice between the lesser of two evils here; I am not interested in promoting Nicki Minaj's "Cuchi Shop" any more than I am in Nelly's "Tip Drill." Yet, there are important distinctions to be made. In "Tip Drill," the narrative is one that very much harkens back to the institution of slavery itself. The infamous "credit card swipe" crossed a line for many of Nelly's fans—as evidenced by the backlash he received from the women of Spellman College. Nelly's rap career never quite recovered from the problems that the "Tip Drill" video presented for him. There is no official video for "Cuchi Shop." But again, "Cuchi Shop" is a woman's narrative, and there is a principal difference between the male gaze versus a woman possessing and/or exploiting her own body. These are different experiences and different narratives. Students must be challenged to draw critical lines of distinction if we are to take the project of Hip-Hop studies seriously. There is a subtle difference between a man exploiting a woman's body (or anyone else exploiting a woman's body) and a woman having agency in the exploitation of her own body. We may not all necessarily agree with that, but critical listeners have to draw that distinction, and I think "Cuchi Shop" represents some of the more difficult discourses that a formal rubric of analysis can produce. The persona that Nicki Minaj assumes in the lyrics of "Cuchi Shop" may be that of a madam, or as someone who is pimping or procuring money for the sexual acts of women, but it is intended *for* women and functions metaphorically in certain lyrics/verses. The fundamental difference here is that there is no explicit male gaze at work. It is narrated solely from the perspective of a woman. This generates a very different narrative than a man smacking a woman's behind or sliding a credit card through a woman's buttocks. In fact, in some ways, those are dichotomous narratives. Nelly swiping a credit card through a woman's buttocks, and Nicki Minaj playing the persona of a madam are contrasting narratives. The twin myths component does not apply to Nicki directly, but we have to be critically attuned to the texts and contexts in order to recognize that.

For Sharpley-Whiting, there is a compelling correlation between what we call sexual tourism and Hip-Hop culture. Sexual tourism is defined by the ways in which people (mostly men) travel to various countries and access local marketplaces (legal and illegal) for transactional sex. While human trafficking has been in existence for centuries, the challenges of human trafficking in the twenty-first century has a complex relationship with sexual tourism, and it most assuredly has been abetted by the visual imagery present in rap music videos that depict exotic-looking women as objects and props. Sexist sexual imagery in music videos shapes and drives the sexual tourism industry if only as advertisements. Within the sexual tourism industry, there is a preference for what Sharpley-Whiting refers to as ethnically ambiguous women. For ready reference, watch Snoop Dogg's video "Beautiful," which is shot in Brazil, and features women that are for the most part ethnically ambiguous.[8] Nicki Minaj's artistic persona is one that feeds into this sexual tourism complex. She often refers to having a multiethnic background. In fact, if you look at her visual presentation, what she does in her music videos, she is almost always representing something "other." She always attempts to position herself ethnically as something distinct from (but not completely unrelated to) what we associate with an African American ethnic identity. What Nicki Minaj does in her music—particularly, the production of her artistic persona—distinguishes her from some of her predecessors who might be better artists, but will not achieve the same kind of popularity that she has in this current moment.

Regarding the DRR, Nicki Minaj is well above average (an eight on the rudimentary scaled rubric at work here). In terms of the ways that she formally interacts with the beats—that is, the percussive elements of her musical production, she has demonstrated great skill. Mind you (again), this is a score separate from any analysis of what she is saying. This is simply about the rhythm of her voice, and how her voice interacts with the rhythm of a track. For all of those elements collectively, and there are many good examples of that for her, she earns an eight in the DRR category. Consider some of her more popular tunes, "Beez in the Trap" or "Anaconda," for example, to hear where the rhythmic virtuosity of her vocals is in full effect. For artistic persona, Nicki Minaj rates (again) in the above average, eight range because she is invested in presenting new and different artistic personas with every album and often from one single to the next on particular albums. In terms of her sense of historical knowledge and respect,

Nicki Minaj slipped on the scale, earning only a six from me. While she is aware of the many successful women that have come before her, I am not sure if she publicly or artistically appreciates the extent to which their styles have informed her own. I know she gives props to Missy Elliot, because Missy is an undeniable influence in terms of the way she sings and transforms herself for a wide range of music video productions. It is less clear if Nicki Minaj is in a place right now (as a pop artist) where she can admit the extent to which Lil' Kim has also influenced her style. Or, perhaps it is more beneficial for Minaj to be at odds with her than it is for her to give due credit. But certainly, Lil' Kim has influenced her style much more than Foxy, Eve, Trina, or any of the other female artists that she has cited in her songs.[9]

For critical listeners, Nicki Minaj initially sounded like a Lil' Kim knockoff. Much of this was about the ways that Minaj's recorded vocals, particularly on her popular mixtape releases, mimicked the tones and tenor of some of Lil' Kim's most popular singles. But the comparisons between Lil' Kim and Nicki Minaj revolve around the extent to which each artist exploited an overt sexuality—both in lyrics and in visuals associated with album covers, promotional materials, and music videos—throughout their careers as rap artists. Moreover, Lil' Kim's willingness to challenge her male counterparts on the record (so to speak) is yet another way that listeners might compare and contrast two of the most popular and successful women MCs in the platinum era of Hip Hop and beyond. The short-lived tension (or beef) between Lil' Kim and Nicki Minaj was fleetingly popular in 2014 but ultimately unsustainable in the way that male rap battles become compelling narratives for media, Hip-Hop fans, and sometimes the artists themselves.[10] Kim simply was past her prime—which for women in Hip Hop can be limited to a few singles and/or a single album in some cases. The limited opportunities for women rappers is one consequence of the male-dominated nature of the music business, the male-centric sensibilities of Hip-Hop culture itself, and the limitations of sexualized narratives produced in the absence of more diverse means of developing artistic personas for women. All of these issues plagued Lil' Kim's career. And yet another comparison bares mention here as well. Both Lil' Kim and Nicki Minaj have cosmetically altered their bodies. While the post-op responses to their sexual/physical presence has been drastically different—few negative comments directed at Minaj and occasionally exaggerated horror at Kim's transformation—the fact that two leading female rappers with some overlap in the construction of their sound and artistic personas both underwent fairly public cosmetic surgeries to better adjust their bodies to further their careers as popular artists is a powerful reminder of what is at stake for women in Hip-Hop culture.

Reading Joan Morgan, Tracy Sharpley-Whiting, or other contemporary feminists reveals an acknowledgment and at times a celebration of a sex-positive political subjectivity that can be grounded within the frameworks of Hip-Hop culture. Morgan's brilliant revision of a famous Malcolm X quote into the title of her groundbreaking tract on Hip-Hop feminism points to the critical consequences of allowing patriarchy—particularly in the Black community and especially within Hip-Hop culture—to dictate the full set of possibilities for the expression of women's sexuality. *When Chickenheads Come Home to Roost*, then is a powerful rejoinder to both the early waves of feminism as well as to the male-centric and misogynistic attributes of Hip-Hop culture. Morgan requires a feminism that "fucks with the grays," challenging the Hip-Hop generation to craft ideologies and practices within feminism that are capable of grasping the complexities (in terms of sexuality and equality) of our contemporary moment.[11] Sharpley-Whiting's work builds on Morgan's, expanding the scholarly discourses on women's subjectivity in Hip-Hop culture and affording scholars (like me) multiple opportunities to make important womanist interventions into the ultra-masculinist discourses of mainstream Hip-Hop culture.

Joan Morgan and Tracey Sharpley-Whiting are a part of a now rich tradition of Black women Hip-Hop scholars (or Black women who have chosen to dedicate significant academic time to researching and writing about Hip-Hop culture), including Tricia Rose, Cheryl Keyes, Imani Perry, Gwen Pough, Marcyliena Morgan, and Monica Miller, among others. My development as a scholar of Hip-Hop culture is simply not possible without the powerful contributions of the aforementioned scholars. Rose's *Black Noise* created academic space and disciplinary placement for my work; Dr. Marcyliena Morgan hired me to assist her and others in her early work to develop the Harvard Hip Hop Archive—later she served on my dissertation committee.

Imani Perry's *Prophets of the Hood* was an empowering call to more critically engage Hip-Hop music and culture with the tools of literary studies; Joan Morgan and Tracey Sharpley-Whiting challenge us to rethink and recast the hypermasculinity so prevalent in Hip-Hop culture (as well as in Hip-Hop journalism and scholarship); more recently Monica Miller has joined me as a colleague at Lehigh University. Professor Miller's work in *Religion in Hip Hop* has deeply informed and influenced scholars' understanding of the role that religion and spirituality must continue to play in our work on a pop cultural form that often seems ascetically secular. These scholars have and continue to make the most important and the most impactful interventions into the academic discourses on Hip-Hop culture. Their work, for me, models our charge as scholars—especially in terms of how we shape and inform what our students are listening to at any given point in the Hip-Hop cultural timeline. In short, scholars of Hip-Hop culture must leverage the popularity of the music (and other forms of the culture) to make strategic interventions into the developing intellectual lives of the students with whom we have the privilege of interacting and engaging. Thus, when students want to discuss Lil' Kim, Nicki Minaj, and/or Iggy Azalea, a moment presents itself for educators to intervene with additional readings and suggested listening.

These are the moments that matter most—especially to scholars who teach courses related to contemporary music: the moments when an academic pivots from thin popular examples toward thicker more populous examples of the musical form or genre in question. This is a move that I often relish making, especially when students are sincerely interested in my opinions of the music to which they are listening.[12] When students want to talk about popular artists like Nicki Minaj, I first explain to them the rich, if brief, history of women scholars/academics who have shaped, informed and (in effect) authored the field(s) of Hip-Hop studies. All of the Hip-Hop courses that I have taught, as well as those that I have visited or in which I have delivered lectures, have featured one or more academic monographs on Hip-Hop culture authored by women of color. After providing this academic context, I then point my students to some more substantive aesthetically enhanced alternative to their popular obsession. And in many cases/classes (recently) the alternative to whom I point has been Rapsody. Rapsody (ne Marlanna Evans) hails from

North Carolina and is currently signed to Jamla Records—an independent label founded and aptly helmed by Grammy Award–winning producer 9th Wonder. Since about 2009, Rapsody has steadily released mixtapes, EPs, over a dozen well-produced music videos and a full-length album in 2012 entitled *The Idea of Beautiful*. Considering the fact that she only signed on with 9th Wonder's label/imprint in 2008, Rapsody has produced a rich and prolific body of work. Her slogan, "culture over everything," a statement that she regularly makes both on record and off, resonates at the heart of the collective body of Hip-Hop "heads." It inspires the sincerest constituents of the culture for whom the notion that culture dominates all underscores Hip Hop's presence and activity in their lives. "Culture over everything" asserts a value proposition with respect to the history and the various elements of Hip Hop. For Rapsody, Hip Hop's originating ethos as a platform for the voiceless, socially invisible, youth of inner-city America must be embraced in Hip Hop's contemporary era. The culture and the history of Hip Hop are more valuable than the music's fleeting mainstream popularity and/or the economic vitality of the entertainment industries that exploit the culture. Choosing the social justice ethos associated with the elements and eras of Hip Hop—over the materialistic pursuits in the music and entertainment industries—is a central feature of Rapsody's rap music offering. Themes related to her penchant for wrestling with substantive issues—Black aesthetic/beauty ideals, Black nationalism, social justice in the era of the Black Lives Matter movement—are often weighed and weighted in her music over and against more shallow popular themes in contemporary rap music. Rapsody is a throwback to a feminist future of Hip Hop; she embodies—through gestures and the overall style of her delivery—a classic lyrical no-frills presentation. And she never trades on the hypersexual or overtly explicit projection of pop sexuality so often depicted via the artistic personas of any number of women Hip-Hop artists like Lil' Kim, Foxy Brown, Trina, Nicki Minaj, and Iggy Azalea.

Rapsody concedes the possibility that her underwhelming popularity within mainstream Hip Hop stems from her desire to write and record songs that embrace the elemental ethos of Hip-Hop culture and her resistance to the popular assumption that women in Hip Hop must promote explicitly sexualized versions of themselves in order to be successful in the entertainment industries. Ultimately, she is comfortable (and successful) with this decision. And in many ways, by dispensing with the trappings of the popular antics associated with explicitly sexualized artistic personas, Rapsody transcends established categories for women in Hip Hop beyond the golden age era of the culture. She projects a mutable subjectivity throughout her body of music. She is lyrically compelling in "Drama" pointing to Billie Holiday's blues and actually claiming "I sing your blues." In the video for "Betty Shabazz," she surrounds herself with Black women wearing the hijab—a powerful visual rejoinder to our nation's Islamaphobia. When Rapsody alludes to Lauryn Hill, Ruby Dee, or Maya Angelou, when she references her conversations with MC Lyte, she instantiates herself within the lyrically discursive pantheon of the greatest voices of both Black culture and Hip-Hop culture. Throughout her artistry, Rapsody is clear in her lyrics about her influences—Nas, Lauryn Hill, and Jay-Z, among others. And these are not just name-drops. You can hear the influences of Nas, Lauryn Hill, Jay-Z, and others in her lyrical styles, but Rapsody is also an absolutely unique artist unto herself.

On 2015's *Beauty and the Beast* album/EP, Rapsody crystallizes the themes and allusions that inform her artistic production. The project's title refers to Rapsody's ongoing deconstruction of the white supremacist and patriarchal manipulation of beauty ideals for women, especially for women of color, especially for Black women. The "beast" refers to Rapsody's unbridled, unmitigated lyrical talent and her unabashed embrace of "black aesthetics" in the sense that Evie Shockley eloquently defines them in *Renegade Poetics*. "The expanded, descriptive conception of black aesthetics … might be understood accordingly as referring to a mode of writing adopted by African American poets in their efforts to work within, around, or against the constraint of being read and heard as 'black.'"[13] For Shockley, "renegade poetics" synthesize notions of revolutionary aesthetics, oppositional poetics, and deliberately complicated multifaceted conceptualizations of Black aesthetics. Rapsody would be considered a renegade within the popular world of Hip Hop simply because she is a woman who raps about Black aesthetically informed beauty ideals, social justice issues and the foundational elements and experiences of Hip-Hop culture as opposed to the more common popular narratives of sexual exploits and material obsession. But in order for her to meet or measure up to Shockley's descriptions of renegade poetics, Rapsody's poetics must enact formal innovations. And here (in the realm of formal poetic innovations in rap music) Rapsody does not disappoint. Note well here that Rapsody's formal poetic styles might warrant a chapter or book of their own. One of her more intriguing innovations is her regular deployment of slant rhyme—also referred to as half rhyme or imperfect rhyme. Slant rhyme is defined as "a rhyme that is not true. It may be deliberate or the result of incompetence."[14] Rapsody's use of slant rhyme is always deliberate, and it regularly relies on Black vernacular pronunciations of certain words in order to make the imperfect rhyme scheme work. Slant rhyme is also sometimes referred to and defined as approximate rhyme: "A term used for words in a rhyming pattern that have some kind of sound correspondence but are not perfect rhymes. ... Approximate rhymes occur occasionally in patterns where most of the rhymes are perfect ... and sometimes are used systematically in place of perfect rhyme ..."[15] The definitions of imperfect, half, approximate, and/or slant rhymes do not fully account for the poetic technique that Rapsody has innovated in her lyrical corpus. When she rhymes the words "style" and "edible," "hurrying and brain," or "Autobots" and "Idlewild," Rapsody slants rhymes that hinge on the phonology and phonetics of southern African American English (AAE).[16] In effect these are not traditional slant rhymes; they reflect an important innovation in Hip-Hop lyricism that forces words to rhyme through pronunciations found in southern variants of Black vernacular English. Thus the "sound correspondence" in Rapsody's slant rhymes is rendered through her vernacular speech—an important empowered poetic move for artists who express themselves in a form—rap—that relies on the sociolinguistic currency of Black speech.

For a one-stop reservoir of the aforementioned features (with examples both in form and in content) spend some critical listening time with Rapsody's "Hard to Choose" on the *Beauty and the Beast* album (2015). "Hard to Choose" finds Rapsody rhyming about the options that have been hard to choose between success and mainstream popularity with respect to her career. She finds it hard to choose the unbridled pursuit of a popular career, one where she would presumably rap about cars, jewelry, and sex. If she chose this path she might be better positioned to support herself and her family. She would be more popular. But she cannot make this compromise as an artist;

the decision is not difficult, but the consequences of her decisions seem to haunt her. And ultimately, Rapsody is "so pro-Black" that her commitment to representing Black folks, especially representing Black girls—that is, proving that a gifted lyrical rapper—who also happens to be a woman—can be successful without sexually selling out—sustains her as an artist. And that, ultimately, is Rapsody's gift to Hip-Hop culture in the twenty-first century; it is why/how she is both a throwback—to the days of Lady B, MC Lyte, and Queen Latifah—and a giant leap forward for underground independent Hip-Hop music. In the official music video for "Hard to Choose" a young Black girl flicks through an analog television set searching for images of herself. What she finds is lacking, but she begins to anchor her identity by performing Rapsody's verses. The video cuts back and forth between the girl's performance and Rapsody's, almost intimating that the girl is a younger version of Rapsody. At one point in the video (at the lyrically appropriate point in the song), the girl searches through a trunk filled with Black Barbie dolls only to pull out the one white Barbie doll. As Rapsody suggests in "Hard to Choose," the scars of white supremacy and the uncritical acceptance of white beauty ideals continue to haunt Black folks in the twenty-first century. Without organically developed, racially sensible and sensitive beauty ideals, Black girls especially will continue to face hard choices about their own identities and ultimately about their own lives. Rapsody's eloquent embrace of complicated issues, such as identity, gender, and beauty ideals, is what ultimately makes her "Hard to Choose" as an artist navigating the popular music world where substance is anathema and where sexism and racism tend to be obscured or blotted out in favor of thin multicultural platitudes.

In 2015, Rapsody's fan base expanded a bit when many listeners discovered her through her guest/feature verse on Kendrick Lamar's "Complexion." Rapsody's guest verse/feature on "Complexion" stands out on Kendrick Lamar's sophomore studio album—*To Pimp A Butterfly*—largely because she is the only other rapper to rap on the record (Snoop appears but he basically sings for his guest appearance). But it is also significant in the sense that this collaboration with Kendrick Lamar introduced Rapsody to many more fans—and she had to have been aware of the platform that a Lamar album presented to her. Yet, "Complexion" functions as a vehicle for Rapsody to present herself to a broader audience as her artistic authentic self. Her verse does not deviate from the themes that she finds most compelling as artistry in her other work recorded for Jamla Records. There are plenty of slant rhymes in the verse; the style is vintage Rapsody. But the concept of the song—a historical confrontation with colorism, intraracial bias, and self-hate—is the perfect vehicle for Rapsody's introduction to a broader audience. Kendrick's verses wrestle with the complex issues related to complexion in the African American community from within the narratives of slavery from the vantage point of a field slave who is trying to "rap" to his lover, but stands at the ready for any opportunity to escape bondage. Rapsody's rejoinder to these verses features allusions to *Twelve Years a Slave*, Tupac's "Keep Your Head Up," and the blues associated with white supremacist skin color/eye color preferences. Rapsody's narrator recalls being twelve-years-old and thinking that her complexion was "too dark." She quickly shifts to a Star Wars metaphor to reconfigure how she embraces her darkness using slant rhymes (stupid/cupid/ George Lucas) to punctuate the point. "Complexion" is more Rapsody's song than Kendrick Lamar's and maybe that was the point of the collaboration on such an important album. Giving Rapsody an opportunity to introduce herself to a broader audience as her self makes an important statement to Hip-Hop listeners—that rap can be pro-Black, conscious, embrace gender equity, and still be popular.

IV

One of the challenges for scholars of Hip-Hop culture has been to generate pedagogies that operate (or can be operational) with an implicit sense of the intrinsic value of Hip-Hop culture within education. But after nearly two decades of teaching courses shaped by Hip-Hop culture, I am not convinced that the ways I have chosen to do so are the most effective or the most prudent. For the most part, I take literary and/or poetic approaches to the teaching of Hip-Hop culture. In fact I do not actually teach Hip-Hop culture. Most of my courses only teach the foundational or elemental history so often referenced in this book. In actuality, I deploy poetic/literary analyses of Hip Hop themes and rap lyrics in order to guide broader and deeper intellectual explorations of social justice and/or human and civil rights issues in contemporary society. Again, I am not convinced that these approaches represent the most effective way to enhance the cultural capital or the educational capital of Hip Hop. Since 1997, when I taught my first Hip-Hop course at the University of Pennsylvania, my abiding sense has been that once Hip Hop becomes canonized, students will be as likely to be alienated by it as they are inspired by it. Generally speaking, my message to students (and all critical listeners) is to be proactive with the time that you spend listening to Hip-Hop music. Be proactive in what you consume. Go discover it for yourself. I make many recommendations throughout this book, but you might not like Fashawn Kendrick Lamar, or Rapsody. I think they are all fantastic, but you have to listen to them and find that out on your own. You cannot rely on mainstream media outlets to choose your music for you, but you also cannot rely solely on professors to do so either (or music journalists for that matter). The processes of exploration and discovery are central components to the practices of critical listening. Only through the determination that musical exploration requires and the tremendous rewards of discovering the lyrics that inspire you by speaking truths to powerful structures in our society, can the essence of critical listening be found.

Critical listening is the predicate for Hip-Hop cultural constituents' collective move beyond the discussions of "who's your favorite rapper."[17] Hip-Hop music often carries more substance when it is localized, and relatively free of the pressures of the corporate world pushing formulaic aesthetics to and into the culture. Consider K'Naan's brilliant ode to his nation, "Somalia," or Kendrick Lamar's day-in-the-life missive, *Good Kid M.A.A.D. City*; there is an organic interface between place/space and substantive Hip-Hop music. Underground artists like Blu or Jean Grae create Hip-Hop music outside of mainstream outlets. They do not need *MTV*, *BET*, Clear Channel, and Radio One to make or distribute their music. They only need the internet, or social media and proactive people who are discerning, critical listeners who will actively and selectively seek what they want to experience in music. In that sense, Hip-Hop music will always be present and available to those who want to listen to it.

More and more I am finding that my students continue to challenge me to be a critical listener. I teach Hip-Hop culture at the college level on a regular basis. At this point, I can admit that I am teaching about/through Hip-Hop culture because I am deeply influenced by the culture and the music it has produced over the course of my lifetime. As a scholar, you must be vigilant about your research pursuits. For me this means listening and reading all things Hip Hop, but my best recommendations still usually come from students. This in turn has made me vigilant about not dismissing the popular Hip-Hop music to which young people have been and will continue to listen. Students regularly encourage me to listen to popular artists that I often think will be of no interest to me, and to (or for) their benefit, I have certainly tried. I will do the critical listening required to assess artists—even the ones that do not appear to engender the substantive approaches to social justice issues that are most appealing to me in terms of my own preferences for Hip-Hop music. I see this work specifically as research—long dedicated hours to listening with and for students so that I might be better positioned to educate and engage them. Ultimately for me, the music must have the substance of the Black musical and cultural traditions out of which Hip-Hop culture has so brilliantly emerged. Without that substance, when the music and/or the lyrics simply subsist in the shallow puddles of popular culture, then I also consider the notion that my work as a scholar of the culture is to broaden the listening pools of my students and challenge them to acknowledge the occasionally limited depths of their own listening experiences.

Part Two

Speech and Beats

From Ashy to Classy

I Ashy is classy

Hip-Hop culture has a complex relationship with class. The postindustrial socioeconomic context out of which the culture emerges is but one starting point along an ongoing trajectory reflective of both the class statuses and the material aspirations of the Hip-Hop generation(s). According to Carlton Usher, "Post industrialism encompasses the changing urban landscape due to gentrification, the loss of manufacturing, unequal access to education/job training, changing immigration patterns, and the shift of industry to a technology base."[1] In light of this socioeconomic complex, the challenge for educators and students is to wrestle with a more comprehensive sense of how the interface between class and Hip-Hop culture might generate more substantive discussions and critical thinking related to the social ills associated with poverty. The title of this chapter, "From Ashy to Classy" is inspired by the spoken prologue to Notorious B.I.G's "Sky's the Limit" on the *Life After Death* album.[2] In it he credits himself for coining the phrase "from ashy to classy." While this may or may not be true, the phrase "from ashy to classy"—a theme that in some ways reflects B.I.G.'s music career—also reflects a prominent theme often used to articulate class mobility among artists within Hip-Hop culture. A simple word search in Genius (formerly known as Rap Genius) yields over 350 results for the phrase—"from ashy to classy." B.I.G.'s referencing of it appears first but many other rappers follow suit, including Big K.R.I.T., Ludacris and Slim Thug who has a song titled "Ashy to Classy." The concept of upward class mobility for rappers is central to their overall commercial appeal in a marketplace where rap music artistry is regularly used to promote more and more conspicuous consumption. This unchecked promotion is often done at the expense of our deeper understandings of structural poverty in the communities out of which most Hip-Hop music has emerged.

The issue for critical listeners of Hip-Hop music is less about the economic mobility of a handful of artists, that is, their transitions from ashy to classy and more about how poverty in the communities (from which many of them originate) has been articulated through the lyrics of rap music. For the most part, listeners are regularly treated to lyrical narratives of *nouveau riche* tails of the classy accouterments of success. Biggie Smalls, later known as the Notorious B.I.G., rose to popularity in his career mostly by rapping about a certain kind of lifestyle that was materialistic and consumerist in nature. On both of his albums—1993's *Ready to Die* and 1997's *Life After Death*—B.I.G. vividly depicts the violent impoverished environment that is often a socioeconomic predicate for the illicit drug trade. *Ready to Die* is semiautobiographical, narrating B.I.G.'s life from inception to suicide. It has been critically acclaimed since its release in September of 1994, and is now included on/in a bevy of superlative album lists, including *Rolling Stone's* "500 Greatest Albums of All Time," *Time's* "Top 100 Albums of All Time," and *The Source's* "The 100 Best Rap Albums of All Time." Critics and critical listeners often commend B.I.G. for his realism—his canny ability to capture the violence, fear, and paranoia that often accompany the fleeting material success so often rapped about in relation to the underground economy of dealing drugs. "Juicy" the lead single for *Ready to Die*, released in August of 1994, crystallizes the "ashy-to-classy" narrative of B.I.G.'s ascension as a rap artist. Over the course of the song he narrates with great detail how he transitions from dreaming about the material success of rappers like Heavy D and Salt-N-Pepa, to becoming famous in his own right. B.I.G.'s body of work demonstrates that rapping about class mobility—via illegal means—has proven to be highly marketable to the consumers of mainstream American popular culture. And one of B.I.G.'s contributions to Hip-Hop culture—through the popularity of his music and the extraordinary spectacle of his death—was to help to situate Hip Hop at the center of the marketplace for popular culture.

The elements of success detailed in B.I.G.'s lyrics, especially how these themes are prominent in the lyrics of "Juicy" and "Sky's the Limit," put into some relief the tenuous semantic relationship between class and classy. In its simplest sociological sense, "class" refers to a society's hierarchy based upon economic status. Classy is derivative from this meaning of social class, but also engenders more subtle meanings of style and etiquette that are supposed to automatically attach to one's class or station in life. The rub here is that conventional meanings of the word "classy" require a classist sensibility with respect to modes of dress, behavior and appropriateness. B.I.G.'s "classy" does not subscribe to the more conventional meanings or understandings of the term. And those rappers that follow him (Big K.R.I.T., Ludacris, Slim Thug, and others) follow his garish interpretation of what "classy" means in Hip Hop. In so doing, the rappers who follow B.I.G.'s invocation of the motif match the in-your-face energy of the "ashy-to-classy" sensibility in its original utterance. *Ready to Die* basically presents B.I.G.'s narrator as having to wrestle with limited life options: selling drugs, being a successful rapper, or dying by either homicide or suicide. Becoming a successful rapper is the classiest of these life options—life options that have been truncated as a result of economic forces and late-capitalist structures barely hinted at in the story worlds of *Ready to Die* or, for that matter, *Life After Death*. Truncated life options, one consequence of the postindustrial world with which many rappers must contend in their real lives, has become an obstacle for artistic exploration. Rappers have, en masse, celebrated their individual transcendence of the limited life options available to those trapped in the postindustrial late-capitalist economy. The rap phrase— "ashy to classy"—appears to capture this artistic sense of transcendence.

If the "classy" aspect of the "ashy-to-classy" motif requires some nuanced sense of how class is operational in a postindustrial capitalist society—and/ or some non-conventional explanation for how/why class mobility has an overstated meaning within Hip-Hop culture—then the phrase's opposite term warrants some additional explanation as well. Anyone can be ashy but as a term in this particular phrase and considering its cultural relevance in African American English (AAE), "ashy" is also a racial signifier. AAE speakers use the term generally when we are talking about Black and brown skin—and the need to prevent it from becoming visibly dry especially before you enter the public space. There is a racialized hint of lower class shame present in the "ashy-to-classy" motif: the sense that maybe one is unable to afford lotion or the resources for personal hygiene necessary to prevent the skin from becoming ashy. This sense of shame—tied to a more subtle sense of how one's skin condition might convey lower class status—resides at the heart of the motif's meaning in Hip-Hop culture. In that one line, Biggie articulates a certain sense of the Black class trajectory for which he is most famous in Hip-Hop culture—an idea that proves its popular appeal via the hundreds of times it has been quoted and or interpolated by artists influenced by B.I.G's work. Ironically, Hip Hop is much more about the Horatio Alger mythology or the ideals of some rugged American individualism than it is about any sense of community progress and advancement.[3] More accurately, the individual's transcendence over economic circumstances is marketable as a pop cultural narrative for mainstream America.

Although B.I.G. came from a single-parent home he was never subjected to abject poverty as a child. His mother worked and for some portion of his education Christopher Wallace attended private school. Of course this has no bearing on whether or not he, as an artist, effectively presented the narratives of abject poverty in his music. Tupac Shakur endured a much more impoverished upbringing than Biggie did. Tupac lived the kind of abject poverty that we often associate with certain narratives of Hip-Hop culture. Yet, as a lyricist, B.I.G. consciously chose to represent the class mobility required to transcend the circumstances of concentrated poverty. In fact, B.I.G. represented the concepts associated with the "ashy-to-classy" motif in very limited ways. He rarely dwelled on the "ashy" in his music; he generally uses narratives reflecting poverty as touchstones from which he launches his tales of success in the music industry—a set of lyrical and sometimes visual representations that clarified and crystallized his success as a rap artist. Listen to almost any Biggie Smalls record and you will hear newly acquired class status—usually complemented by behaviors often associated with conspicuous consumption. He paints a very materialistic portrait of his success. In this way, B.I.G. was not a unique artist. As an artist he bore the burden of a low-class existence (despite coming from a middle-class background) but he also achieved unprecedented fame by articulating the transition from "ashy to classy" that is regularly referenced within Hip-Hop culture. B.I.G. then is a useful case study for us to critically engage the concept of class especially in the peculiar way that it is present in

Hip-Hop music. The "ashy-to-classy" motif teaches critical listeners about the different kinds of masking and misdirection that occurs (with respect to class issues in Hip-Hop culture), but it also underscores the celebration of conspicuous consumption and mass materialism in the culture. Note well here that American culture is (and continues to be) a hyper-consumerist one. It should not come as a surprise that Hip Hop represents and reflects that more readily than many other forms of American music.

It would be both parochial and inaccurate to indict Hip-Hop culture for the complex globalized late-capitalist economic system in the United States. Hip Hop's materialism, rappers' ongoing efforts to promote conspicuous consumption, even the echoes of poverty in the lyrics of the music are all important factors in any analysis of the "ashy-to-classy" motif in Hip Hop, but some better understanding of how the motif maps onto and through the culture is warranted here. In its origins, Hip Hop was very ashy. In fact, most folks believed that it would peak and fade by the 1980s. It was not until 1979—when "Rapper's Delight" achieved some commercial success—that the music industry took note. It would not be until much later in the culture's short history before the music industry actually took Hip Hop seriously. "Rapper's Delight" is an interesting example to note, because it communicated some of the familiar messages of materialism that we tend to associate with contemporary Hip-Hop culture while also maintaining a specific class setup that mirrored Biggie's ashy-to-classy evolution.[4]

"Rapper's Delight" was, for the most part, written by the working-class and middle-class members of the Sugarhill Gang, but as I discuss in Chapter 1 a member of the Sugar Hill Gang pilfered lyrics from a well-respected artist by the name of Grandmaster Caz. Caz never made much of a career for himself in terms of the mainstream music industry, but he was well known in the early developments of Hip-Hop culture and remains well respected as a pioneer of the culture itself. Unlike the Sugarhill Gang members, Caz did come from an impoverished background. So, here, at the very moment that Hip Hop develops, you have a conflict over identity, class, and authorship—at least according to the dictates of authenticity in rap music and Hip-Hop culture. This is not to diminish the talent of the Sugarhill Gang or their historical importance. Instead it underscores the masking and misdirection that Hip-Hop culture and the music industry entail, especially as they are directly related to class narratives and discourses in the music.

The first era of the culture, what I have been referring to as the old school era of Hip Hop, began in the early-mid-1970s and ended in the mid-1980s. This was the *ashy* era of Hip-Hop culture (so to speak). The old school era was characterized by ingenuity, improvisation, and the dramatic repurposing of any and everything—from the turntable to cardboard boxes and brick walls.[5] It may seem too intentional here to refer to the old school era as "ashy" but the sensibility of that moment in Hip Hop's history was the definition of grittiness.[6] The golden age or era represents that signal moment of transition and transformation of the culture. It is when Hip Hop was both musically diverse and economically emergent in the American pop culture industries. Hip Hop's relationships to brands developed expediently and the potential for artists to access material success developed exponentially.[7] The golden era saw Hip Hop's fusion with fast-paced technological developments—a fusion that would last into the contemporary moment but at the time saw Hip-Hop music benefiting from new ways of consuming popular culture. The platinum era was all "classy" in the most conspicuously consumptive sense imaginable. Some folks jokingly refer to that moment as the "shiny suit" era of Hip Hop but the point of that joke is to critique the convoluted notions of a fleeting sense of wealth or riches that artists attached to definitions of class and/or classiness that were ultimately antithetical to both the origins of the culture and the elitist definitions of classiness.

II The phrases of poverty in Hip Hop

Yet in each era of the culture, there were artists (and songs) that were wholly committed to the project of articulating the narratives of poverty that persistently plagued inner-city life in America's postindustrial economy. "The Message" (1982) by Grandmaster Flash and the Furious Five opens with the indelible lyric: "Broken glass everywhere ..." From that point on, through five verses, Melle Mel, the only rapper to actually rap on the record, poetically paints the imagery of poverty in America. Rats and roaches, homeless people, and drug addicts all populate the world of "The Message." The eroded public education system, an incapacity to pay utility bills, and the desire to hustle a way out of the impoverished morass leads to incarceration, rape and eventually suicide. Melle Mel's message on poverty is a dramatically bleak peak at the world within which Hip-Hop music was produced. For all of its pinpoint images depicting the limited options for the poor who subsist in the wealthiest society in the world, critical listeners are compelled by the simile in the refrain of the song. The notion that living the life of poor folks in inner-city America is akin to living life in a jungle captures our imagination by producing a figurative but tangible survival model—the Darwinian idea that, via natural selection, the most fit to survive will survive and reproduce. If impoverished inner-city living is like living in a jungle (sometimes), then critical listeners will also note that the simile—the figuration, if you will, while compelling and powerful—is not wholly accurate or appropriate to the concrete jungle to which it analogically refers. Unfortunately, America's concrete jungles do not operate based upon the principles of natural selection and therefore those who are most fit do not always survive. In fact, with over 1.5 million African American men "missing" from some of America's major population/urban centers we could argue/conclude that some segments of the African American population most connected to Hip-Hop culture/the Hip-Hop generation(s) actually are not surviving at all.[8]

A community where there is "broken glass everywhere" is likely to be a community where Broken Windows' police policy and practices will be in effect. The credibility of what social scientists refer to as the "Broken Windows" model of policing continues to diminish as protesters across the United States have sustained collective calls for a more just and equitable legal system. In January 2014, critical race theorist and legal scholar, Patricia Williams was calling for an "end to Broken Windows policing" (in *The Nation*). Professor Williams' insights were accurate then and in the extraordinary aftermath of grand jury decisions from two separate states failing to secure indictments of law enforcement officers who killed unarmed Black men, many Black Americans have come to terms with the fact that our justice and legal systems are more broken than our windows.[9] Wilson and Kelling (1982) first defined the concept of policing minor crimes of loitering and disorderly conduct as a means of reducing major crimes. The theory being that if a community had fewer "broken windows," it would also ultimately have less serious violent crime. Whether or not this policing tactic or others can account for the precipitous decline in violent crime across the United States is difficult to prove. For example, some social scientists attribute the fall in violent/serious crime to access to reproductive rights for poor families. We simply cannot prove that "Broken Windows" policing works the way that theorists or law enforcement leadership suggest to us that it does.

Here is what we do know. The data from Stop and Frisk, alone, suggests to us that in the hearts and minds of law enforcement it is often people of color, especially Black men who actually are the broken windows. Their presence (their bodies) in certain environments like street corners, streets themselves, or in front of convenient stores compels police to police them—sometimes with excessive force. Too often this policing of the "broken windows" is itself a broken policy that continues to break the trust between the community and law enforcement.

One way of radically re-ordering policing and law enforcement tactics is to apply the basic principles of the "broken windows" model to the American criminal justice system itself—to aggressively police the minor infractions of conduct that police officers get away with regularly. Since the exoneration of Zimmerman, activists, organizers and a growing segment of the American citizenry have become desperate to challenge our broken justice system. Many of these calls for help recount the struggles with the petty tyranny of law enforcement. At a pool party in Mckinney, Texas, one law enforcement officer physically assaulted a fourteen-year-old Black girl and pulled his gun on other teens in order to diffuse a situation which may have only been exacerbated by his presence and behavior.[10] Aggressive policing is but one component of the criminal justice system that claims to address the "broken glass everywhere" but does more breaking then crime fighting. Add to this the long wait times, predominately white court systems with all Black and brown defendants, the hassles of being stopped and frisked multiple times at different times by the same officer; and the picture of the relationship between the broken glass lyric and Broken Windows policing is apparent. This is the substance of petty tyranny and too many Black folks have suffered under its boot for too long. Sadly these minor infractions will rarely bubble up to the national/ international level that the recent spate of murders of unarmed civilians has. And rightly so, but what if "broken windows" theories actually work best on "broken systems" of policing and meting out justice.

We have to wonder if a "broken systems" approach taken by the officers who murdered Tamir Rice in Cleveland; or Officer Pantaleo, who choked Eric Garner; or Officer Wilson, who shot and killed Mike Brown, could have saved the lives of their victims. If we had aggressively policed police with minor conduct infractions, then Tamir Rice would be alive right now. Eric Garner would be alive right now. It is tragic to deal in "what if's" when so many families and communities are and have been in pain. But it is equally urgent to consider that if what law enforcement thinks is so effective at managing crimes in our communities might be equally if not more effective at managing crime in theirs. Ultimately, "The Message" in its opening phrase/line points to an ongoing social outgrowth from the persistent poverty that has been one feature of the postindustrial economics of Hip-Hop culture. In too many inner-city neighborhoods, "broken glass" is everywhere; it can be an indicator of concentrated poverty and more often than not it is also an indicator of extreme social (and economic) neglect—a neglect that cannot be healed nor resolved through more aggressive policing.

The pervasive presence of social neglect—especially as it is reflected by and through the actual presence of broken glass in the 'hoods of America—points to another phrase of poverty that develops over/across a range of lyrics but was crystallized in Ghostface Killah's "All that I Got is You" featuring Mary J. Blige and produced by The Rza for Ghost's 1996 *Ironman* album. In "All that I Got ..." Ghostface flashes back to his (or rather, his narrator's) childhood. Through a series of lyrical remembrances he nostalgically reflects on a childhood marked by abject poverty. For Ghostface, whose rap personas often indulge in esoteric ruminations on the materiality of urban drug trafficking, the lyrics of "All that I Got ..." offer some of the MC's most class-conscious reflections on record. Images of four children sleeping in one bed, roach infestations, food stamps, visits from state case-workers, and the no-frills brand food products all populate the impoverished story world of "All that I Got is You." Ultimately, Ghostface's tone is more anguished than nostalgic—awash in the oceanic forces of inner-city poverty. Somewhere between "sugar water" and the viewing of "Saturday morning cartoons" Ghostface's narrator begins to look to his mother as the sole reason for his capacity to survive the travails of concentrated poverty. "All that I Got ..." transfers particularized narratives of poverty into the lyrical discourses of and on Hip Hop. It also translates itself as an ode to the maternal figure in rap music—a figure nearly deified by Tupac in "Dear Mama" and (later) by Kanye West in "Hey Mama"—songs we can now listen to on a loop during our nation's perennial celebration of Mother's Day. For Ghostface, it is only through his mother's unbridled love that he and his siblings, including two brothers with muscular dystrophy, are able to survive the intense social neglect that concentrated poverty requires in inner-city communities across America.

If the presence of broken glass and the protection of heroic single mothers are important phraseological signifiers of concentrated poverty expressed lyrically in/through Hip-Hop music, then certain responses to concentrated poverty have likewise been coined in spectacular fashion through some of Hip Hop's greatest wordsmiths. Jay-Z's "Minority Report" begins with yet another indelible Hip-Hop phrase and opening lyric: "My people were poor before the hurricane came ..." The line states a simple fact about the conditions of poverty that existed in certain neighborhoods of one of America's most culturally rich cities, New Orleans, Louisiana. "Minority Report" from Jay-Z's somewhat underwhelming 2006 album, *Kingdom Come*, focuses on a multilayered critique of individual, media, and government responses to the Hurricane Katrina disaster, a natural calamity induced by the political neglect of climate change and exacerbated by governments inattentiveness to the consequences of our rapidly changing environment. "Minority Report" also (in its very title) signifies on the popular 2002 Tom Cruise film of the same name. *Minority Report*, the film, was directed by Steven Spielberg and based on the Phillip K. Dick short story also of the same title. The film centers on the ethical and philosophical implications of a "precrime" unit that uses enslaved people with the mental capacity to "see" the future in order to preempt violent crime. Jay-Z's "Minority Report" signifies on this doctrine of preemption, challenging the media, the government, fellow rappers, and ultimately even himself about what we knew about New Orleans before the storm and in general what we know about poverty in our own communities. The sense of Jay's opening line is that poverty is a structural problem, always already on the precipice of becoming a societal disaster. The media and the president fly over the destruction and the human carnage, taking images (snapshots) but leaving American citizens stranded in the aftermath of the flood. Jay-Z takes all to task here, suggesting that "Minority Report" is also leveraging its literal meaning as lyrics that are reporting on the impoverished living conditions of minority populations in America. Again these are all issues about which we do not need superhuman prophets to inform us. Jay's critique of himself (in the song) is that although he donates money to the recovery effort, he does not give his time—which for him means that he (like us) really does not care about the poor. This is doubly troubling for Jay-Z's narrator in "Minority Report" since he was himself poor and because he acknowledges that giving his personal money to organizations like the Red Cross may not guarantee that those resources will actually be used to help poor people and/or rebuild the community in a way that makes space/places for them to return.

"Minority Report" also frames an issue—a concept really—that continues to haunt Hip-Hop generations in this extended moment of state-sanctioned violence against unarmed citizens and what has become the (mostly) well-organized demonstrations in response to that violence. There has actually been very little looting or what some media outlets have referred to as "rioting" in community/grassroot responses to the murders of young women and men of color over the last several years. "Minority Report" questions and revises the impulse to loot if you do not have loot—that is, how can we define rioting and/or looting as pathological behavior by citizens who live in communities that suffer from extreme social neglect and concentrated poverty? Or to put this another way: How do we as a society value property over humanity? One answer to this question stems from American history where Black folks were treated, traded, and sold as property as well as the variety of systems over the long history of this nation that have attempted to structurally sustain the oppression of Black folks. For Jay-Z and other Hip-Hop artists who have survived violent underground economies and have gone on to find success within the music and entertainment industries, the "loot-if-you-don't-have-loot" phrase signals the arbitrary meaning that attaches to some semblance of moral economies in the wealthiest nation in the world where concentrated poverty continues to live and breathe across a broad set of underserved communities.

Lupe Fiasco regularly writes lyrics that reflect on the social consequences of poverty in urban communities. The first single of his career, "Kick, Push" is an optimistic narrative about a young man who teaches himself how to ride a skateboard in an urban setting/environment. Generally speaking, skate culture and skateboarding has/had not been a topic of choice for rap artists to take on as subject matter in their lyrics. Lupe defamiliarizes the genre of popular rap by fusing figurative themes of grinding, kicking, and pushing in Hip-Hop culture and skate culture in his initial foray into mainstream rap prominence. In "Kick, Push" skate culture offers both a figurative and literal alternative to pushing drugs in poor neighborhoods (presumably in Chicago) or eking out a materialistic existence via the grind of the underground drug economy. For Lupe Fiasco's narrator in "Kick, Push" this is a false choice, of sorts, that is ultimately predicated on a false collective consciousness, but in the end, the lifestyle of the skater maintains as a critical alternative to the lifestyle of the drug pusher. At the time of the release of *Lupe Fiasco's Food & Liquor*—the full length album featuring the single "Kick, Push"—fans, critical listeners, and critics who had been following Lupe's emergence as an artist, were becoming more and more aware of his complex radically progressive politics. See/hear "American Terrorist" for ready reference. Near the end of the album, "Kick, Push II" proffers a deliberately dark coda to Lupe's now-famous lead single, "Kick, Push." In the second version of the song, Lupe's narrator dispenses with the light figuration on pushing a skateboard past the drug pushers in the 'hood. Instead he narrates a much darker world, where a young man skateboards to a location where he can beg for food for himself and his younger sister. When he passes by the hustlers and drug dealers who offer him work he still turns them down, but he also reflects on the fact that one of the reasons why he must beg for food is because his mother is one of their best customers. In the original "Kick, Push" the rap narrator's love interest is a skateboarder of equal skill to the narrator. She boldly responds to Lupe's narrator's suggestion that she ride with him by telling him that she has her own skateboard and her own set of skills to grind and push. In "Kick, Push II" the narrator's partner is a poor white girl who is pimped by her mother who is abused by and contracts

HIV from her stepfather. The girl and the panhandling narrator are a part of group of misfits and derelicts from a variety of class backgrounds who are circumstantially thrust into the brutal materiality of a late-capitalist globalized America where everything is for sale and human compassion is the rarest of commodities. Lupe's dark rejoinder to one of his most popular singles, signals his career-long commitment to wrestling with complex class issues and themes of consumption and materiality in his music. "Kick, Push" and "Kick, Push II" both avoid the more trite celebration of the luster of conspicuous consumption that much of rap music finds appealing. Instead, each song attempts to push for alternative perspectives on the "ashy-to-classy" ethos so prominent in and significant to Hip-Hop artistry and industry.

III Bursting the bling bubble

In a short but incisive article titled "Bling was a Bubble," Chris Holmes Smith argues that "while the middle classes binged on a heaping larder of cheap credit—barely pausing to acknowledge catastrophic turns of events like 9/11, Hurricane Katrina, and Abu Ghraib—hip-hop's mavens of extravagance provided the guilt-free soundtrack for the feast."[11] Through the essay, Smith traces the term back to an artist by the name of B.G. (Baby Gangsta), who was a member of the No Limit camp in New Orleans. Smith's discussion hints at the irony inherent in the fact that B.G., an artist who comes from the Calliope Projects—one of the most poverty-stricken neighborhoods in one of the poorest cities in this country—coined the term "bling." This is the kind of relative complexity that the ashy-to-classy phrase intimates. For Smith the term "bling" enters into the American discourse, providing a Black vernacular soundtrack—in/for mainstream Americans—to negotiate the unchecked debt and aggressive overspending that became a prominent feature of early twenty-first American consumerism. He establishes ties between the credit crisis and overconsumption in the United States to the discourses generated by/through Hip-Hop culture. Bling is a signifier of the conflation of "ash" and "class" in the context of Hip Hop's own love affair with materialism and consumption. "Bling Was a Bubble" gives the reader a sense of the power of language, but the essay also points to the ways that Hip Hop wrestles with, and often intervenes in, issues of class. The narrative of the eras of Hip-Hop culture underscores several of these interventions. From that old school ashy era where Hip Hop was mostly grit and technological innovation, the culture underwent a transition in the 1980s that featured more popular exposure and consumption and the musical diversity that characterized the golden age era. Hip Hop in that particular moment—lasting from about the mid-1980s until 1998—was tremendously diverse in terms of the music. The extraordinary economic potential of the culture was still not quite realized and thus the formulaic imposition on the content of the music had not yet taken shape in the industry. The golden age/ era was arguably the healthiest era in Hip-Hop history from a perspective of how Hip Hop interacts with class. The era was not without its share of violent and consumerist narratives, but there was also a marked shift toward more conscious production—evidenced in the lyrical work of BDP, X-Clan, Public Enemy, De La Soul, and many others. There was a fair amount of socially conscious and class-conscious music in that particular moment of Hip Hop and only more recently has Hip-Hop music featured several acts committed to social justice principles in their music and in their lives.[12]

From the ashy, old school era, through the transitional, golden era of Hip Hop, it was economically logical then that the Hip-Hop music industry would enter the platinum era. The fact that it became a sound track for a "a successive series of asset bubbles that have ranged from property and credit to commodities and emerging market equities" indicates the far-reaching force of Hip-Hop music and the need for audiences to engage the critical listening directives of *Hip Hop Headphones*.[13] Holmes Smith effectively argues that economic bubbles are driven by popular misconceptions that can often be aided by popular culture. There is no small amount of irony that a form of Black culture that emerged from economically challenged circumstances served as a soundtrack to the materialistic follies of Wall Street and the mainstream middle class. Dick Hebdige's early claim that "rap is rooted in the experience of lower class Blacks in America's big northern cities" resonates here because it was a truth that initiated an ongoing tension in the ashy-to-classy transitions of Hip-Hop music.[14] The steady repetition of the "ashy-to-classy" phrase and themes in Hip Hop suggest that Biggie Smalls (aka Notorious

B.I.G.) became an ambassador of the unchecked materialism and conspicuous consumption that characterized Hip-Hop music during its platinum era. But these transitions were not unchallenged, and Hip-Hop music's development into its more materialistic/capitalistic form was not without its tensions and rejections.

For their second major-label album project The Roots wrote and recorded "What They Do" on *Illadelph Halflife* which was released in September of 1996. The lyrics for "What They Do" offer a powerful critique of the (then) contemporary trends that glorified materialism. The Roots, front man, Black Thought (ne Tariq Trotter), characterizes his 1996 contemporaries as a "lost generation" of rappers who have forsaken the roots and origins of Hip-Hop culture for material gain.[15] For Black Thought's narrator in "What They Do" the onset of the platinum era in Hip Hop is accompanied by a deluge of bling-ed out rappers who lack lyrical skills and are corrupting the culture through hyper-materialistic imagery. The music video for "What They Do" directed by Charles Stone, III, is among the group's most popular music videos. It offers a diagrammatic critique of the platinum era Hip-Hop music video. In it, The Roots hang out in a mansion, have a pool party at that mansion, drive expensive cars, and generally reproduce the stock scenes of the platinum era Hip-Hop music video. But the text/subtitles for each scene—in tandem with Black Thought's lyrics—reveals all, as the mansion and the car are rented; the models are all hired, and the materialistic absurdity of this particular brand of Hip-Hop imagery is continuously called into question. Popular discourse about the "What They Do" video was characterized by rumors that Biggie was personally offended by the video and its critical message. After all, the rented mansion in "What They Do" was the same mansion that was rented for a popular Biggie Smalls' video—"One More Chance"—the same setting, except for the important fact that Biggie's video was not a satirical critique of Hip Hop's ashy-to-classy conspicuous materialism; it was a celebration of it. Ahmir "Questlove" Thompson (drummer and front man for The Roots) writes candidly about these tensions in his memoir, *Mo' Meta Blues: The World According to Questlove*. He writes that "a civil war was brewing in hip-hop; the tension between the haves and have-nots that I sensed at the Source Awards was now at a fever pitch."[16] Thompson refers to the 1995 Source awards show as "hip-hop's funeral." He responded viscerally to each award that *Ready to Die* (Biggie's debut album) won over *Illmatic* (Nas' debut album). "For every award Biggie got I watched Nas wilt in defeat, and that killed me inside."[17] Thompson subtly suggests that the song and video for "What They Do" was in some ways The Roots' response to this civil war in Hip Hop. It was not directed at Biggie necessarily but upon reflecting on Biggie's public response—quoted in the *Source* (of course) that his feelings were hurt by the video—Thompson has second thoughts. "In retrospect it seems obvious. There was no good way to isolate and critique the direction hip-hop was heading in without targeting the videos that Biggie was making with Puff and Hype Williams."[18] The critique of the ashy-to-classy ethos in Hip Hop may not have fallen upon deaf ears in 1996, but it surely cannot claim victory in terms of the content of Hip-Hop music over the last decade.

Still, bling was as much a bubble for Hip-Hop music as it was a signifier for the various economic bubbles in the era of globalization. Music videos continue to be ostentatious with some artists reveling in materialism, but Hip-Hop music does not readily claim materialism and conspicuous consumption in the same ways that it did during the zenith of the platinum era. Materialism, speculation, and conspicuous consumption have consequences for national economies as well as the popular cultures that portend to reflect certain economic realities (and fantasies). There remains no question about the classic nature of Biggie Small's coining of the phrase "ashy-to-classy." It has put into some relief the critical class tensions within Hip-Hop culture—especially that schism between the communities out of which many Hip-Hop artists emerge and the fantastical materialistic realms to which their artistic success sometimes entices them to aspire. Yet for all of the class consciousness that ensued (lyrically) in the golden and platinum moments in Hip Hop's history, artistic and philosophical reflections on poverty, the economics of globalism, and the striking nature of income inequality in our contemporary moment are still not the normative mode for Hip-Hop musical production.

Best Never Heard: Playlist Pedagogy in the Hip-Hop Classroom

Although Hip-Hop music continues to wrestle with the ideological gaps between its humble origins and the fantastic materialism to which so much of the music over the last four decades has been subjectively committed, its pervasive global popularity and presence is undeniable. In a 2015 article in *The Independent*, Christopher Hooton writes "that hip-hop is the world's top genre, showing up on playlists more than all others, regardless of geography or language."[1] Hooton's assertion is based on an analysis of over twenty billion songs for a "musical map" generated by the popular streaming service Spotify. For at least a decade now, playlists have been a staple feature of the pedagogy that shapes and informs Hip-Hop classrooms. For example, I have an "Ashy-to-Classy" playlist that features many of the songs of the same title and several of the songs that quote the phrase or specifically allude to the themes outlined in Chapter 3. The brief reflections in this chapter point to the utility of the playlist as a tool in the Hip-Hop classroom.

Playlist pedagogy in the Hip-Hop classroom raises the possibility that certain ubiquitous learning environments exist for Hip-Hop culture. Tech-education researchers have been charting advancements in learning environments that have become more and more pronounced in the twenty-first century. The progression from electronic learning to mobile learning to the potential for ubiquitous learning has largely been the by-product of advancements in computer and mobile/cellular telephone technology.[2] "A ubiquitous learning environment is any setting in which students can become totally immersed in the learning process.... So, a ubiquitous learning environment (ULE) is a situation or setting of pervasive (or omnipresent) education (or learning).

Education is happening all around the student but the student may not even be conscious of the learning process. Source data is present in the embedded objects and students do not have to DO anything in order to learn. They just have to be there."[3] Given the proper tools—an mp3 player or music streaming service, a pair of headphones, some basic critical listening techniques and approaches—the playlist can become a tool that extends the potential for learning well beyond the traditional classroom space.

Hip Hop is ubiquitous. The culture itself has spread its tentacles throughout the world and its artistic products have been the subject of or soundtrack for everything from advertising and film to news productions, Broadway plays and high school curricula. The question of whether or not ubiquitous Hip-Hop learning environments exist is an issue that I am not out to prove or disprove here. My sense is that one feature of the globally pervasive presence of Hip-Hop culture is the implicit challenge that educators leverage and tap into the heart of the culture in order to access the learning environments therein.[4] Again, it is useful to consider the four elements of Hip-Hop culture and to briefly examine how each element offers its own set of ubiquitous learning tendencies and pedagogical environments. For ready reference/example, DJs have to teach other DJs how to be DJs, and MCs have to teach other MCs how to be MCs, and graffiti artists teach each other—so on and so forth. Apprenticeship is an important context for the discursive energy that exists around the ULEs of Hip Hop, especially within the old school era. The fact that Hip Hop's artisans learned their crafts from established practitioners helped to generate the spirit of the nontraditional learning environment cultivated by and for constituents of Hip Hop. By the mid-1980s, when you have Run–D.M.C., and other more prominent Hip-Hop artists and groups, Hip Hop enters into the beginnings of its golden age, around 1986/87. At this point, vinyl and cassette tapes are enjoying the last vestiges of their industrial moments as primary recording technologies for popular consumption. CDs and MTV were (more and more) responsible for transmitting the music, a paradigmatic shift in the music industry. The discursive ULEs of the golden age era embraced specific subjects: knowledge of the self, of Hip-Hop history, of the streets, and of the music industry. Already, we have shifted away from the apprenticeship mode of the old school era, into the digital mode of the contemporary eras. Obviously, we cannot shift the culture without simultaneously altering the kind of learning environments that exist therein. One can see this most clearly in the content of the music, where the music is geared toward themes of self-knowledge and Hip-Hop history—BDP, Public Enemy, Queen Latifah, Native Tongues, etc. The music also promoted knowledge about the streets, and encouraged awareness about the issues plaguing urban environments. Also, very subtly, the music was beginning to critique the industry's commodification of the culture. Now the critique of certain social, racial and economic systems are running through a lot of the ULEs within Hip Hop—a practice that gestated in the golden age environment. Many of these ULEs exist in predominantly Black public spheres such as barber shops, classrooms, on the street corners, and in the public spaces where Black and brown folk are interacting and talking about the music and the culture most frequently.

Over the course of the third era—the platinum era—the murders of Tupac and Biggie, occurring in 1996 and 1997, respectively, drew immense media attention to Hip-Hop culture. In the aftermath of those murders, a couple of important developments occurred. First, Hip-Hop culture was elevated to a new stature of popularity. Second, those two artists, in terms of popularity and presence, left a gaping hole in the musical world of Hip Hop through which other artists gained access to the upper echelons of the music business. In the platinum era, Hip-Hop artists' record sales reached unprecedented numbers. This was in stark contrast with the golden age era where if you sold just one million records, it was considered exceptional. By the time we reached the platinum age era, one million or two million records was much more common. Hip Hop began to develop in various regions across the nation and the globe. Two of the many defining attributes of the platinum era were pop cultural dominance and ubiquitous digital transmission.

By the end of the platinum era, most consumers are engaging the music through some type of digital platform. We primarily consume music visually and digitally, as opposed to through analog and/or the immediacy of live performances. The ULEs that emerged during the platinum era developed online. There are plenty of Hip-Hop sites where you can see how these learning environments operate virtually. Ubiquitous digital transmission includes all of the above. Along the developmental arc of Hip-Hop culture, we can identify several potential discursive subjects where ubiquitous learning environments might intersect and these topical considerations intersect through the technology of the playlist. Just for clarification, there could be three-hundred ULEs (or more) within and/or related to Hip-Hop culture. I do not mean to suggest that the three I am employing here are the most prominent ULEs, or that they holistically represent how ubiquitous learning environments operate within Hip-Hop culture. I am only offering three, because these are the three that I use in my own speaking engagements in the classroom and in learning environments for Hip-Hop culture to which I have access. That is, I use these three playlists in order to teach certain aspects, themes, and forms within Hip-Hop culture. The environments of these discourses or discursive communities vary greatly. The potential for them to exist or thrive is contingent upon the community's engagement with Hip-Hop culture. As such, Hip-Hop culture has a lot of diverse learning communities. Constituents of Hip-Hop culture in youth communities move freely in and out of the culture and this fluidity is one predicate for the potential of nontraditional learning environments to develop around Hip Hop–related subjects. Hip-Hop ULEs exist where young people listen to, love, and critically engage Hip Hop.

One playlist that I use often in courses and in my writing is a list that I almost jokingly refer to as the "Inquisitive Discourses on the Origins of Samples." Essentially, this list consists of a dozen of the most sampled songs in Hip Hop. For reference, some of my work takes cues from Joseph Schloss' *Making Beats: The Art of Sample-Based Hip Hop*.[5] Schloss relies on his in-depth ethnographic research—working with and interviewing Hip-Hop producers in order to decipher the ethics and the aesthetics of sample-based musical production. Music production in Hip Hop which is interstitially related to DJ-ing and the manipulation of turntables, is a complex and sophisticated craft; DJs and Hip-Hop producers have to in some cases have the knowledge of and function as musicologists and/or music historians. DJs and producers from around the world use their extensive knowledge of (usually) Black music to teach audiences a bit of music history through sampling. Depending upon the generational makeup of an audience, the most-sampled songs playlist can generate vastly different educational and/or discursive responses. If it is a younger demographic, they will have heard many of the rifts and every drum sequence in these songs without ever having heard these songs, specifically or directly. The notion of being the "Best Never Heard" comes into play here in order to account for the dissonance between hearing and listening to sounds or samples of previously recorded, sometimes unheard material. If the audience or classroom consists of older, first-generation Hip-Hop folks (born in the 1960s and 1970s especially), you may have heard every single one of these songs and know that they have been sampled hundreds, if not thousands, of times. Younger audiences, may not be aware of the repetition and sampling that pervades old school era and golden age Hip-Hop music.

Constructing playlists based upon sampled songs is an important educational exercise for Hip-Hop music. Given the fact that repetition figures deeply within Hip-Hop culture, playlists that capture the original songs/sounds from which Hip-Hop music is made serve the purposes of the scholar/researcher as readily as the student or "normal" listener. There is a kind of "zero hearing" effect produced by music that relies heavily on samples and excerpts from previously recorded music where you can have young people who have heard the sample/excerpt but have not really heard the full composition/recording. This is one of the more powerful pedagogical moments that scholars can leverage within the ubiquitous learning environments of Hip-Hop culture. Young people understand that much of the music they listen to is sampled, and often, there is a desire to find out from where. Unfortunately, however, we do not always have enough music historians or pedagogues in these learning environments to access, leverage, and get the potential out of them. Playlists, and the capacity to share them online and on social media, function in the gaps of these educational environments.

Another playlist that has been useful in the classroom is one that catalogs Hip-Hop music's penchant for alluding to film and/or literary works. It presents an opportunity for a second ubiquitous learning environment that revolves around the interface between literature and Hip-Hop culture or film and Hip-Hop culture. Various discourses on the discovery of allusions in the lyrics of rap music constitute a range of educational and academic discourses that fuse reading and viewing audiences with the critical listening audience. The "Allusive Discoveries Playlist" is not exhaustive but through it educators can begin to collate the themes of Hip-Hop music, certain albums and certain lyrics with their literary and cinematic counterparts. A quick gloss of some examples from this list will bear this out. The first example from the playlist is The Roots' "Things Fall Apart" from their 1999 album of the same name.[6] There may have been some fans of The Roots who were not fans of Nigerian literature and who might not have ever heard of Chinua Achebe. Note well that reading Chinua Achebe's *Things Fall Apart* is not a prerequisite for enjoying The Roots' album or vice versa.[7] Conversely, there are a lot of people who have read Chinua Achebe's *Things Fall Apart*, but do not listen to The Roots. Essentially, The Roots are participating in the construction of a learning environment whereby their allusion to Chinua Achebe gives us a deeper understanding of how they view themselves as artists within Hip-Hop culture. They also give the Hip-Hop generation a point of entry into the sophisticated nuances of colonialism and to the missionary struggles that Chinua Achebe documents so well in *Things Fall Apart*. The Roots are a live band from Philadelphia. Despite being the house band for *The Tonight Show with Jimmy Fallon*, they have not achieved extraordinary commercial success. For most of their career, The Roots have been more successful touring the world and performing live than they have been at selling albums/records. They make their money by—from their own perspective—staying true to a certain authenticity of craft within Hip-Hop culture. This is not to say that live bands are more authentic than artists who rely heavily on sample-based production, but the production on a typical Roots album is more musical, organic/original, and from the group's perspective, more substantive. For The Roots, the *Things Fall Apart* allusion is a poignant reference to their position within a commodified industry that pushes the corporatization of the music and the culture that in turn results in formulaic popular artists who follow more than innovate. Despite their great talent, they will not likely ever be multi-platinum selling recording artists. And at this point, given what they have achieved through live performance and their permanent residency as the Tonight Show Band, they do not have to be. They will never sell a million records simply because they have not been interested in making the kind of music that sells within the pop culture framework. Their relationship to the music business has been a tentative one where they are constantly wrestling with the paradigmatic shifts that commodify and colonize what they consider to be their culture—Hip-Hop culture.

Another example from this playlist is Ghostface Killa's "Motherless Child," an important rejoinder to the litany of versions of this classic Negro spiritual from a member of the Wu-Tang Clan. Ghostface's "Motherless ..." is a powerful allusion to a classic African American spiritual.[8] More specifically, it is an allusion to a slave spiritual where the enslaved child laments the loss of his or her mother, pointing to the systematic dismantling of the Black family that was one of many evil tools of oppression in the transatlantic slave trade. Ghostface's version of "Motherless Child" highlights the brutal (and murderous) reality of inner-city life, especially when that life is subject to the underground economy of substance abuse, robbery, and illegal drug sales. The connection between histories of the oppression of Black folks and the contemporary conditions of inner-city life so regularly detailed in the lyrics of Hip-Hop music suggests the purpose of allusions in Hip Hop. Single-parent households led by women are regularly demonized in the contemporary public sphere. Ghostface's lyrics do not directly touch on this phenomenon but his allusion to the history of slavery (in the title) here suggests that contemporary challenges in African American life have roots and reflections in the history of slavery. Ghostface's version of the motherless child reads the historic alienation from the mother in the institution of slavery as one of the inputs to the abject poverty and the ruthless response to such poverty detailed in the story worlds built in the recordings of Wu-Tang Clan. This is a strategic allusion. To reflect upon the alienation within the institution of slavery and suggest ways that the modern world inherits systems of oppression from that history is a significantly educational move by an artist who is not regularly associated with the pedagogy of his lyrics. In these examples, allusions contribute to the capacity for ubiquitous learning environments to exist for the constituents and consumers of Hip-Hop music and culture.

MCs regularly reference parents—present or absent—in their lyrics. Jazzy Jeff and the Fresh Prince's "Parents Just Don't Understand" (1988) was an instant classic that went on to become even more famous as the opening theme music for Will Smith's 1990s sitcom, *The Fresh Prince of Bel-Air*. Extolling or condemning the actions of one's parents has become staple content in the lyrics of Hip-Hop music. Jay-Z's "Meet the Parents" features some of the artist's richest lyrics in terms of the number of allusions.[9] Hip Hop artists make substantive songs but when an extremely popular artist does so the message may have more potential to reach more people. Jay-Z does not do this often, but when he does, the results can resonate. The narrative of Jay-Z's "Meet the Parents," not to be confused with the popular movies starring Ben Stiller, depicts the life of a young couple who become pregnant. The father is a hustler, and the mother is a young woman who is fascinated by him in the inner city. As the song progresses, the mother births their child and the father denies the son. The father continues to deny his son and continues to hustle drugs in the same neighborhood. The mother grows gradually depressed as the father continues hustling. Inevitably, the son grows up—fatherless—and becomes a hustler as well. At the conclusion of the song, the father unwittingly kills his son, although they do not know each other. Not only is there an obvious Oedipal intimation in the song, but there are also certain aspects of Egyptian mythology that are alluded to in the lyrics of the song as well. The narrative of "Meet the Parents" may surprise some listeners who only expect Jay-Z to rap about money, drugs, and women. The song concludes with Jay-Z's narrator lamenting the fact that too many fathers do not know their sons and that this in some ways is killing them as if they were shooting their sons themselves. Again, this is not Ben Stiller's *Meet the Parents*. This is a poignant urban reflection on fatherhood and fatherlessness that is significant for critical listeners of Hip Hop. Not only is it valuable for audiences to know that Jay-Z is capable of making socially substantive music, but it is also valuable in the sense that it helps us understand the subtle mythological and Egyptian elements interpolated into it. Learning environments are constructed via the discourses generated by the lyrics of Hip-Hop music. Identifying them can be as simple as building playlists. The greater challenge is, can we tap into, and ultimately leverage, the lyrics of Hip-Hop music to access the learning environments that exist in and around them?

Immortal Technique's lyrical version of the spy thriller film *Point of No Return* presents yet another example where Hip-Hop artists realize and invert the metaphor of painting pictures with poems.[10] Within this song, Immortal Technique references the title of the film to reflect the mindset of an alienated individual in a late-capitalist, culturally eroding society as told from the perspective of a disillusioned narrator who is deeply depressed and also incensed by his alienation.[11] Consider also, "Minority Report" which is another socially relevant lyric penned by Jay-Z.[12] It signifies on the Steven Spielberg film of the same name, but conveys a different message about Hurricane Katrina. In this song, he not only details how he felt about the destruction but also offers a scathing critique of both the media's and the government's response to it. Audiences have seen quite a few of Jay-Z's music videos, but music videos for socially relevant tracks like "Minority Report" are rare. Additional examples on the "allusions" playlist include "Welcome to the Terrordome," which is Pharaoh Monche's remake of a Public Enemy song that is similar to "Point of No Return," in that it offers a critique of a late-capitalist society and the kind of alienation and restlessness that capitalism breeds for inner-city inhabitants in that situation.[13]

The three versions of "Lost Ones" are significant contributions to this playlist. The subsequent versions (by Jay-Z and J. Cole) allude to and signify on the first version penned by Lauryn Hill. Hill's version poetically merges her tumultuous relationship with the music industry with tumultuous personal relationships.[14] Jay-Z's version of "Lost Ones" signifies on Lauryn Hill's version, grappling with his own relationship to the industry and ultimately lamenting the tragic loss of his nephew who died in a car accident, in a car that was purchased by the MC and gifted to his nephew.[15] The most recent iteration of this Hip-Hop standard is J Cole's version that contemplates pregnancy and abortion as well as the economics of child-rearing. Each version of "Lost Ones" centers thematically on some powerful experience with human loss and as such the lyrics work together (across each version of the song) to establish the concept as a subjective standard within Hip Hop—producing versions of the song across three different decades from three outstanding but stylistically different artists. Also included in this list is *The Miseducation of Lauryn Hill*.[16] Lauryn Hill's first solo album was critically renown, winning five Grammy Awards and capturing the imagination of Hill's fan base; the record's title is also alluding to and signifying on Carter G. Woodson's classic text, *The Mis-Education of the Negro*.[17] Here again is an educational opportunity to critically engage/consider Lauryn Hill's artistic decision to situate her work as an artist within the context of Carter G. Woodson's discussion of (mis) education in America. Carter G. Woodson is the founder of Black History

Month, and his book, *The Mis-Education of the Negro* is all about the ways in which public education systems alienated and culturally conditioned young people. For Hill, the experience of alienation is one of many by-products of public education that also mirrors certain experiences with the Hip-Hop music industry. Again, the examples of instances where Hip-Hop music compels substantive educational engagement—easily accessed through thematically arranged playlists—abound throughout the canon of popularly released music. The question remains: Are we in a position to leverage these opportunities?

I have also compiled a "Tellability Playlist" featuring songs that explicitly tell stories and feature explicit references to a narrative's reportable base—or the foundation for why a narrative or story must be told in the first place. It is a playlist that can be paired with complex texts or essays on narratology and deployed in learning environments that feature multimedia narratives on various platforms, traditional stories or fictional texts, as well as the everyday narratives that we exchange in human discourse. Two entries on that list work together to defamiliarize ways that students approach narratives of crime in inner-city America. Certain stereotypical narratives abound in the popular media with respect to crime across urban America. Even though the data show that violent crime rates have dropped precipitously since the 1990s, news media coverage of violent crime has increased sixfold in that same time frame and the emergence of certain forms of Hip-Hop music have contributed to certain stereotypical perceptions of urban communities. One of several classic lyrics penned by Slick Rick is found in the lines of "Children's Story." "Children's Story" is one of the earliest examples of Hip-Hop noir, an anticrime parable that is framed as if it were a bedtime children's story. In it the narrator raps a story about two "stick-up kids," one who becomes addicted to robbing people, robs an undercover cop and is eventually pursued by law enforcement. After a series of experiences, the "lil boy" is eventually cornered by police and shot to death. The song ends with a warning directed at children to follow the "straight and narrow" path. Upon closer (critical) listening, Slick Rick slips in the fact that the "lil boy" actually drops his gun once he is cornered. According to the order of the narrative, the "lil boy" actually should not have been shot by the police officers that "surrounded" him. The fact that he was and that this bit of information is largely unremarkable in the litany of discourses that attend to this, one of Slick Rick's most popular songs, suggests some inconvenient truths about state violence against alleged criminals and the socially accepted nature of these kinds of narratives. While the instance of the cops shooting a "lil boy" dead may appear to be the most tellable aspect of the narrative, the hidden piece of the narrative—the fact that he was unarmed when he was murdered—suggests a more subtle reportable base to Slick Rick's "Children's Story."

Earl "DMX" Simmons' foray into the narratives of robbers in the 'hood, "Crime Story," finds another "stick-up kid" found out and pursued by law enforcement. "Crime Story" recounts a narrative of a criminal on the run—inflected with some eerie resonances with Richard Wright's *Native Son*—Bigger Thomas. After evading intense pursuit by law enforcement for criminal activity narrated in the song—possibly suggesting some inherent criminality—the subject of "Crime Story" transforms himself into a human bomb and detonates himself in a New York City police precinct.

Through playlist pedagogy, I have learned how young people want to talk about what they are listening to, and I have found that I can be more productive from a pedagogical standpoint—talking about their music—than I can from my educational standpoint trying to get them to talk about "my" music.[18] The combination of those things—coming to that realization and also gaining a deeper appreciation for the ubiquitous nature of those conversations—is the inspiration for many of the playlists that populate my iTunes library. Of course, the lists referenced here are abbreviated playlists, and the technology that I am talking about is iTunes, essentially. When you look at iTunes, it will tell you that there is much more information they can provide than this. In fact, one of the more important features it provides is the number of times you have played a particular song. In keeping track of my own record, all of the songs mentioned in this chapter are played a minimum of forty-four times. The two artists that are prominently featured on my most played list (at this time) are Lupe Fiasco and Kendrick Lamar. Now, that is not necessarily shocking to me, but it seems to suggest that the discourses around who your favorite artist is take on a certain tone and tenor within the mainstream. Not surprisingly, the artists that I am listening to are more socially conscious in their lyrics and music than many other mainstream/popular artists. I reference the lyrics of these artists throughout this project and regularly in my public speeches and in my classrooms. In order for us to have access to the ubiquitous learning environments within Hip-Hop culture, we have to be prepared to learn a little bit about the music in the culture, the technologies through which we access and listen to it, and an eager willingness to learn more and more through critical listening.

Part Three

Scholarly Reviews

5

Angry Black White Boyz

Angry Black White Boyz

The very first Beastie Boys recording that I ever listened to was "Slow and Low."[1] I absolutely loved that record (and still do). Back then, circa 1985/86, the Beastie Boys adjusted the rhythmic pace of Hip Hop for all of us who were kinesthetically challenged. I did not know it then, but it turns out that "Slow and Low" was a cast off from the recording sessions of my favorite group at the time, Run–D.M.C. Run–D.M.C.'s *King of Rock* was an instant classic.[2] It makes sense that "Slow and Low" captured some small modicum of that essence, and in turn, put the Beastie Boys on my energetically unfolding Hip-Hop map.

I can still remember the night my brother Rob told me that the Beastie Boys were white. I could not believe it. Of course, listening to it now, "Slow and Low" may not sound so Black (whatever that means), but my listening comprehension of that record in the mid-1980s occurred in the vacuum of whiteness that was the assumed predisposition of rap music. I simply could not wrap my head around the fact that the Beastie Boys were white. Like many Hip-Hop heads, I often relied upon my older brothers, cousins, and friends as expert guides in the culture that was beginning to totalize my existence. Still, I chalked it up to a rumor—a ploy to get folks to talk about the record and the group. Clearly there was no MTV or visual representation for me in my Hip-Hop worldview in Newark, New Jersey. Perhaps I was not old enough or connected enough to radio or TV to figure this out on my own, but when I heard "Fight for Your Right to Party" I finally realized that what Rob said was true. The Beastie Boys were white and I had a love-hate relationship with "Fight for Your Right."[3]

Early on, I simply could not fathom a white voice in what I believed was an utterly Black and/or brown creative form. However, none of this really mattered after the first time I heard "Paul Revere" by the Beastie Boys.[4] For me, "Paul Revere" put the Beastie Boys on par with Grandmaster Flash and Run–D.M.C. at least by the official standard of memorizing all of the lyrics to a tune. The song's reverse anthropomorphosis—transforming the colonial legend into the horse—signaled all of the irreverence that the Beastie Boys came to represent in that burgeoning moment in Hip Hop. Arguably, that irreverence was part of the racial camouflage that positioned them as the first significant white group in Black rap music. The three Beastie Boys, Ad Rock (Adam Horovitz), MCA (Adam Yauch), and Mike D (Mike Diamond), began their careers as separate, but overlapping, punk rock entities. In 1981, Ad Rock played in a band called The Young and the Useless, and the original punk rock incarnation of the Beastie Boys included Yauch, Diamond, drummer Kate Schellenbach, and guitarist John Berry. By 1984, Schellenbach and Berry had moved on and Horovitz had joined Yauch and Diamond to form the group that has since become one of the few indelible groups in Hip-Hop history.

The debut album of the Beastie Boys (including each of the three aforementioned songs), *Licensed to Ill*, was the first rap album to be number one on the Billboard 200 chart and has (to date) sold over nine million copies.[5] Its initial success was never duplicated on successive attempts by the Beastie Boys: *Paul's Boutique* (1989),[6] *Check Your Head* (1992),[7] *Ill Communication* (1994),[8] *Hello Nasty* (1998),[9] *To the 5 Boroughs* (2004),[10] *The Mix-Up* (2007),[11] which won a Grammy Award for best Pop Instrumental Album, and *Hot Sauce Committee, Pt. 1* (2010).[12] Aside from the musically aesthetic continuity of *Check Your Head* and *Ill Communication,* the Beastie Boys consistently charted new territory and/or discovered new ways of imagining their artistic personas on various albums. Their most recent effort, *Hot Sauce Committee, Pt. 2* was alleged to have a working title of one of the album's songs entitled "Tadlock's Glasses," a somewhat obscure reference to Elvis Presley. In a 2009 interview with BBC, Adam Yauch claimed that the Beastie Boys once had a tour bus driver named Tadlock who had also driven Elvis Presley's backup singers. Even more amazing, Presley had given Tadlock a pair of glasses of which he was very proud.[13] As a relevant digression, it is important to note that white rappers in

Hip Hop have often had to (and might always have to) wrestle with the specter of Elvis Presley. Not that Presley has anything to do with Hip Hop directly, but his relationship to rock music and his uncanny ability to ape blackness (more so in his dance moves and performance than in his sound) render him a sort of whipping boy/cultural obstacle for white rappers who feel a desire to distinguish their style from his. Although Presley became the most famous rock star in history through his appropriation of Black sound and movement, he is famously and regularly quoted as having said that "the only thing a Black person can do for me is shine my shoes."[14] The Beastie Boys have not really been on record as having confronted the ghost of Elvis' past, but this Tadlock reference is an interesting reflection of their artistic autonomy. It denotes a creative confidence that allowed them to deftly navigate the rap music domain as the first white guys in the genre.

It is fairly telling (and indicative of their success and longevity) that the Beastie Boys, as an artistic entity, have never tried to sound Black or even be Black. No contemporary rock-fusion group (Limp Bizkit, Linkin Park, Kid Rock, or even Portis Head and/or Beck) can claim to have absconded their musical influence, and no white rapper that followed in their wake would enjoy the identity markers of whiteness (or lack thereof) so effortlessly in the world of Hip Hop. This includes Hip Hop's next (or maybe first) great white hope Robert Van Winkle, also known as Vanilla Ice. He is widely considered to be the most infamous rapper in history, but certainly, he is the most infamous white rapper in history. He is, in effect, Hip Hop's wannabe Elvis Presley. When "Ice Ice Baby" hit the airwaves in 1990 it was an insatiable party and club smash[15]— more so as a result of its crafty interpolation of "Under Pressure" than Vanilla Ice's lyrical ability.[16] Although the Beastie Boys did not necessarily have street credibility, they were from New York and they had Run–D.M.C. and Def Jam behind them. They were also completely comfortable in their own skin which showed through in the music. Vanilla Ice had none of the above. No artistic camaraderie with either Def Jam or Run–D.M.C., no street credibility, and, as would become painfully obvious, no confidence or conviction. To give him a little slack for his self-constructed predicament, Vanilla Ice came along at a time in Hip Hop when the music was shifting from its boastful roots to a much more sinister and critical reflection of the postindustrial environs of American inner-city life. In that cultural context, Vanilla Ice was probably fated to fail. Still, *To the Extreme*, his 1990 debut album, sold over seven million copies, proving once again that there were millions of white fans waiting for the right moment to step into the Hip-Hop arena.[17]

Despite all of *To the Extreme*'s fleeting pop-cultural cache, Vanilla Ice, born in Miami with no violent street ethos to which he might refer, conceived some cockamamie story about his own gangster past. Gaping holes were immediately poked into the fabricated narrative of Van Winkle's past, and by the time his 1990 film, *Cool as Ice*, was released in the fall of that same year, Vanilla Ice was known as the biggest fraud in Hip-Hop history.[18] He committed the cardinal sin of constructing an inauthentic identity at the very moment when the politics of Hip-Hop identity were consuming the foundational essence of the culture. True to his own fraudulent form, Vanilla Ice followed his debut with *Extremely Live* in 1991, a desperate attempt to salvage the final vestiges of his manhood, by reinventing himself as a gangster rapper.[19] How could a white boy named Ice possibly compete with the likes of Ice-T, Ice Cube, and N.W.A.? One important distinction to note between Vanilla Ice and the Beastie Boys is that although some of us might have thought that the Beastie Boys sounded Black, theirs was merely a by-product of the utter absence of white voices in Hip Hop. Vanilla Ice, on the other hand, actually tried to sound Black on too many of his successive albums which was (and is) simply unacceptable in the authenticity-driven worlds of Hip-Hop culture.

In the ill-fated aftermath of Vanilla Ice, there was MC Serch and 3rd Bass. Just prior to Vanilla Ice's meteoric uprise and demise, MC Serch (Michael Berrin) and Prime Minister Pete Nice (Peter Nash) joined forces with DJ Richie Rich (Richard Lawson). This interracial trio, a Black DJ with two white New York–bred MCs, proved that white boys could do Hip Hop respectfully and authentically. Their Def Jam debut, *The Cactus Album*,[20] featured one of Hip Hop's greatest singles, "The Gas Face."[21] In one verse from that now classic cut (and video), MC Serch solidified himself as the most respected white rapper of all time: "Black cat is bad luck, bad guys wear black/Musta been a white guy who started all that. (Make the Gas Face!) For those little white lies/My expression to the mountainous blue eyes." Some folks might recall that Serch reprised this verse as the sole white rapper in the revolutionary group, the Mau

Mau's, featured in *Bamboozled*, Spike Lee's poignant treatment of the legacy of blackface minstrelsy in American popular culture. Ironically, he ended up being the sole survivor of that fictional Hip-Hop group.[22]

MC Serch's critical consciousness, on brief display in these simple, yet powerful lines, not only underscored his connection to the plight of blackness but also his willingness to speak the truth even at the expense of his white brethren. This lyrical insight put into bold relief the deepest meanings of Serch's rap moniker. Unfortunately, 3rd Bass only held it together for two albums. On their second record, *Derelicts of Dialect*, released in 1991, they demonstrated, once again, their potential as rappers (white or black) who were committed more to the elements of the culture and perfection of the verbal craft of rapping than they were to the pop charts or mainstream success.[23] More so than the Beastie Boys, and much more effortlessly than Vanilla Ice, the MCs of 3rd Bass sounded Black (whatever that means) in ways that were not an affront to Hip Hop's traditional sense of blackness. "Pop Goes the Weasel," a pointed and hilarious jab at Vanilla Ice, was not only their most successful single, but also single-handedly spawned the demise of Vanilla Ice's career.[24] There was no way for Vanilla Ice to exist in the same Hip-Hop world that produced MC Serch. Serch went on to pursue a solo recording career, releasing *Return of the Product* in 1992 and eventually served as the midwife for Nas' career.[25] He still produces music—he released *Many Young Lives Ago* in 2007[26]—and delivered several standout performances as the host of VH1 and Ego Trip's *White Rapper* reality TV series.[27]

For all of the debates and discourses surrounding white rappers generated via the careers of the Beastie Boys, Vanilla Ice, and MC Serch, no one could have anticipated the advent of Marshall Mathers/Slim Shady/Eminem. If we imagine these rappers (Beastie Boys, Vanilla Ice, MC Serch) as the pillars of white Hip Hop, then Eminem must be the centerpiece. Eminem, born Marshall Mathers III in St. Joseph, Missouri, but who lived his formative years in and around Detroit, is something more than the next or latest "great white hope" since that term suggests or implies some impending failure to meet expectations. On almost all accounts, Eminem has done just the opposite. His success as a rapper is unparalleled, although his career has not been without its challenges and failures, controversies and tragedies. Mathers grew up in abject poverty, nomadically shifting from one home to the next. His father abandoned him early and (as has been brutishly chronicled through his recordings) his mother was addicted to drugs and abusive. At an early age, Mathers was inspired when he saw the Beastie Boys perform on the Run–D.M.C.-headlined "Tougher Than Leather Tour." He was already a Hip-Hop head but seeing the Beastie Boys and listening to *Licensed to Ill* was an affirmation of sorts. In his riveting (*New York Times* bestselling) photo-autobiography, Mathers says: "I liked the Beastie Boys because they were themselves—they weren't fronting …. It was them being themselves that helped me figure out how to relax and be me."[28]

Although the blockbuster film, *8 Mile* (2002), is a semiautobiographical depiction of Mathers' personal and musical journey through the Detroit underground Hip-Hop world,[29] *Eminem: The Way I Am* is an uncensored autobiographical account of his own life told from his own perspective.[30] Named after the single from his 2000 album, *The Marshall Mathers LP*, the documentary resonates with its nominative predecessor in significant ways.[31] In the song "The Way I Am," Eminem's pulsating lyrical delivery is seething with anger.[32] His anger is primarily targeted at his newfound fame, fans who hound him in public, and a controversially inclined media eager to attach his name to any scandalous headline. Although these attacks are equal parts veiled and explicit from one verse to the next, it is pretty clear from the song as a whole that Eminem's anger is mainly directed at white people and white social institutions. In this sense, "The Way I Am" becomes sort of a super signifier for Eminem's relationship to whiteness.

There are at least two prevailing themes that repeat themselves like a refrain throughout *Eminem: The Way I Am*. First, foremost, and throughout the narrative, Eminem pays homage to Proof, his closest friend, and the first Black man who made it possible for a white boy like him to navigate the Black world of underground Hip Hop in Detroit. According to Eminem: "Proof was the key to my whole game. He was the only reason I stopped getting my ass whipped. I'm not going to sugarcoat it—he was my ghetto pass."[33] Proof was Eminem's attestation of authenticity. He paved a path for Eminem to hone his skills in the battleground of Detroit's potent underground universe. Without Proof, there might not be an Eminem (or, at the very least, not the mainstream success that we know Eminem as today). Proof's integral role in Eminem's development was but a precursor to the authentic credence lent to him via his ongoing association, friendship, and creative collaborations with the inimitable Dr. Dre. Sadly, and maybe from Eminem's perspective, tragically ironic, Proof was murdered in an altercation gone awry outside of a Detroit nightclub in 2006. Eminem depicted Proof's murder in the 2004 music video for "Like Toy Soldiers."[34] Although he had nothing to do with Proof's murder—he was not even there the night it happened—Eminem still had to (and has to) question the role that the video plays in the narrative of Proof's life and tragic death. His honesty about the ways in which Proof proved his authenticity in Hip Hop only further serves to endear Eminem to all of his fans and his peers in Hip-Hop culture.

The other central theme of Eminem's autobiography is the abiding anger that informs all three of his identities: (1) Marshall Mathers: angry at his family, his impoverished and isolated upbringing, and tumultuous personal life—especially his volatile relationship with his twice divorced wife, Kim Scott; (2) Slim Shady: angry at the industry and the pop culture icons it produces and promotes; and (3) Eminem: angry at the world—targeting dominant social institutions like the media, the government, and the music industry generally. Through all of the manifestations of his identity, Marshall Mathers/ Slim Shady/Eminem, he is still unsure of the primary source of his anger. He poses the question to himself throughout his autobiography but a satisfactory answer never emerges. Seemingly, there is not a singular source for so much angst and anger.

I find it difficult to categorize Macklemore within the context of other rappers who preceded him and also happened to be white. Like so many Hip Hop and pop music listeners I was first introduced to Macklemore via the super-successful "Thrift Shop" single in 2012. Generally speaking, I do not listen to mainstream radio so much these days. I prefer a more proactive approach to deciding how I spend my precious listening time. When a new popular artist comes to my attention it is usually because some young person, a student, insists that I listen to "fill in the blank" because she/he is the hottest. Ironically, it was my own children—my daughter especially—who put "Thrift Shop" on the aural map for me. This is a weird phenomenon—that my children listen to variations on the form of music that I listened to growing up. And because I have had significant impact on how they listen to Hip Hop and what kind of music they listen to period, I now have great respect for their individual musical preferences as teenagers. I know what the inputs are with respect to their musical tastes so I am inclined to listen to their suggestions. But the first time I heard "Thrift Shop" was no such sophisticated affair. We were in the car driving and they blasted it and bopped their heads to it, singing along with that infectious chorus that stays with you for hours—if not days.

Interestingly enough, I had already heard of Ryan Lewis—one former student of mine was so excited about Lewis' artistry that he cornered me one day and made me watch YouTube videos of Ryan Lewis producing beats, playing instruments, and performing. This is how an aging Hip-Hop head comes to "discover" new (at the time unknown) artists. It is an interesting process—this coming to terms with new music and new artists via community advice, and ongoing discourse about the music seems to me to be authentic to Hip Hop—not exclusive to it, of course, but authentic to it, in the sense that the word-of-mouth phenomena within Hip-Hop cultural discourses are vital components of the culture itself.

I copped *The Heist*, marveled at its independently produced mass appeal, and basically kept it movin'. I do not indulge too much in the debates about appropriation in Hip-Hop culture—white, Black, Asian, or otherwise—because a chunk of my time as a scholar within the culture has been spent defending Hip Hop against attacks of it being an appropriative form—a derivative of greater Black and/or American musical forms. Seeing Hip Hop expand its reach across the globe over the course of my lifetime has been an incredibly empowering experience and researching, writing, and reporting on it up close has challenged me to develop sophisticated models for assessing the culture, the music that derives from the culture, and the slippery questions of authenticity in the artistry of the culture.

When my good friend and colleague, Georgia Roberts, presented me with an opportunity to meet Macklemore and Ryan Lewis, I was delighted to take her up on it. Macklemore and Ryan Lewis immediately struck me as humble and thoughtful artists. Before our conversation about cultural appropriation, white privilege, and other critical topics on "The Remix," I knew Macklemore would be an engaging interviewee. He is effortlessly self-reflexive and deeply committed to learning more about the particular subject position he inhabits as a successful pop star who set out to make good Hip-Hop music. He also happens to be white—an existential fact that is almost as much plague as it is privilege in the world of authenticity games in Hip-Hop culture. My conversation with Macklemore on "The Remix" attempts to wrestle with these issues in a short-form interview, but give a listen to his pre-"Thrift Shop" days music, especially "White Privilege," to get a better understanding of his complex lyrical engagement with identity within Hip-Hop culture and some of the social justice issues that he has been thinking about for some time now. Going forward, my sense is that when the debates on race, cultural authenticity, and Hip Hop converge in the public sphere, the dialogue on "The Remix" can serve as a primer on how we might advance the discourse about race and pop culture beyond the "gotcha" polemics to which our conversations often devolve.

In an edited collection of essays entitled *White Reign: Deploying Whiteness in America*, Michael Eric Dyson suggests that the traditionally unmarked identity known as whiteness has been "outed" in the late twentieth and early twenty-first centuries.[35] According to Dyson, whiteness "in the context of race in America," is deployed through three interlocking elements: whiteness as identity, whiteness as ideology, and whiteness as institution.[36] Surely the Angry Black White Boyz of Hip Hop have exhibited each of these elements, and, to varying degrees, deployed whiteness both strategically and not so strategically in order to emerge as superstars within the world of Hip-Hop culture. That said, it is those Angry Black White Boyz that sincerely love Hip Hop and genuinely appreciate the ways in which whiteness is inextricably linked to blackness (not identical to it or subsumable by it). The same Angry Black White Boyz who are quick to critique and lyrically dismantle the dominant institutions and ideologies that Hip-Hop culture emerged in response to, the same Angry Black White Boyz that Hip Hop has come to know and to generously and unabashedly love.

6

A Review of Mansbach's *Rage is Back*

By the third time that Adam Mansbach's narrator, in his novel, *Rage is Back*, refers to himself as "your boy here," Kilroy Dondi Vance will have utterly ingratiated himself to even the most uninitiated reader.[1] Dondi's endearing narration is the anchoring thread for a novel that both (re)constructs and reaffirms the mythos in and around Hip Hop culture's lost element: graffiti art or writing. Cultural knowledge and history are at the forefront of Mansbach's latest foray into the collective conscious of the Hip-Hop generations. Knowledge is power for Hip-Hop heads and in *Rage is Back*, Dondi drives the narrative through the artistic archives of graf art, DJ-ing, underground Hip Hop, and the literal underground itself. Mansbach achieves these feats by showcasing the breadth and depth of his experience(s) within Hip-Hop culture, coupled with an encyclopedic, liberal deployment of relevant literary allusions to everything from classic alternative drug use to Homer's Odyssey.[2]

Dondi's journey through New York City circa 2005 (and the 1990s via crafty, intermittent flashbacks) is a frame through which readers will follow the prodigal return of his father, William Vance, also known as Billy Rage. Rage leaves and returns some sixteen years later to New York City after a series of tragic incidents, including the murder of his best friend and partner in the graf artistry, Amuse, by the evil antagonist of the novel Officer Anastacio Bracken. In addition to leaving his son, Dondi, fatherless for most his life, Rage's odyssey includes a stint in the Amazonian rain forest where he learns the shamanic arts of healing and mind alteration.

Mansbach's reverent insight into the little-known world of authentic graffiti artists is the most compelling aspect of the novel's multilayered narrative and a stunning achievement unto itself. This sensibility seeps into each and every sentence about graffiti crews, train bombing, and selling in Soho. The fictional graffiti crew around which the narrative centers, The Immortal Five, a "… name long smudged with irony …"[3] consists of Dondi's dad, Rage, his murdered friend, Amuse, Dondi's blind friend and mentor, Ambassador Fever Dengue, Sabor, who commits suicide soon after Amuse's murder, and the resident hustler of the crew, Cloud Nine. What remains of the crew in 2005—a discombobulated Rage, a nearly blind Fever, and a recently paroled Cloud—work with Dondi and his mother (also a former graffiti artist) to avenge the cover-up of Amuse's murder in the most spectacular fashion possible for a washed-up crew of old school graf artists.

If the novel's education on the world of graffiti writers is somehow lacking, *Rage is Back* also features condensed, but equally intense courses on DJ-ing via an ode to Kid Capri's masterful record selection skills, and a testament to MC-ing or rapping through a dizzying array of allusions, metaphors, analogies, and similes. Dondi's frenetic narration skillfully features more similes than the oeuvre of a rapper who has been in the rap game for over a decade. Some, "like the first guy who jumped from the North Tower,"[4] will haunt the reader well beyond the solitary experience of reading the novel itself. Many more serve to imbue Dondi's storytelling prowess with greatest-of-all-time status in the discourses that continue to drive much of the talk about Hip-Hop culture.

For any aficionados of underground concepts in the literature, Mansbach's craftily constructed underworld will not disappoint. In addition to situating the lived realities of risk-taking graffiti artists within the context of lost New York City subway tunnels and the near mythic homeless underground dwellers popularly referred to as the "Mole People," Dondi's self-reflexive and intermittently self-conscious narration produces meticulous imagery of the seedy underbelly of New York City. In a direct shout out to the "silent oppressed" of the Hip-Hop world and to the annals of Black literary history, the underground passages of *Rage is Back* will surely become the substance of graffiti lore for the foreseeable future.

7

Gangsta Scholarship: A Review
of *Nuthin but a "G" Thang*

Eithne Quinn's exceptionally executed study, *Nuthin' but a "G" Thang: The Culture and Commerce of Gangsta Rap,* signifies the fullest potential of Hip-Hop scholarship and its undeniable place in the fields of American Studies and Cultural Studies proper.[1] At the onset, Quinn situates her argument squarely within one of the longstanding and ongoing debates in cultural studies. On the one hand, oppression resulting from the social invisibility, unchecked globalization, and postindustrialism that plagued the West Coast urban environs (from which gangsta rap emerged in the late 1980s) can cultivate a critical consciousness. Indeed, the kind of social critique found in powerful rap lyrics like N.W.A.'s antipolice brutality anthem "Fuck the Police"[2] or Tupac's redemptive "Dear Mama" inform this consciousness.[3] inform this consciousness. Yet more often than not, gangsta rap also reflects a pervasive false consciousness in the Marxist sense where ideology is posited as "a kind of 'veil' over the eyes of the oppressed."[4] False consciousness is reflected in much of the misogyny that runs rampant through the lyrics of gangsta rap, where women have become the axiomatic scapegoats of choice for too many rappers and songs to name here. More importantly for Quinn, is the shameful consumerism reflected in the "blinged-out" era of gangsta rap where spending hundreds of thousands of dollars on ornamented jewelry is commonplace for artists who supposedly represent communities in desperate need of economic resources.

According to Quinn, gangsta rap inhabits the deconstructed spaces between these two pillars of argumentation among scholars and researchers. She posits:

> Gangsta rap tends to represent false consciousness and at the same time reflect on it; to angrily spout antiprogressive sentiments, and to see the

pitfalls and despair of this stance; to verbally abuse women in the most offensive terms, while registering the power of the opposite sex; to enact marketable stereotypes of black masculinity, and then to critique these very depictions.[5]

Her writing eloquently ushers the reader into her discourse. Her opening parable brilliantly analyzes and examines gangsta rap's precarious relationship to commercial culture through an incisive interpretation of an Ice Cube malt liquor "advert" and that same brand's requisite product placement in the film *Boyz n the Hood.*[6] She characterizes the shift from the flagrant promotion of malt liquor to the more subtle product placed mode thusly: "The shift in emphasis can be summarized as the superseding of commodified authenticity with a new subcultural articulation of authentic commodification."[7] From there, she establishes her framework based upon the politics of representation—a triangulation of structuralism, culturalism, and Marxism—that allows her to expertly excavate and explicate "the wider structures and deeper determinants that shape the popular-culture terrain."[8]

Some of these determinants are the forefathers of gangsta rap such as Stackolee (or Stagolee) and other "Bad Nigger figures" that precede the Tupacs and Ice Cubes of the genre.[9] Quinn's objective handling of African American folk and cultural history suggests an academic expertise unparalleled thus far in studies on gansta rap music and culture. Her chapter on Tupac Shakur stands as the single most reflective historical explication of one of the most frequently written about figures of Hip-Hop culture. Unlike others, she does not betray herself to be a fan of the genre or as one of the misguided haters attempting to censor that about which they know little. Her sole misstep may be that she directs too much attention to the politics of representation as tools of empowerment for the artisans and entrepreneurs of this fading subgenre of Hip-Hop music. But, considering her astute management of one of pop culture's most complex and conflicted forms, *Nuthin' but a "G" Thang* is by far the definitive scholarly work on gangsta rap music and culture.

A Review of *Beats, Rhymes and Life*
(ATCQ Documentary)

Beats, Rhymes, and Beef

Twenty years later, I still find it difficult to qualify or quantify the formidable and formative impact that A Tribe Called Quest (ATCQ) had on Hip-Hop culture and its most loyal constituents. In the early 1990s, Hip Hop was caught in the crossfire of what would eventually become a binary battle between good and evil. Public Enemy, due to social and market forces beyond their control, had passed the proverbial Hip-Hop baton to N.W.A. This change in the content (and form) of Hip-Hop music was, at the time, much more subtle than it seems when looking back through decades of musical meandering in the muck of misogyny, consumerism, and violence that has appropriated the content of rap music at the mainstream level since the 1990s.

A Tribe Called Quest represented a third space. A space where Hip-Hop enthusiasts could carry on their love affair with the culture without the baggage of globalized Americana. In short, ATCQ made Hip-Hop intellectualism (and its attendant discourses) cool without pumping fists, glaring sounds, or trite nationalism. To call them Hip-Hop hippies though was to gravely miss the point. ATCQ carved out identities for maturing listeners of Hip-Hop music. They were an indelible example of the ways in which we might engage Hip Hop as adults. Since I was (at the time) just legally becoming an adult, I felt their vibe viscerally.

You can imagine, then, that I was beyond excited about the advent of Michael Rapaport's documentary film, *Beats, Rhymes, and Life: The Travels of A Tribe Called Quest.*[1] Like so many other Hip-Hop fans, this film's screening was an extraordinary event for me; an opportunity to relish in the nostalgia of what Hip Hop was, what it could have been, and (for me) what it still can be. Many of my fellow Hip-Hop aficionados and colleagues had similar or comparable experiences with the film.

Rapaport's film unabashedly addresses the tensions and conflicts between Q-Tip and Phife Dawg, a conflict well known (albeit externally) by many die-hard ATCQ fans. For some, the film's focus, (a director's choice for sure), delimits the real impact and import of ATCQ. For others, just seeing ATCQ on the big screen in some of their glory and much of their conflict is a narratological vindication. Indeed, we are so starved for our own stories that almost any narrative, positive or negative in perspective, is an irresistible morsel for those of us whose disgust with the present pop dominance of formulaic rap seeks to unseat the music from its throne in our collective imagination. It is painfully ironic that the film signifies on the title of ATCQ's fourth full-length album, *Beats, Rhymes, & Life* since, for well-versed fans, this album fatefully signaled the beginning of the end of ATCQ.[2] By the time *The Love Movement* dropped, we knew that ATCQ was anything but loving in terms of the group's interpersonal dynamics—a point that Phife reifies for us in the film.[3] Still, Rapaport's documentary does seek to answer a burning question about the lack of ATCQ music in the new millennium. The long anticipated answer (as to why there have been no more albums) is that ATCQ does not get along. Q-Tip is the plagued perfectionist, Phife is the reluctant artist, Jarobi is the culinary artist, and Ali Shaheed Muhammad is the distant objective DJ. Given their polarizing personalities, it is no small feat that they were able to keep it together for three magnificent albums—miracles to Hip-Hop music if we consider how many albums since then measure up in quality and/or playability.

In short, we still need an ATCQ documentary that more intently spotlights the music and explores Q-Tip's knowledge of musical history and sound selection. We still need a Hip-Hop documentary that focuses on health issues and more deeply explores the chronicles of addiction to legal food substances—sugar in Phife's case—and the ways in which our knowledge of nutrition (or lack thereof) is literally killing us. Finally, we still need a Hip-Hop documentary that more holistically surveys the group dynamics of

crews, homies, DJs, and ancillary folk who form the very backbone and/or
identities of some of our favorite Hip-Hop acts. This documentary does not do
all of those things, because it simply cannot. Rapaport's sole mission is to offer
an explanation as to why our favorite Hip-Hop group no longer makes music.

Over the course of this explanation, he offers some very candid (albeit
unsatisfying) answers: (1) Q-Tip is the musical and lyrical foundation of
ATCQ. Although he is somewhat reluctant to admit it, he is largely responsible
for what we think of as the ATCQ ethos. However, he apparently has been
very effective in letting Phife know this fact which leads me to ... (2) Phife
is a reluctant member of one of the greatest groups in Hip-Hop history. He
quite literally had to be coaxed into the studio. His health issues certainly
complicated matters and reordered his priorities, but the bottom line is that
sometimes he just did not want to be part of the group. While many, including
Q-Tip himself, will come away from this documentary thinking that Q-Tip
is some kind of pretentious performer, those of us who know artists (or are
artists ourselves) know that his posture is sometimes par for the course of
musical greatness.

In the end though, I left the Ritz Theater in Philadelphia thinking about
the crazy possibility that all beef in Hip-Hop culture could be this nonviolent.
Imagine, for example, if Tupac and Biggie could have settled their differences
the way that Q-Tip and Phife have, or if Jay-Z and Nas had not needed to
assassinate each other on record before they could form a tentative, temporary
alliance. What if EPMD could have stayed together (throughout the 1990s)
without splitting up or burglarizing the other? If all Hip-Hop groups or
competitive adversaries worked through their issues in the turbulent, but
relatively nonviolent manner in which Q-Tip and Phife have, then rap music
and Hip-Hop culture would be all the better for it.

What Conservative Men Think … A Review of "What Black Men Think"

After a screening of "What Black Men Think" at the Gettysburg College Africana Studies program, I declined from responding to Mr. Janks Morton immediately following the film.[1] Although I enjoy spending time with, and intellectually engaging, my colleagues, Morton's film left an awful taste in my mouth. To its credit, it is (I would argue) fairly well produced and fairly well edited for an independent project. That said, "What Black Men Think" is tacitly misogynistic, blatantly homophobic, and ideologically contaminated by some of the most self-hating troglodytes of the Black political right. Let me exemplify each of these issues (misogyny, homophobia, and ideology) in turn.

The balance of pundits in the film panders to men; which, given that it is a film about what Black men think, I begrudgingly accepted. However, the question of what women think about Black men is explored and resolved around three key points of the film:

(1) Black women are unduly influenced by Oprah and the media into thinking that more Black men are on the "DL" than there actually are. Statistically, what Morton depicts for us on his board of (mis)education is that "only" thirteen percent of Black women who contract HIV from a heterosexual partner are exposed to the virus because of their heterosexual partner's closeted bisexual or gay behavior. Conversely, sixty-four percent of Black women who contract the disease contract it from substance-abuse-related issues. Aside from the inability of the numbers to accurately quantify the subtleties of the main issue here (hint: that Black women are contracting HIV at rates higher than any other segment of the American population), how dare Morton ignorantly suggest that thirteen percent is a statistically insignificant number.

Morton's tactics here are flawed by-products of the same kind of divisive gender politics he is supposed to be critical of in this very film. Instead of thinking pragmatically about the main problem (that Black women are dying from HIV) he wants to first, minimize the "down low" phenomenon (of course, without ever considering the ways in which repression and violent homophobic attitudes produce these closeted behaviors to begin with) and second, tacitly redirect the blame onto Black women themselves. This is not even the grossest example of how the film lavishes hate on Black women. His subsequent portrayals of interracial marriage are equally shameful, and indeed, infuriating. Even by his own selected statistics written on the board of (mis) education, the numbers have doubled over the period in question. To suggest that more or less interracial marriage provides a better or worse lens through which to view Black men is absurd, and I would also challenge Morton to look into the parental and marriage backgrounds of his beloved pundits for more on that score.

The gravest miscarriage of statistical evidence occurs after Morton's felonious, overly contrived buildup to the numbers on the number one killer of Black people. After dismissing the serious facilitators of Black mortality—HIV, cancer, homicide, and heart disease—he sensationally and disingenuously juxtaposes these numbers with the number of abortions (I assume/hope for Black folk only and during the same year but this remains unclear). I am not sure where exactly to begin with this or even how to address it. I do not believe, though, that this is about religious beliefs, when life starts, or any of the attendant debates around choice or life. This is Morton's covert way of once again proclaiming that what is really wrong with the Black community is the behavior of Black women. Beyond that, how on earth can we rectify the fact that nearly a million Black men are in jail (many more are in the system either through probation and parole), divorce rates are at about fifty percent, public schools systems are collapsing and/or being closed, joblessness in the Black community is at times twice the national average, and just about every disease on the planet affects our community to a greater degree than it does the mainstream community. Given these statistics, how can we possibly remedy these issues with Morton's suggestion that we have more children? Why do we have to rob women of their reproductive rights in order to save the Black community? I would honestly appreciate answers to either of those questions.

(2) Certainly the scenes from "Passions" and the various clips of Black male actors portraying female, transgender, or cross-dressing characters are intentionally designed/positioned for us to hate those images. Suffice it to say that while I believe we need to be suspicious and critical of figures like Martin Lawrence and Eddie Murphy who mask their personal misogyny and femiphobia in the prosthetics and heavily weighted accouterments of Hollywood costume design; I also think that clear distinctions must be made between the portrayals offered by Murphy/Lawrence and Flip Wilson.

(3) Please be aware, make your students aware, and anyone else who spends their time watching this film that most of the major pundits in the film including Shelby Steele, Armstrong Williams, John McWhorter, Jesse Lee Peterson, Juan Williams, and Mychal Massie are all birds of a right-wing feather. The film critiques the National Association for the Advancement of Colored people (NAACP), Jesse Jackson, and Al Sharpton for race-baiting and prostituting themselves for money. These critiques may in some cases be totally warranted. However, to not direct the exact same critique at several of the aforementioned stars of the film is subservient to conservative power brokers and the Republican Party. Moreover, it is a direct and unforgivable insult to the audience. The Manhattan Institute, The Hoover Institute, and think tanks of their ilk engage in the same pay-to-play politics that this film is allegedly critical of. How dare Shelby Steele or John McWhorter open their mouths in a film that attempts to denounce Black intellectualism and identity prostitution when they serve white racist interests. How can we possibly believe anything that Jesse Lee Peterson says when he is coonin' daily on his radio program and one of his most proud and prominent supporters is Sean Hannity! To add insult to injury, Juan Williams works for Fox News.[2] How can we possibly dignify the remarks of Armstrong Williams when we know that he took hundreds of thousands of dollars from the Bush administration to feign objectivity and endorse the No Child Left Behind Act?

These pundits project sincerity as they ask (in opening sequences of the film) what happened to the Black community between 1965 and now. Their answer is that the Black community bought into government handouts.

Allow me to diffuse this loaded sentiment for a moment. First, this is not ignorance, and aside from Jesse Lee Peterson, these guys are all pretty smart. Second, the institutions, platforms, and entities that make all of them millionaires certainly want to dismantle all social safety nets. But, to be clear, faith in the American safety net is not what has destroyed the Black family. Indeed, underfunded public school systems that serve Black folk, along with the CIA who purposefully plagued our communities with crack, guns, and other social challenges have played a role. What has happened since 1965? Globalization, postindustrialism, and the outsourcing of working-class jobs from our communities are just a few factors. This is what has contributed to the so-called destruction of the Black family. If you couple joblessness (as a result of globalized shifting economies) with the rise of the underground economies (crack/CIA) and the privatization of the prison system (what is often referred to as the prison industrial complex) then you can begin to understand the systemic underpinnings of the challenges we face.

Do these problems cause an erasure of agency in the Black community? No, they do not. After years of working in the prison systems and the public school systems of New Jersey and Pennsylvania of my own volition (i.e., voluntarily and without pay) I have found not one Black male who blames the system, white privilege, or even white supremacy for the challenges he faces. To bring a long-winded (but extremely warranted) criticism to a close, let me say this: Maybe it is okay for Mr. Morton that the number of Black men in prison is nearly equal to the number of Black men in college. But for me, the fact that over 800,000 of our brothers are locked in chains after having been vigorously prosecuted by an unjust system is a new manifestation of oppression eerily reminiscent of our slave history. That most of them are not there for violent crimes but for petty transgressions and substance abuse is yet another oversight utterly lost in this film.

For me, though, the gravest oversight of the film is this: I am a Black Man. I am married to a Black woman and we have two beautiful children. I was born and raised in Newark, New Jersey, and I earned my Ph.D. in the Ivy League. This film, "What Black Men Think" does not in any way represent me, where I come from, or what I think. In the interest of uncensored truth, Mr. Morton should humbly rename his project, "What Conservative, Well Paid and Well Trained, Black Men Think."

Part Four

Rap Around the Table

10

Race Theory and Gender in Hip Hop's Global Future Roundtable Participants: Treva Lindsay, Regina Bradley, and Scott Heath Moderator: James Peterson

This roundtable discussion wrestles with the conceptualization of Hip Hop as African American, masculine music, while critically considering ideas such as "post-race" and "gender trouble," in the contextual realities of globalization and US cultural imperialism. One frame of this discussion centers on Scott Heath's "Head Theory." Heath makes two important arguments for unpacking the global tenants inherent in discursive enterprises aimed at redressing the limitations of assertions generally made by and about Hip-Hop culture. (1) That Hip-Hop discourse is faced with the challenge of transcending its own historical narrative. A gendered narrative that limits the understanding of the culture to its performative elements and the sui generis histories of a handful of "authentic" forefathers and cultural protectors and (2) that Hip-Hop discourse might take a more theoretical turn that requires discursive participants in the culture to consider the language (and attendant narratives) of technology, what Lawrence Lessig might refer to as "remix culture" and what Heath explicates as "repurposing found objects, rededicating public space, redeploying assorted cut-and-paste methodologies, and rerouting regular cultural and historical narratives." The discussion was organized around a series of prompts, several of which precede the participants' discourse below.

1. Clearly race will be a vital (if less "visible") aspect of Hip-Hop culture looking forward. Consider how/if the discourses on race can expand in discussions of Hip Hop globally. To what extent have American notions of race shaped Hip-Hop culture? Is Hip Hop responsible for exporting

notions/narratives/histories of race to the broader, global audiences of
the music and culture? One inspiration for this roundtable was Toure's
much-critiqued NYT article on emerging white "femcees." In it he makes
certain assumptions about the African American-ness (and maleness) of
the culture. How did the audience of Hip-Hop scholars/writers respond to
his claims? How do/did you? Particularly for Regina: How has whiteness
factored into the discourses on Hip-Hop culture—especially in media
and/or in the music industry? And finally, does the concept of "post-race"
have any purchase in Hip-Hop culture—does it have more or less valence
with domestic or global Hip-Hop culture?

Regina Bradley: Postracialism is the latest blip in post-Civil Rights America
that suggests we as Americans have a reached the mountaintop of racial
tolerance. It is arguably a strictly American cultural phenomena. It is the public
dismissal of race as a marker of identity and privilege. The reality, however, is
that postracialism is a dystopic construct that relies upon the ambiguity of
white supremacy as an indicator of the achievement of racial tolerance. Instead
of blatant practices of racism like Jim Crow, Americans currently practice what
Eduardo Bonilla-Silva calls "colorblind racism," where everything but race is
why there is a difference in the treatment of ethnic groups. Tensions between race
and privilege that exist in this currently colorblind racist America frequently
play out in popular culture—especially rap music. Although global Hip Hop
permits a complexity and mingling of protest, entertainment, and identity,
U.S. rap remains tethered to a rigid and capitalistic definition of blackness
that suffocates any attempt to illuminate the complexities of a contemporary
Black experience in the United States. Conversely, it is important to point out
the role of Black American complicity in the dominance of the current Black
narrative in the American popular imagination. Because a Black middle class
exists/existed and there are a few more nonwhite people of color in prominent
positions, there is the acceptance that Blacks have "made it" in this post-Civil
Rights and thus postracial moment of American history. Postracialism is
mistaken for antiracism, which is not the case.

Aaron McGruder's animated version of *The Boondocks* comic strip is a
great tool in mapping the trajectory and treatment of (post) racial politics in
Black popular culture. The Freemans, moving from Chicago to the fictitious

suburban city of Woodcrest, grapple with being the representation of the Black middle class who made it: the token Black face in a predominantly white setting. This is further signified in the dichotomies of racialized space: urban is Black, suburban is white. There is also the toying of the play on emigration and displacement, a theme that runs which plays out throughout the entire series. In the first two seasons, McGruder exudes a lighthearted but heavily exaggerated representation of race and class relations in America. As the seasons progress, however, McGruder takes the gloves off. There are biting, darker, more "in-your-face" discussions of race and class that scream: "I don't care! I'ma tell you why I'm mad!" What immediately stands out to me is McGruder's brilliant depiction of the election of Barack Obama in the "It's a Black President, Huey Freeman" episode. There is a horrific scene where "stans" (stalker fans) celebrating Obama's election hold up a burning effigy of Huey Freeman. These Obama supporters become a literal and figurative lynch mob. They figuratively LYNCH a young Black boy who was not sold on Obama being president simply because he's Black. It's a powerful scene where Obama's election not only implodes current postracial racial politics but dismisses the suggestion that race is no longer relevant in America's sociopolitical exchanges.

James Peterson: Treva, would you like to respond?

Treva Lindsey: Post-racial-ness serves as a complicated, ahistorical, and mythical lens through which some in the United States grapple with a profoundly violent and unjust history of race relations.[1] The conflation of "racial" with "racism" further encourages many people to identify U.S. society as postracial. Consequently, and according to this particular logic, U.S. society thrives as postracist. Those invested in postracial/postracist logic use stories such as the election of Barack Obama, the unparalleled success of entertainment moguls such as Oprah Winfrey and Tyler Perry, and the appointment of a Latina woman to the highest court in the land as substantive examples of racism's "rapidly" dwindling presence in the fabric of American democracy and capitalism. Although arguably entering a new chapter in U.S. race relations' history, this current chapter builds upon stark legacies of white supremacy, slavery, imperialism and colonialism, antiimmigration efforts targeting specific racial and ethnic groups, and the genocide of U.S.

indigenous peoples. The incessant recollection of and reliance upon these exceptional "success stories" of individuals from racial minority communities reveals a more accurate framing of our contemporary socio-cultural-political moment- hyper-raciality.

Hyperracial more adequately describes current iterations of U.S. race relations. A hyperracial reality becomes blaringly evident when exploring U.S. popular culture, and more specifically, rap music.[2] Hip Hop and popular culture more broadly mirror the extant hyperracial moment. Although one could argue that hyperracial dynamics always existed in the U.S.—particularly because spaces where domination, oppression, and exploitation thrive require racialized and racist logics to sustain these spaces, the current emphasis on being postracial demarcates a distinct historical and cultural moment. Hip hop is an essential cultural component of this moment. Once identified as the Black CNN by Public Enemy founding member and lead emcee, Chuck D, Hip Hop serves as an expressive vehicle for black, brown, and other marginalized voices. Rap music, in particular, enjoys commercial success at a global level. An increasing number of non-black and non-brown voices from around the globe use Hip-Hop forms such as emceeing to self-articulate and to illuminate their individual or shared realities and stories. On radio stations and music television stations in places throughout the world, one can hear rap music.

Mainstream rap music in the U.S., however, continues to serve as a site predominated by African American, heteronormative masculine expressivity.[3] Despite the very recent commercial success of Afro-Trinidadian-American, female artist, Nicki Minaj, the songs of Black male artists dominate the sonic and visual airwaves. The hypercommodification of particular performances of Black masculinity prove profitable amidst turbulent economic times. Content and lyrical dexterity vary among the artists amassing mainstream attention, and yet, Black masculine expressivity as commodity propels these artists' commercial viability. From a "post-racialist" standpoint, the success of these rappers and their appeal to multiracial and multiethnic audiences substantiates postracial claims. Conversely, however, I would argue that this success reveals a hyperracial truth in which the mass consumption of specific performances, iterations, narratives, and images of Black masculinity further racialize Black male bodies. Furthermore, this racialization contributes to a sociocultural landscape that supports the criminalization and mass incarceration of Black boys and men as well as state-sanctioned violence against Black male bodies.

Scott Heath: I'm very happy to be here. Lately I've been mincing the hyper and the post, thinking about the postracial. During the Obama campaign and after his election, we started hearing this "post." There was this conversation about race and racism being over. Now I've chosen to think about it in a different way, use that "post" in a different way. I guess much like you're [Treva] using the hyper when we talk about race and raciality. I think of postracial moments and postracial sites as these instances in which we're called to question and reevaluate the ways that we are processing and operating through race. For instance, the emancipation in the United States might be considered a postracial moment in the way that I'm thinking about it. The assassination of Martin Luther King might be considered a postracial moment. Moments that make us step back and say, all right, what does race mean now and what are we doing with it? And in that sense, I think of Hip Hop as a postracial site, in a sense, because throughout the last forty years, we have been asked by Hip Hop—music and Hip-Hop culture to consistently, constantly reconsider race.

And Hip Hop has changed over that time as well. You know, just the other night we were talking on NBC about the untimely passing of Adam Yauch of the Beastie Boys. Thinking about the Beastie Boys and their rise to prominence, when they begin in the early eighties and when they came into public light, they—I would argue—did not meet the same level of criticism that a non-black or white emcee has met since in coming to that same level of public light, partially because I think that Hip Hop itself was in something of an experimental phase—still trying to figure out what it wanted to be. Naturally, people in various communities were defensive of the culture and the way that it was being shaped. But I think that the Beastie Boys, f as a crew, maintained a high skill set, a high level of acumen with regard to their representation of a specific art form. And they were satirical. When it comes to white emcees, you have two strains. You have the consciously satirical, which gestures toward the Toure article since I think some of these women that he's talking about have a satirical edge. And I don't know that every listening community or every community of readers of culture takes that so kindly right now. On the other hand, you have someone like Paul Wall, right? Who is very consciously white, but not attempting to be satirical in any way. He's performing. He's performing the culture as he's known it. Wouldn't you say there's a difference between these sorts of white emcees? For instance, I think in this moment it's impossible to talk about race, not to mention gender, sexuality, class, in any comprehensive way right now in the twenty-first century without talking about Hip Hop and talking about how race has been shaped in Hip Hop. And the challenges that we see now I think have to do with the calcification of a certain strain of racial thinking inside Hip-Hop culture, and in a lot of ways, Black American-ness is very specifically represented through Hip-Hop culture around the world. Let me stop there for a minute.

James Peterson: One quick follow-up, and Regina, you can piggyback on this as well. I was at 30 Rock (NBC Studios) the night that you [Scott] appeared on the Ed Show on MSNBC, and everyone was talking about the Beastie Boys. They were playing the Beastie Boys in the studio. Then you did the national segment about MCA, and it forced me to consider how many Black rappers or rappers of color we have lost over the last several years that do not garner that kind of national news attention. So I wonder—how you felt being interpolated into that particular discourse when you know we have lost …

Scott Heath: We've lost many.

James Peterson: We have lost so many rappers without a single acknowledgment from national cable news networks. And again, this was not just the show that you were on. The entire building was abuzz about MCA and The Beastie Boys.

Scott Heath: Yes. I think his whiteness definitely has to do with his acclaim. He was shaping himself into a bigger sort of political figure. I have to give him that. And he was defining himself as a freedom activist with his work in Asia and other efforts. But this is what happens, and maybe this is what's happening now. His whiteness allowed more access to audiences who would themselves be a little apprehensive about approaching Hip Hop or announcing themselves as fans of Hip-Hop music and culture. So I think quietly he's celebrated for that very thing, as are the Beastie Boys. But notice if you follow that group's career or Adam Yauch's career, you'll know that they began as a punk outfit. And listening to some of their later work, you see these returns to punk strains or more rock-oriented music. I mean, I can't argue with it because that's what they were sort of doing all along, but there was some more deliberate and vocal returns to that aesthetic later on. So on that level, I think that Yauch, the Beastie Boys, and their whiteness has indeed contributed to the sort of broadening accessibility of Hip Hop, and the explosion of things that were once considered more or less private culture spaces into something much more publicly accessible and immediate.

James Peterson: What are your thoughts on this, Regina?

Regina Bradley: Scott makes some great points that help me frame how death and Hip-Hop intersect with these current moments of post-color, post-racial, post-whatever. I do believe that death is celebrated in Hip Hop. There's something else there, too. Look at the craze surrounding the hologram of Tupac Shakur. That freaked me out. I couldn't watch the clips people were posting on Twitter and Facebook like they were introducing him to me for the first time. I was there when he was alive and had new hits. But I would classify Tupac's hologram as not only a celebration of death in "post-racial" Hip Hop but also as a "post-life" moment where Tupac is highly regarded and representative of a nostalgic yearning for the 1990s. Technology plays a significant role in sustaining Tupac as a postracial figure: he's a hologram being consumed by a multicultural audience that is simultaneously memorializing and revitalizing him in this aggressive Black masculine discourse almost twenty years after his death. In my current research, I employ Nicole Fleetwood's theorization of *iconicity* to frame Tupac.[4] I'm curious about how this hologram image of Tupac perpetuates him as not only an icon but how he represents shifting negotiations of Black agency and empowerment today from the height of his fame in the early and mid-1990s. Why are we struck by Tupac as a hologram to the point that Dr. Dre's camp is considering taking the hologram *on tour*? What does he represent? Why can't we let Pac go? The man's been dead over a decade and I heard he's in New Orleans now.

Treva Lindsey: He's in New Orleans?

Regina Bradley: He's in New Orleans now.

[Laughter]

Regina Bradley: Heard he's doing a gig in New Orleans which is particularly suiting considering the connections to New Orleans and death, ... but something I'm currently grappling with is how Tupac's iconicity situates him as a "messy" organic intellectual for post-Civil Rights generations. What I mean is that aside from Tupac's hyperawareness of a Black nationalist agenda passed down from his mother and godfather Geronimo Pratt, he was also very Hollywood, literally a rapper, actor, and connoisseur of commercial blackness. He openly grappled with this in his music and poetry. He was not easily pinpointed. And that's what adds to the mystery and allure of Tupac Shakur. He wasn't just a "studio gangsta": He punned and engaged violent discourses while living and making art out of it. Look at his use of acronyms like T.H.U.G. L.I.F.E. (The Hate U Give Little Infants F**** Everyone) and O.U.T.L.A.W.Z. (Operating Under Thug Law Az Warriors). People interpreted literal meaning where he was trying to ascend, if not layer, the norm. In order to get folks' attention, he attempted to pun the norm. Unfortunately, many times this was overlooked and dismissed. So in thinking about the layered image and iconicity of Tupac Shakur, it becomes even more interesting to consider Shakur's prodigal-like return to social-politically charged rap—very much on display in the *Makaveli* album. His connections and attempts to embody Nicolo Macchiavelli's *The Prince* while sustaining a hyper-violent, pathological, and conventional Black masculinity are striking. He puns the Illuminati, an underground and powerful group of intellects and heavy hitters in sciences and math, with the Killuminati. He renames himself Makaveli. In a way, this album can be seen as Black pathology with purpose. And, of course, there's the play on Christianity where Tupac makes a promise of returning in seven days. He's not considering himself Christ here; Christ rose from the dead in three days. But the emphasis on seven in Christian ideology suggests coming full circle, becoming whole. So, there's a lot to play with and deconstruct. Still, bringing Tupac Shakur back as a hologram? What is that suggesting about cultural memory? Why is there a need, an *urgent* and capitalistic need, to bring Pac back and not somebody like Biggie, for example?

Now, as far as whiteness and Hip Hop is concerned, accessibility immediately came to mind. Touré suggested that there was a lack of space and accessibility for white femcees to exhibit talent and be taken seriously. I was really bothered by his constant description of white women rappers as "cute." It brings up this pesky, ever present dichotomy between Hip Hop as a hyper-sexual space—that Treva talked about earlier—and visibility. What makes women visible or show up less frequently on Hip-Hop wavelengths? How is that troubled when we think about whiteness in Hip Hop diasporically and internationally? He references Kreayshawn, from Oakland, K.Flay from Britain, and Iggy Azalea from Australia. Touré makes no distinctions in white femininity, internationalism, and Hip-Hop influences. He clumps his representations of white women rappers altogether, taking away any distinguishing factors or complexity. I'm getting up on Iggy Azalea. She hasn't made the playlist, yet. Azalea was the first woman rapper to make *XXL* magazine's annual "Freshman Class" of on-the-brink rappers. She was the viewer's choice. When asked about her start in rap, she said her classmates thought of her as an outlaw, like Tupac. She asked them to associate her with 50 Cent's G-Unit because that's what she was more familiar with. I dropped the magazine for a second. It was interesting how she associated rap's blackness and, ultimately Black cool, with these generational Black rap figures. And she is making her rounds on Black cool. She's currently being endorsed and "protected" by rapper T.I. He made some comments in her defense after catching wind of a developing beef between her and a Black female rapper which caused quite an uproar. I first heard about it through Twitter. You know, good old Twitter. That's the new Black folks' CNN, and you can quote me on that.

[Laughter]

Regina Bradley: But T.I.'s comments [in defense of Iggy Azalea] caused this huge uproar, because people are wondering why are you downgrading and throwing shade on Azealia Banks. Is it necessary to degrade her in order to support this white female rapper from Australia who talks about being a slave-master in her music? Have a row of seats, Tip. So, the best way that I can describe this idea of Hip Hop globally and postracially, is that it's murky. There are no clean-cut barriers between consumerism, production, and expectation.

And because it's post—racial, you want to be able to say "I'm post-racial and I believe in the human race. I'm a humanist. We're all human." But then when you're behind closed doors, you're no longer a humanist. You're really talking about how you really feel. There is a fear that speaking about race publicly makes you a racist. That's a problem. Talking about race doesn't make you a racist, contrary to popular belief. There is misrecognition in race and supremacy.

James Peterson: I want to move beyond the race piece, with a couple of follow-up questions about the Toure article. Am I correct in my assessment of your comments that part of the response to the article was that it was not global enough in terms of its thinking? That some of its limitations were based upon the fact that he centered too much on the domestic and then allowed that to unfold into what we may think of as a (racialized) gender bias on his part by not acknowledging other artists? Is that a fair assessment of the Twitter and social media response to Toure's article?

Treva Lindsey: Toure's piece depicted a domestic, narrow understanding and framing of racial and gender contexts of rap music. He ignored any kind of translocal, transnational dynamics in an effort to seemingly affirm and embrace white female emcees. What becomes apparent through the article is how Toure understands what "black culture" is and whether he fits in and can speak in this racialized cultural space. He provides a distinct understanding of what Black spaces are. One response I had to his article was whether I cared if white women are "allowed" in Hip Hop or not. Another response I had reverted back to my understanding of rap music in the U.S. as a site predominated by African American male expressivity. Consequently, viewing rap music as a potential site for white female expressivity proved challenging. While certainly not opposed to listening to and supporting white female emcees, I began contemplating the roots and routes of Hip Hop through the racial, ethnic, gender, and sexual identities of emcees. This reflection also brought about questions of authenticity, sincerity, (mis)appropriaton, and cultural ownership. Unquestionably the roots of Hip Hop reside in black and brown, disenfranchised communities; nevertheless, its historical and contemporary routes are expansive, dynamic, and resist limitations and boundaries.

Hip Hop is constantly in its own process of self-definition and evolution that moves and flows through spaces and through roots and routes that give people opportunities to define themselves and their communities. Although I appreciate any attempt to highlight the contributions of emerging, talented emcees who do not fit neatly into racial, ethnic, sexuality, nationality and gender identity expectations, Toure's piece did not discuss what it means to have people who fall outside of this idea of "authentic" Hip Hop participating in Hip Hop as emcees. He also did not engage with how these white female emcees use particular racial narratives to insert themselves into the space. Whether through using "nigger" or rapping about being a slave-master, the cadre of white female emcees he highlighted employ racialized rhetoric that rely upon racial histories and narratives.[5] To defend their usage of certain words, references, and imagery, some of these white female emcees invested in this mythical idea of a postracial/postracist society in which Hip Hop exists.

Scott Heath: It was also I think poor cherry-picking. I thought the article was rushed. I think it was problematized by Toure's attempts to be funny, tongue in cheek in different places. But there are any number of white female emcees that he could have included. I mean, the first that comes to mind for me is Invincible out of Detroit.

James Peterson: Yes.

Scott Heath: You want to talk about somebody doing—like really doing good work, and she's arguably less popular and been around a whole lot longer. I knew—I saw Rhonda when she was sixteen in Ann Arbor, Michigan. You know, and so to choose these, talk about them as sort of the white woman's entrée into Hip Hop, you know, it's just I think a bad choice if you're not going to talk about why these women work, why these women are, I don't know, presumably blowing up. I don't know that they're entirely that popular, but—

Regina Bradley: They're YouTube superstars.

Scott Heath: Right. But you take a look at those that he picked, and once again, you've got these emcees who are poking fun at Hip Hop itself and the conventions of Hip-Hop culture. And a meta-critique is fine. But there's something else layered there. They're not always smiling. There's a critique, but a critique with this affectation of African American tonal speech—sort of sounding Black, if you will, or at least attempting to, and playing off of that. I don't know that they're going to do so well with that.

James Peterson: For folks who are not so familiar with this Toure article, it was in the December 25th edition of *The New York Times*. It was published in 2011, and titled, "Challenging Hip Hop's Masculine Ideal?" In it Toure briefly glosses three emerging white female emcees, at least one of which (actually two out of the three), were fairly controversial in terms of the imagery and the kinds of lyrics and symbolism that they depicted in or through their artistic personas. People love to attack Toure anyway, but social media became critically responsive around some of these issues and/or some of these artists. I think for our purposes, as we are trying to push the conversation forward, we want and need to be more global in our thinking. I believe that thinking globally in this particular context would have allowed him to at least mention Invincible in this piece. We have several more prompts to discuss, so I want to try to move us ahead, at least to our second one, especially now because we are talking more inclusively about gender.

I spent some time in Nigeria earlier this year, and Hip-Hop music is thriving there. Although many of its most popular artisans are indigenous, much of the content echoes the materialism and sometimes the violence often reflected in the mainstream iterations of domestic Hip-Hop music. I went to several beauty/cosmetic stands at local market in Yola. One beauty stand had scores of skin-lightening products. When I asked one of my student hosts about this, she explained to me how prevalent the use of skin-lightening creams were among her peers at the American University of Nigeria, and how she felt the culture (and Nigerian Hip-Hop music) facilitated youthful aspirations to Eurocentric beauty ideals. Now this is especially for Treva, because it relates to your work. Is this a future for global Hip-Hop culture? How can we account for this kind of trend, and to what extent are gender norms or ideals in American Hip Hop shaping, reflecting, or paralleling these beauty trends in a place like Nigeria? Are there counter-narratives, domestic and/or abroad? Most importantly here, what do we know or what do we need to know from the history of the use of skin-lightening creams and other cosmetics that can help flesh out the reasoning behind certain cosmetic aspirations or choices? As an addendum, let me just say that I was stunned by this realization. Not that the skin-lightening creams were there, but that so many young people were using them, and that these students are associating that with popular culture and Hip-Hop culture more specifically.

Treva Lindsey: Part of my work looks at skin-bleaching practices in U.S.-based Black communities from the late nineteenth century into the mid-twentieth century.[6] In particular, I focus on the New Negro era and how skin-bleaching became a practice through which a number of African Americans attempted to assert themselves anew and to imagine themselves in this new and modern space. Skin-bleaching was a popular practice among some African Americans because of how racial, gender, color, sexual politics and ideologies linked lighter skin to greater "upward" mobility. Skin-bleaching was an integral, selective practice within the context of New Negro expressive culture.

Contemporarily, we see skin-bleaching practices become more and more common in certain spaces with legacies of slavery, colonialism, and imperialism. These legacies are important factors that we must consider when we think about skin-bleaching products being massively exported to particular countries. In recent years, a substantial number of people in India use skin-bleaching products and practices. This growing phenomenon undoubtedly has its roots in both India's colonial past as well as an increasingly global popular culture market that trumpets fair and/or lighter skin as ideal and desirable. Globalization produces a context in which places with unprecedented access to expressive cultures derived from other places and communities reproduce extant narratives about racial and color hierarchies. Even within Hip Hop, a U.S.-rooted, but globally routed expressive culture, skin color ideals prevail. Most U.S.-based popular culture forms implicitly and explicitly promote a lighter skin ideal. Not surprisingly, the images exported by the U.S. via popular culture sites such as Hip Hop to other countries combine with these countries' racial/cultural histories and hierarchies to usher in evolving beauty ideals. These ideals reify the power of white cultural hegemony at translocal, transnational, and transglobal levels.

Beauty ideals, while affecting people of various gender identities, have particular set of consequences for female bodies. Ideals are often tools that regulate female bodies. At the same moment that we have amazing possibilities for what popular culture brings to the table in terms of its global reach and its functioning as a site of creative expression, we also confront the reality that popular culture creates ideals and standards to which we ascribe and aspire. These standards and ideals can reproduce harmful narratives, which spark cultural movements such as skin-bleaching among people of color. It is also fascinating to read skin-bleaching as a practice rooted in desires for mobility.[7] Skin color politics play an integral role in how people move through the world. Skin-bleaching is often not just about achieving a beauty ideal, but is a tool of mobility. We must think critically about skin color as social and erotic capital in our comprehension of skin-bleaching practices among people of color. Although similarities exist between preferences for lighter skin in the U.S. (particularly as expressed within rap music) and in a country such as India, we must exercise care in our analyses of the aesthetic practice and not generalize what skin-bleaching means to certain individuals and communities. We cannot posit generalized claims about cultural and expressive practices thriving in different locations. We must explore skin-bleaching with translocal, transnational, and transglobal lenses to uncover the similarities, differences, and distinct features of skin-bleaching practices used by people of color across the globe. Using these lenses, we can connect the ways that certain race-based ideologies function and trickle down. We can also examine how race, gender, and sexually based ideologies function within globalized popular culture spaces such as rap music.

James Peterson: Are there other ways—perhaps more positive ways—of reading or interpreting the use of those kinds of cosmetic products, I mean, other than the way that I have. Does anyone else have thoughts on this?

Regina Bradley: What she said.

  [Laughter]

James Peterson: Scott?

Scott Heath: I haven't been to Nigeria, but a decade ago I spent some time in Accra, Ghana, and the skin-bleaching products were prominent there. I'm pretty certain they still are, especially in the marketplaces. Something a little stronger than what we have in the States, I believe. Just to help you picture the urgency of it, we're talking about products that take time to chemically lighten your skin. It's not like people smear it on and suddenly they're that much lighter. It's a process. It takes time. But the result of the process, or at least part of the process, is that the originally dark-skinned individual doesn't end up looking like a naturally lighter-skinned individual. There's this orange hue. This is what I saw.

Regina Bradley:	Yes.
Treva Lindsey:	Like a Sammy Sosa.
Scott Heath:	This orange hue …
James Peterson:	Yeah.
Scott Heath:	… still dark around the eyes. So there's this kind of a raccoon effect going on.
Treva Lindsey:	Yes.
James Peterson:	Yeah.
Scott Heath:	And a smell …
Treva Lindsey:	Yes.
James Peterson:	You can smell the chemicals.
Scott Heath:	Yeah.
Treva Lindsey:	Yes.

Scott Heath: So there's this visceral element to it. When you think about the lengths to which someone is going to in order to achieve this certain aesthetic, but it's an aesthetic that represents access to materials. In some sense, it's an aesthetic that represents opulence. I think to bring it back to what we've been seeing for the past twenty-five, thirty years in Hip-Hop videos in the United States, often times lighter-skinned Black women are just another sort of item on the set. If you listen to some rap songs—actually, more recently, I've been hearing red bone less and hearing yellow bone more, especially coming out of the South. So I have this kind of car; I got this kind of watch, and I got me a yellow bone girl, too. These are signs of objectification in the context of material possession/materiality. And it's interesting and terrible that this phenomenon is very global, and it's not just Black people, you know what I mean? So it's across the world. I mean, they did a number on us. They really did a number on us.

James Peterson: Regina?

Regina Bradley: I'm a literature person by training. That's my thing. And I really couldn't help but think about George Schuyler's *Black No More* in this part of our conversation. For those of you that aren't familiar, Schuyler is an early twentieth century satirist that is arguably the predecessor for today's Dave Chappelle or Aaron McGruder. Schuyler wrote the essay "The Negro-Art Hokum" for *The Nation* in 1926. Langston Hughes responded a week later with "The Negro Artist and the Racial Mountain." Schuyler, an extremely conservative Black journalist argued there was no such thing as African American art. There is nothing African about the art and writing done by people of color in the United States. It's all American. He later comes out with this brilliant satire *Black No More* in 1931. There's a Dr. Frankenstein-esque thing going on. He comes up with this machine where Black people can "turn" white. Considering the harsh social-cultural climate of the U.S. at the time, turning white was a viable option. Of course Black folks would be like "Hell yeah! We're going to go white!" This part of the novel was like reading an early draft of Chapelle's skit on reparations. Everybody went to the bank, took all their money out, and went to this guy who invented the process Dr. Junius Crookman, like, "make me white." And they were Aryan white: blonde hair and blue eyes. There was a very specific type of whiteness that granted access to white privilege and respectability. Schuyler brilliantly punned this idea of self-worth and pity and race.

Now that I think about it, this procedure is similar to the "whiteface" seen in post-Civil Rights comedy performed by Black comedians like Richard Pryor and Eddie Murphy. Blacks perform whiteness by redressing their skin in chalky white makeup and light colored contact lenses. The exaggerated look that they achieve is always chalky and peculiar. It never looks natural. This is a developing part of my research because it's a visual demonstration of the peculiarity of postracial culture. If Black people were to perform what we understand as whiteness and exaggerate it to a point where it makes one uncomfortable, what is being talked about publicly that is taboo in public? It's only entertainment, right? If I lighten my skin and we're postracial, it's all good. I'm just imitating my human brother. But the implications behind acts like whiteface are indeed racialized: "No, for real, I'm pretending like I'm white, but I still don't have the same access that you kind of have on a daily basis." So it's really fascinating, not only because of the beauty aesthetic that Treva was talking about, but its cultural currency and how we understand power and privilege. And that's the most interesting and entertaining aspect about the book is the treatment of white privilege. Now that everybody is or could be white, "naturally" white people are like, "Wait a minute, wait a minute. You're whiter than me, and I'm *white* white." The question now becomes, what are the levels of white privilege? These different levels of whiteness equivocated different levels of social privilege and respect. If one didn't have this specific type of whiteness, then they were still considered inferior. So Schuyler is playing with these ideas of not only a white beauty aesthetic but what we understand to be impositions of Americanized and Eurocentric beauty. What privilege or lack thereof is attached to this aesthetic? Further, if everybody had this Eurocentric beauty standard, blonde hair, blue eyes, how do we maintain this functionality of how race in social-capital and class discourse?

Scott Heath: I like the Schuyler novel, too, and it's interesting that it's considered one of the early Black American science fiction novels. And because there's this technological element—the invention of this machine and all that. And it's written as a true story. You know, it's one of those novels that's framed as though you're entering some version of our reality.

Regina Bradley: He gives a disclaimer at the beginning of the novel.

Scott Heath: Right. He gives a disclaimer. In it he talks about what he based the novel on which was inspired by an actual Japanese scientist who came to the States in part to conduct research on the possibility of skin lightening. He was researching this and so Schuyler took that news report and sort of ran with it. Just one other interesting point, though, is that—and you were touching on this—is that the whiteness that was achieved through the machine was too white, right?

Regina Bradley: Too white.

Scott Heath: It was—and it was detectably so. After a while you could see like a natural white person and a person who was just trying to be white, and you were able to tell the difference. So it gets a little tricky. But these ideas of performing whiteness persist in a lot of Black American literature. And I think about a part that people don't talk about that much in Richard Wright's *Native Son* near the beginning. Bigger Thomas and one of his buddies says: "Let's play white. You know, let's play white." And they start—they're trying to act white. There's also some discussion of Martians or aliens or something early in there, too. There's really interesting little bits. But yeah, you know, there's this reification of whiteness as a certain type of cultural capital that is emulated and is sometimes deemed inauthentic or not, depending on context.

James Peterson: There is a rich conversation still to be had about *Passing*, or if you think about Adam Mansbach's *Angry Black White Boy* which inverts the Schuyler novel in some ways. But we have to keep it moving. One more gender question: part of what we are discussing here are the ways in which— and we cannot make too many conclusions here, but the ways in which shared experiences have similar outcomes around gender and certain racialized aesthetic ideals. I wonder if there is a way for us to turn this discussion toward a more constructive or forward-thinking direction and I want each of you to respond to this as briefly as you can. Can we talk a little bit about where Hip-Hop culture is in terms of gender politics right now, and how we should be moving forward, or what moving forward looks like in terms of gender and sexuality within Hip-Hop culture? Give an example of something that you are seeing in the culture around issues of gender that is interesting or compelling, (or maybe not interesting or compelling at all), and then give us a sense of Hip Hop's future. What are the parameters of "moving forward" that we are establishing and how do they manifest within Hip-Hop culture? If we have this shared set of experiences around some things that I might be casting as negative, are there ways for us to rally these same global experiences around something more constructive and positive?

Scott Heath: Misogyny's played out. It doesn't make sense. But the way I talk about postracial, I think I'd also want to talk about post-gender moments. And I think Hip Hop is coming into what could really be that. I guess we're going to talk a little bit more about access and things, and especially access due to new information technology and technologies of exchange. In other words, we're cutting out the middlemen, and I do mean the middlemen in a lot of ways. And so as we lean toward a bit more conversation about globalization, part of what's driving it (and I actually may have a bit of a critique about how we're talking about globalization now), but part of what's driving it is this—the immediacy of access, and that is possible through new technology, our YouTubes, and our Twitters, and Instagrams, and all these things.

I think we're at a moment where a lot of women producers of work classified as Hip Hop have the tools of access in front of them, and I like to think that what we're going to see is something that someone might call underground, but definitely something that skirts the traditional production models. I'd like to see more women artists and thinkers around Hip Hop really taking advantage of the things that say, you know, the young Chinese emcee is taking advantage of when he produces a song and puts it on YouTube and pushes it to a viral status. I'd like to hope that some of the challenges to some of the sadder conventions of Hip-Hop cultural production—I hope that some of those— some challenges to those conventions can really be raised. That's aspirational, but I think—I'd like to hope we're headed there.

Regina Bradley: Well, something else that I like to play with on the side— my side piece research—is identifying alternative ways of looking at race and gender. One mode of analysis I'm currently invested in is sound theory. Plugging myself a little bit here, but I have an article coming out in *Current Musicology* where I theorize what I call Hip-Hop sonic cool pose. It's the use of traditional and nontraditional sounds like laughter, grunts, wails, and moans heard in commercial rap music to provide an alternative discourse for how we consume and understand Black cool. I'm especially interested in sounding trauma and Black masculine cool, those kinds of feelings and emotions that are supposedly unavailable to men in color within this hyper-commodified, hypermasculine space. My work in sonic studies of Black masculine cool puts me in conversation with work like Michael P. Jeffries' theory of complicated cool found in *Thug Life*.

One of the things that I argue is that when we think about sound as an alternative medium of gender expression there is no rigid, particular formula of interpretation. Sound allows for alternative definitions of how we understand, for the sake of my own interests, Black masculinity. How do Black men advertently and inadvertently utilize sound to gives themselves room to talk about emotion and themselves in nonnormative ways?

Returning to Tupac for moment. Tupac's laugh is striking. He laughed a lot. It wasn't necessarily like that "ha ha, it's funny" laugh. His laughs were frequently awkward and more so "I don't really know how to explain my angst here, so I'm just going to laugh." These sonic cues are important for complicating Black manhood and its surrounding discourse. I'm not suggesting that Black cool is limited to men of color. Rebecca Walker's *1000 Streams of Black Cool* is a great example of that. In Hip Hop, Nicki Minaj's performance of Black cool immediately comes to mind. Its fascinating how she changes her voice to represent these alter egos that are helping her function and navigate through these commercial expectations upon her; not only her blackness, but her femininity. So she creates these literal and sonic alter egos that can directly confront what she doesn't like. Her character Roman, for example, allows her to exact revenge on her naysayers. There are a lot of tropes and memes Minaj plays with in her music that shine through her delivery. The theatric shifts in her voice reflect not only a mastery of her lyrical content but the agency needed to validate her role as an emcee. Minaj pivots between gendered understandings of aggression—the idea that aggression is reserved for Black mal rappers—and sexual profitability. I find it interesting how sound is used, and I think that's a way to progress. It's not necessarily looking at lyricism, but more so the actual musical accompaniments, the nonmusical factors, which is something that I'm playing with as well.

James Peterson: Treva, do you want to talk at all about gender futures?

Treva Lindsey: I remain cautiously optimistic about the gender futures, while simultaneously witnessing a larger war on women and genderqueer individuals that is occurring and not solely located within Hip Hop. It is difficult for me to think about the possibility of eradicating patriarchy, misogyny, and transphobia within Hip Hop when systemic gender-based discrimination and disparities thrive in many countries throughout the world. Nevertheless, I am encouraged by what technology can afford to individuals and communities seeking to create and disseminate gender-progressive and anti-patriarchal cultural products. Within technology, however, inequality and uneven access exists. Some conversations about access to technology discuss a race divide within digital technology, but do not necessarily address gender and sexuality divides.[8] Who has access to creating and utilizing digital technology? Who receives training for technologies which produce music, and specifically Hip-Hop music? When we discuss and laud Hip-Hop producers, how many women do we mention in these conversations? This question circulates in a larger discussion about women's access to any number of cultural and political arenas.

In the face of this "War on Women," I still view Hip Hop as a space in which marginalized and disenfranchised individuals and communities, from various locations can find a voice. From transgender Hip-Hop artists to queer Hip-Hop artists, to artists who come from spaces that push our boundaries of thinking about race and class and force us to think very differently about gender and sexuality. Artists such as these gaining traction signal that Hip Hop remains a malleable force that is capable of growth and self-reflexivity. I also see the possibility of radical sexual politics rooted in pleasure being embraced among some in the Hip-Hop generation. This possibility, is perhaps the most intriguing for me because of my interest in gender futures that engage a politics of pleasure that does not police, regulate, or deny any consenting persons healthy, pleasurable experiences.

James Peterson: Clearly, I have been a bad moderator, because we only got through two of our four prompts, and we do need to open it up and invite the audience to participate. In the last two prompts we were going to talk more about sound, some of the things that Regina was hinting at in her penultimate response here, just to think about what the direction is from a phonographic perspective for Hip-Hop culture. For the fourth prompt, we were going to dive deeper into considerations around theory, because our panelists have done some really exciting work around theory in Hip-Hop culture. But we are going to open it up to the audience now and begin to take some questions, and maybe we can circle back to some of those prompts as we progress through the Q&A part of the session.

Audience Member: With respect to Nicki Minaj, I'd be interested in hearing your perspectives on the way that queer sexuality has functioned with/forNicki Minaj, because I think it's significant that when she was doing work that was much more Caribbean-based or Caribbean-focused, like her feature on Gyptian's "Hold Yuh," where she represents her queer sexuality, but then now that she has become a megastar—it is so much less a part of her discourse [especially as she became more popular in the U.S]. What do you think this suggests about U.S. Hip Hop versus world Hip Hop?

Treva Lindsey: Minaj is an Afro-Trindadian-American woman. Given her racial/ethnic/cultural background, masquerading must become part of how we think about her. Minaj is an African diasporic subject. Consequently, she should not be read in a solely U.S.-based context. She incorporates Trinidadian cultural tropes and signifiers, with which U.S.-based audiences may not be familiar. Minaj's body of work speaks to a masking culture and carnivalesque dynamics that embrace women's bodies doing very different things than U.S.-based spaces and popular culture allow for female bodies.[i] Varied responses to Minaj's genderqueer performances also speak to a larger sense of discomfort with genderqueerness. Hip Hop encompasses some spaces for gender queer performances. And yet—similar to other areas of popular culture, gender normative strictures pervade Hip Hop.

Scott Heath: Yeah. I was thinking about her assumption of different characters, different personas, and it's very obvious, in a way, that—a way that says "yes, I am playing a role." You know we were talking about the categories. I think there's already (with Nicki Minaj), there's already sort of a queering of the conventions around what a woman emcee looks like or should behave like. I think she walked the line a little bit with her considerations of queer sexuality. I remember earlier interviews where she was hedging her bets and not really speaking unequivocally on her own sexuality. And I think that might even just have to do with—either a maintenance of character or an attention to fan base. Also, her sound is interesting. You know, at least in Washington, DC, you know, Nicki Minaj sound appeals quite well to audiences going to the gay clubs, gay night clubs. Her near drag aesthetic appeals quite well to those audiences.

Treva Lindsey: Yes.

Scott Heath: And I think she's benefited from that, and I won't even say in an entirely mercenary sense. I am crediting her without too much criticism at this moment. But I think she's busting up a few—busting up a few things. I like the role play. I like the acknowledgment of role play. I think MF Doom does it best.

James Peterson: Yeah.

Scott Heath: I think he—I think he does it so well with the mask, and then he went on that streak for a while where he was having different people perform as Doom—

James Peterson: As Doom.

Scott Heath: You know, some people got pissed off because they paid money to see this particular guy, but his point was, you know, Doom is there. I'm in New York and you're in Indiana, but Doom is Indiana. You know, I'm just—I'm just not there today. And then of course he has other—other personae that he would adopt along the way, his Viktor Vaughn and these other things. I hope you guys are somewhat familiar. If not, check him out. Hip-hop artists have been doing that without much acknowledgment of that part of the craft for quite some time, the discussion of oneself in the third person. I'm telling a story about a character. This is what—this is what Prodigy is about to do. This is what Jay-Z is about to do. You know, this sort of conversation, constant statement of one's own name, and that sort of thing. One slippery moment that I love, old one, is when Rakim says—he says—he says, "Eric B gets stronger as I get older." And I'm trying to figure out whose voice he's talking in. Sometimes I wonder if he's talking in my voice, you know. Because Eric B gets stronger as I get older, too. And there's just these switches of character that I think Nicki Minaj has gotten a hold of and really used carefully, you know, protectively.

James Peterson: Yes, sir?

Audience Member: A very interesting and very informative panel there. Thank you very much for your contributions. I wanted to point out one question and make a comment. The question—I'll start with the question. The question is that whether it is actually advisable that we consider linking—I'm a sociolinguist—linking the sociolinguistics of globalization to the sociolinguistics of colonization. You know, the power structures that are set up under the sociolinguistics of colonization are those that globalization is actually using now. And I tie this to the comment you made about Yola in Northern Nigeria. There are multiple centers of cultural influence, and Northern Nigeria grew a lot from the Arab world, and the question of skin complexion in Yola could be an influence of a Northern African and Middle Eastern experience in colonial times.

James Peterson: Well, first, thank you for the question on Nigeria. That is so important, and I think it dovetails perfectly with many of the questions that I am asking right at this moment. It is very helpful to understand how the geo-politics operate within Nigeria historically to give us multiple answers to the skin-lightening question. I think for me, and maybe for some of the panelists, too, this is a challenge or an issue that requires a global response. In order for us to really understand the sociolinguistics of globalization, we have to have a comprehensive understanding of the sociolinguistics of colonization, and that is what you gave us there in that example in terms of understanding how the North in Nigeria is influenced by Arabic and by Islamic culture, and how other regions might be more influenced by European culture.

The Toure comment is equally interesting. I do not know if anyone here on the stage really called him out, but at the time, a lot of folks called him out based upon this implicit premise that he did not know enough about Hip Hop to talk about the things that he was talking about in the way that he was talking about them. Those limitations were painfully revealed in his discussion of these three white female emcees. I think if we did not make that clear in our discussion about it, I should make it clear now, that part of what I see when I see him calling Piers Morgan to task for not having a right to speak—or not having enough sensibility of the pain and history of the African American experience with respect to violence and profiling and so on and so forth to talk about the Trayvon Martin case as a journalist is his way of giving Piers Morgan what he has gotten in other venues based upon his book and also based upon this particular *New York Times* article. I do not know if Toure thinks of it that way, but that is the way that I saw it. It is an engaging irony to think about it from that perspective.

Regina Bradley: I just wanted to speak to the travesty of the Piers Morgan-Toure showdown, and bring into this conversation Trayvon Martin. I really think it's important to keep him present tense and not past tense. And one way to do that that really hasn't been discussed is through not only looking at the roles of activism that have been played out, but actually listening to the 911 tapes. Going back to my earlier conversation about sound as an alternative means of understanding the Black experience, for people who aren't familiar with a contemporary "black experience," the 911 tapes provides an alternative space that humanized Trayvon for people that might have fallen into those kind of polarized assumptions about his Black masculinity that George Zimmerman imposed upon him. He has the hoodie on. He has the thug appeal. But when I listen to the tapes, I hear something else. I don't see the hoodie. I don't see the thug. For the record, I'm on that side that believe the person screaming on the tapes is Trayvon Martin. His sonic imprint of screaming humanizes him before it racializes him.

Scott Heath: And horrifies the listeners.

Regina Bradley: Right. It allows for that empathy that the listener feels for whoever it is who's screaming. And it happens to be a young Black man. Yet that empathetic notion overlooks the conflict of racial politics that doesn't really get teased out enough. When people talk about the Trayvon Martins of the world, the Oscar Grants of the world, it's really important to think about how these incident trouble our notions of racialized authenticity in not only popular culture but critical discourse. How do we address this in such a way that we allow for these conflicts of emotion and criticism to exist?

We've tried to make a unionized response to Martin's tragic death. Everybody needs to feel bad for Trayvon Martin, without really speaking to *why* are we feeling bad about Trayvon Martin. Is it from a racialized epicenter? Is it from this idea that he was a youth? Is it this idea that he was American? If you globalize Trayvon Martin, what is his cultural currency? What does he represent? And that's something that's starting to kind of be teased out now, because I have friends in Ghana who are seeing graffiti pictures of Trayvon Martin. What's the connection? Is there a diasporic appeal to the distress behind the Trayvon Martin situation? Are they relating to him because he's a young Black man? Are they relating to him because of what his American-ness stands for in a transnational perspective and how that oppression plays out within an American construct? America is supposed to be the greatest superpower in the world. Everybody tries to come here for this freedom, the dream. Martin is a wakeup call to this idealized American identity. A lot of this goes back to what Dr. [Marcyliena] Morgan was talking about earlier in her keynote in terms of segregated bodies, and sound being an integrated space. Listening to the 911 tapes provides an integrated space that allows for complicating Martin's humanity and not restricting him to a politicized and criminalized Black male body.

Treva Lindsey: Rhetoric is integral to how we understand and discuss Black masculinity. For example, in this current moment we say the "Trayvon Martin Case." Cases are usually named after the accused party. This is the "George Zimmerman Case." Trayvon Martin is a victim. As of 2012, we are twenty years past the LA uprising. We still remember the catalyzing event as the "Rodney King Case." But what of the four cops who committed the crime of police brutality? We do not have a language to see Black males in the space of being a full victims. The names of cases in which Black men and boys are victims imply that these men and boys are assailants. We have the Trayvon Martin case, the Rodney King incident, the Oscar Grant case or Sean Bell case as just a handful of examples. This rhetorical violence quite detrimental to affirming the humanity of Black men and boys. We must think about the possibilities of language in terms of dictating who is a victim and who is an assailant. By addressing this rhetorical violence, the necessity of making Trayvon Martin "the perfect victim" dissipates. The rhetoric frames him as an assailant, regardless of the reality that he is a victim.

James Peterson: That is the sociolinguistics of colonialism versus globalization issue that we have been discussing.

Regina Bradley: Just the use of "the," real quick. It suggests an all-encompassing, monolithic term of endearment. Right? So like THE Trayvon Martin case makes it sound like it's only going to happen once. Like it's a singular occurrence.

James Peterson: We isolate the occurrence.

Regina Bradley: The Oscar Grant case? Oh, Oscar Grant's not going to happen anymore. The Sean Bell case? Sad. Sean Bell's not going to happen again. The use of "the" adds that sense of urgency that people are looking for when traumatic experiences happen like these tragic occurrences, but it covers and skips over the root of *why* there continues to be these different the insert-your-name-here cases? That gets overlooked and is problematic.

Scott Heath: Well the one I always go back to is the Negro problem. You know, I teach Dubois through Harlem Renaissance, and this idea of the Negro problem comes up. And I always ask classes, well, whose problem is the Negro problem? You know, why is the Negro—is the Negro being called a problem or does the Negro have a problem? You might even take it back to the white man burden. You know, whose burden—Who's burdening whom? For instance. So no, I think it's a sad statement on the entrenchment of this idea of really unfortunately Black people and Black bodies are something that need to be dealt with, in some way or handled.

Audience Member: Thank you for your conversation. I thought it was really provocative and telling. And I really want to try to complicate this idea of global and the way that we're using it, because I feel like—I'm coming from dance studies, and we kind of have dealt with our own problems with how things are classified as world or [global] and this kind of colonialist experience that gets replicated, although not intentionally. So I feel like there's this import of a black/white binary that is present with the examples of the speaking back of the colonized to what American Hip Hop is or is not, because there's really—there's a multiracial society, there's ways that the state uses Orientalism to present a solution to the quote/unquote problem of blackness. And I want to ask how do you see a more critical way of interpreting the paradigm beyond the U.S. centricity, beyond the U.S. empire/hegemony being the dominant model, and still not letting go of the terms that we use, like diaspora and global and—I mean, we're just talking about postracial as a very U.S. conversation. Nobody talks about postracial in the Philippines. Nobody talks about postracial like in Canada. And they do have their local indigenous and local and racial ideologies. So I just wanted to kind of ask that question to you, and do you see it in more like—how do you see it?

Scott Heath: I can respond by speaking for my project which is called *Head Theory: Hip Hop Discourse in Black-Based Culture*. And I named it Black-based culture for a reason. I think that obviously when you talk about something like Hip Hop, and a lot of people are generating Hip Hop, consuming Hip-Hop cultural products, but at its heart it's still Black-based. You know, I'm thinking about its originary points. And I've said that Hip Hop is always already Black, always already American, you know, as it has been globalized, and I think—I mean, I think it's not being globalized. It's already globalized. I think that you see these—I guess these formulative moments in which say there's a local group, a local population, that takes on Hip Hop, begins to generate its own things called Hip Hop, and in its initial stages typically rappers sound very American, or people who don't speak English very well are rhyming in English. And oddly enough, it takes a while for it to get around to someone rhyming, for instance, in their indigenous language. I'm thinking about hiplife in Ghana. I did some—there's highlife music and then hiplife music, right? So I'm thinking about the invention of hiplife, which came about when Reggie Rockstone, he's credited with this, had the bright idea of rhyming—he's an emcee—rhyming not in English, like most people were doing, but actually rhyming and tweeting in his own language. You know, just this crazy idea. Why don't I just rhyme and tweet? The strangest thing, but you know, strange because he was butting against the convention that said that Hip Hop was Black American art, right? But talking with Reggie Rockstone then, I wonder what his conversation would be today. It's been a while, but one of his concerns as a art maker was that his music, if it did get outside of Ghana, or as it got outside of Ghana, would be classified not as rap or Hip Hop but as world music. And that's something he really wanted to avoid, but that's something that had been the pattern. He's like, we get out, but because it's not from the U.S., they put us in the world music group. I want to be in this group right alongside Gang Starr and the Fat Boys. I think one of your prompts was pointing in this direction. *I'd* like to think that some of these newer technologies that I was talking about, the new access, is going to let us skirt that problem a little bit, or at least make it a more democratic situation for audiences who want to choose what they listen to. I mean, so much of—I don't know who really watches music video shows that much anymore. I mean, most videos I see are on YouTube, right?

So—and I'm led to them in different ways. It's easier and less easy to find good things because it's not thrown in my face as much. You kind of have to look for it. Hopefully in that looking, we'll begin to access things and hear things that we wouldn't normally hear from other places outside the United States. I mean, again, aspirational. Can I say something else, too? I meant to say Rakim is stronger as I get older.

James Peterson: I want to add a couple of things here just very quickly. Part of the reason or part of the challenge of moving beyond a U.S.-centric discourse for some of the things we are thinking about for this roundtable is that globalization itself is U.S.-centric. So, in some ways, you have to escape the paradigm of the discourse of globalization to move toward the kind of conversations we want to have. For young scholars, in particular, there has to be a very deliberate return to, and investment in, ethnography that takes you to the places where Hip Hop is emerging and developing. I want to be in the community that I am thinking about or writing about in terms of culture, and that is not from an essentialist perspective. That is only from a perspective of doing exactly what you are asking, which is how do we move beyond a sort of U.S.-centered sensibility with respect to how we think about, speak about, and write about Hip-Hop culture, because when you go there, you can discover a host of different complexities and different ways of viewing the world.

A colleague of ours who is an African historian, has talked about how the term "world" is used sometimes in a colonial sense. One of the things he said to me is: "I don't want to teach world history at all." I do not know if using the term "world" is necessarily the best move going forward. For me personally, what I want to do, or where my tendency lies, especially when it comes to pedagogy, is to reclaim the world and make it what you want it to be. So if you want it to be an African diaspora world, then make the course match that. I believe scholarship has to operate within those master houses. Repurposing language with the trajectories and the paradigms that we want to see in those globalized or world terminologies should be the goal.

Treva Lindsey: Quite often, when someone says global Hip Hop, the automatic assumption is that the person is speaking about Hip Hop happening somewhere besides the U.S. This notion reproduces U.S. cultural hegemony.

If we re-establish global to mean certain things, which take root in very problematic constructions of globalization, the U.S. stands as an exceptional site. We run the risk of reproducing this exceptionalism in our work and how we frame and study "global" Hip Hop. We must imagine "global "meaning something very different than what it means at this very moment to disrupt U.S. cultural hegemony.

James Peterson: Well folks we are going to have to leave it out on that note as we are out of time. Special thanks to: Dr. Regina Bradley, Dr. Scott Heath and Dr. Treva Lindsey.

Part Five

Rapademics

These Three Words

Censoring and interpreting Hip-Hop culture in the public sphere

My career as a media contributor began as a result of two controversial events in recent history: (1) Don Imus, while commenting on the 2007 Women's NCAA National Championship game, referred to the Rutgers University Women's Basketball team as "nappy-headed ho's." (2) After receiving too many solicitations from cable news producers, Dr. Michael Eric Dyson began recommending me to speak on the various emerging issues that Imus' debacle had thrust into the public sphere. The confluence of these variables afforded me the privilege of an all access pass to America's latest attempt to incite a moral panic around issues of language and speech in rap music. Hip-Hop or rap music is only one element of a (sub)culture that includes styles of dress, sociolinguistic variations, graffiti art, modes of dance/movement, entrepreneurial sensibilities, and DJ-ing or turntablism.[1]

Rap music and Hip-Hop culture were interpolated into the discourse by Mr. Imus himself when—in response to insistent questioning and critique— he deflected the discourse to Black athletes and rappers. Imus asked, "Why isn't the same kind of outrage, let me ask you, in the black community when rappers and other people in the black community, athletes in the black community defame and demean black women?"[2] This peculiar exchange fueled mainstream media's demand for my work as a Hip-Hop scholar. For a few weeks, my phone rang regularly with requests to comment on Hip-Hop culture's role in all of this. As evidenced by a series of media events (including Russell Simmons' appearance on *The Oprah Winfrey Show* and a preexisting, powerfully predicated media discourse on misogyny in Hip-Hop culture)

Hip-Hop music videos and rap lyrics were once again under fire for provoking and promoting society's ills. One of the key distinctions regarding this particular moment in this intermittent, yet ongoing debate is the reemergence of issues pertaining directly to the First Amendment and the legal limits of protecting free speech.

There were several narratives and/or incidents that directly shaped and impacted the issues of free speech, rap lyrics, and their relationship to misogyny and obscenity in the public sphere. These include, but are not limited to: Don Imus' comments, Simmons' appearance on *The Oprah Winfrey Show* and his subsequent initiation of a ban on three words: "nigger," "bitch," and "ho" in rap lyrics; the music video for Nelly's single entitled "Tip Drill," a pointed response to this video by both Essence Magazine and undergraduate women of color at Spelman College; and a documentary film on concepts of Black masculinity for the Hip-Hop generation by Byron Hurt entitled *Beyond Beats and Rhymes*.[3] Each of these incidences (and the subsequent narratives developed in and through them) function as separate but dovetailing dialogues designed to confront, critique, and censor public speech that summons the discourse on the First Amendment of the Constitution of the United States.

The earliest and most prominent case of rap lyrics challenging, and by extension redefining, the boundaries of free speech occurred in 1990 just five years after the formulation of the Parents' Music Resource Center (PMRC).[4] According to Claude Chastagner, "Deeper motives for the PMRC's actions are suggested by the fact that its most frequent targets were heavy metal and rap music, two genres traditionally (though erroneously) associated with minority groups, working-class youth and the black community."[5] Any cursory gloss of PMRC's targets will regularly yield certain politicized motives: "As Lawrence Grossberg put it, the PMRC aimed at reasserting control over the cultural environment of children: the moral fabric of the United States, its personal and family values had to be rescued through the regulation of youth's cultural consumption."[6] That the PMRC's denizens are usually personally related to various political figures is also a well-known fact. Political and cultural biases notwithstanding, the PMRC was the legal and political entity most notably engaged in free speech/censorship issues with respect to rap music.

"In June 1990 a US District Court judge in Fort Lauderdale, Florida found the 2 Live Crew album *As Nasty as They Wanna Be* to be obscene in the three counties under his jurisdiction."[7] This ruling, in turn, prompted the arrest of at least one record store owner who dared to keep selling the obscene rap album in question as well as two members of 2 Live Crew for performing the material in Broward County Florida. Since many other scholars[8] have rehearsed the elements of the case and dissected numerous aspects of it from legal, literary, and cultural perspectives, I will not retread those discussions here. Some salient points to bear in mind, though, is that the dubious distinction of being the first rap album ever banned by a federal judge served mostly to promote and endorse 2 Live Crew in a manner not attainable by them based on the merits of their own skills as producers, recording artists, and/or lyricists. Moreover, public dialogue between scholars such as Gates, Baker, Crenshaw, Binder and others was largely ignored by the Hip-Hop generation and the artists producing and writing Hip-Hop music.[9]

Nonetheless, Houston Baker offers some keen insights on how we might wrestle with this current discursive upheaval. First, Baker warns against taking too seriously the opinions and comments from "expert witnesses" who reveal themselves to be "middle-of-the-game" scholars of Hip-Hop culture.[10] That is, be wary of those who would condemn—or in the case of Henry Louis Gates' defense of 2 Live Crew—summarily defend the lyrics of any particular artist. Indeed, especially, artists who are so clearly mediocre and generally not representative of a holistic sense of the culture. Baker's call here is for scholars and scholarship that more seriously and more thoroughly engages Hip-Hop culture. Especially since "controversial rappers are some of the most ardently political musicians. Many drive home a message of non-violence, social justice, and racial equality. Admittedly at its extreme, rap seems consumed with violence, but the First Amendment surely protects violent speech. To deny, or even threaten rappers' speech rights mocks the First Amendment and suggests racism."[11] Arthur K. Spears' insights are particularly instructive here:

> Even among rappers, the style of 2 Live Crew represents a minority. Many rappers infuse their music with social critique, strategies for community self-help, and sociohistorical remembrances seeking to instill group pride and initiative. It is disgraceful yet expectable that so much media attention

in the United States has focused on one corner of the rap industry to almost whole-sale exclusion of mainstream media coverage of what is on the whole—in terms of uplift, business acumen, grassroots orientation, and critical depth—among the most progressive institutions in the African-American community.[12]

This approach to scholarship and criticism has the potential to ameliorate the rampant misinterpretations of the lyrical language of rap music. Yet, the prevailing perception and popular portrayal of rap music and Hip-Hop culture is still thoroughly consistent with the gangsta-oriented misogynistic and consumerist narratives repeatedly (dis)played on two to three mainstream musical platforms. As with the 1990s case involving 2 Live Crew, these issues finally rest upon interpretive perspectives. In short, "If music serves as an emotional looking-glass, then it must reflect the entire palette of human feelings—among them anger, aggression, and sexuality. Works of obvious human passion stand among the greatest musical achievements in the western tradition."[13]

II

Interpretation or rather "a theory of interpretation" has become an essential touchstone for debates surrounding the protection of questionable forms of speech. If, as according to Professor Amy Adler, "any theory of censorship must have a theory of interpretation," then one thing that has been sorely missing from the most recent discussions about rap music, language, and its effects on, or reflections of, society (misogyny, violence, etc.) is the theory that must coincide with new classifications of censorship.[14] I will make some mild suggestions for interpretive approaches later with an expressed focus on how to read/listen to Hip Hop going forward and how best to place into proper perspective the most egregious instances of misogynistic rap lyrics. For now, though, suffice it to say that the occurrence of so many instances of misogyny in the public sphere of Hip-Hop culture warrants an outlining in order to first understand what prompted this most recent call for censorship and to highlight the new directionality of the call.

For my inaugural appearance on MSNBC, I sat on a panel of two during an early Saturday afternoon segment entitled, "What's OK to Say?" on MSNBC news in April 2007—barely a week after the initial fallout from Imus' comments. My co-panelist, T. Denean Sharpley-Whiting, authored *Pimps Up Ho's Down: Hip Hop's Hold on Young Black Women*.[15] The segment was framed around comments from a New Jersey minister, Reverend Deforest Soaries, who, like so many others during this period, tied Imus' comments directly to the lyrics of music industry artists, especially those artists who happen to rap (and most of whom also happen to be black). Reverend Soaries exclaimed, "You can't be angry when Don Imus says negative things about people and not be angry when your favorite athlete or artist says the same thing."[16] First, as a point of clarification, I have no recollection of any athlete or rapper using the phrase "nappy-headed ho's" to characterize African American women. Secondly, when Snoop Dogg (or any other rapper for that matter), uses the phrase or some portion of it, they are engaged in the misogynistic project that so much of American popular entertainment produces and promotes. It should be noted, however, that this phrase is not lyrically common in any genre of rap music.

There is no need to excuse Snoop Dogg (or any other rapper), but Snoop's comments in response to the Imus controversy revealed a deeper sense of hatred directed toward poor Black women than any of his lyrics from any of his songs. In response to a prompt from a reporter connecting his music to Imus's comments, Snoop replies, "We're talking about ho's that's in the 'hood that ain't doing sh–, that's trying to get a n—a for his money."[17] The ignorance inherent in this statement reverberates throughout Snoops' oeuvre with respect to how he references women.[18] More recently, and (I would argue) as a result of recent public pressure on rappers using misogynistic lyrics, Snoop sang a reformed tune on Larry King Live. A brief excerpt from their revealing interview will make this point clear:

> KING: Have you—have you been [one of] those—a lot of the other rappers accused of rap music that's insulting to women?
> DOGG: Yes, in the past I've always made music that was very insulting to women, because that's what I was taught. That's what I was brain washed not to know. As I get older, and with my wife and my daughter and my

mother and my grandmother, I tend to make more records that are, you
know, aimed at telling the woman how beautiful she is and how she's
appreciated and how I apologized for being so brain washed and not
knowing that I'm supposed to respect a woman.

KING: Well said. In December of 2006, "Rolling Stone" had you on the
cover in a Santa hat, with a headline describing you as America's most
lovable pimp. What did you make of that?

DOGG: They wasn't lying. They told the truth, Larry. I am the most—I'm
the player into making in progress. That's what pimp means to me,
P-I-M-P, Player into making progress.

KING: That's a different derivation.[19]

Snoop's feminist conversion notwithstanding, none of this justifies or in any
productive way sheds light on the comments made by Imus. Snoop is simply
a well-known figure, a self-proclaimed gangsta rapper, who helps to frame the
media discourse on Imus and its expressed intent to use the Imus situation to
initiate a critique of Hip-Hop culture that seeks to censor rap music. The very
framework (or lack thereof) of the "What's OK to Say?" segment on MSNBC
attempted to forego any serious critique of Imus in favor of a full-frontal
assault on Hip-Hop culture.

The irony of the "What's OK to Say?" segment is that MSNBC proffered
Fergie's hit single, "My Humps" as a plausible example of how women might
collude in their own oppression—a theme that will resurface later. "My Humps"
is a pop song in which Fergie's narrator revels in her ability to trade/tax on
her "lady lumps" for various material accessories.[20] Not only have we swapped
white male supremacy for Black male supremacy (two related ideologies
vastly different in power and scope), but we have gone one step further and
implicitly asked the question: Do women desire to be called ho's? The fact that
Fergie is white should likewise not be lost in this controversial quagmire. The
MSNBC segment has essentially deracinated Imus's patently racist comments
and deferred any culpability on his part onto/toward the artisans of Hip-Hop
culture. Fergie is a weak example set to explore women's roles in misogyny
and exploitation. When I pressed the host, Contessa Brewer, about the lack of
positive and/or constructive examples when referencing Hip Hop she calmly
replied, "But you know what we like to do we like to point out what's wrong
with society not what's right?"[21]

In this particular case, the media's proud penchant for hyper-focusing on the negative or offensive displaces some of the more productive dialogues that occur around issues of misogyny in rap music. In September 2007, BET premiered a town hall-styled talk show intended to explore Hip-Hop culture through dialogues between artists, activists, journalists, and various authors including: MC Lyte, T.I., Stanley Crouch, Reverend Al Sharpton, Michael Eric Dyson, Nelson George, Diane Weathers, Farai Chideya, and too many others to list here.[22] As a part of the promotional effort, I spoke at several advanced screenings. At the Howard University screening held on September 20, 2007, a group of panelists including the executive producer of the program, Selwyn Hinds, fielded questions from an audience of college students, faculty, administrators and the CEO of BET, Debra Lee. The exchange was equal parts engaging and intense as a Spelman graduates challenged the gender balance of the panelists on the program for being indicative of the silencing of women within the culture. Her question gets at the heart of an internal and internecine struggle among people of the Hip-Hop generations over gender roles, representations, and relations.

Unsurprisingly, the first episode of "Hip Hop vs. America" attempts to address the misogyny in Hip-Hop culture.[23] In some of the most riveting segments, renowned rapper Nelly makes several ineffective attempts to defend his salacious music video for "Tip Drill."[24] The video features crass, hypersexual strip club scenes that generally degrade women (and deliberately emphasize notions of consumerism and commodification) by promoting body parts on display for dollar bills. This is featured most prominently in the penultimate scene of the video as Nelly swipes a credit card down a young woman's buttocks—signifying that everything, including sex and sexuality, is reducible to a monetary transaction. There is no need to revisit the backlash that Nelly received from the media (Essence Magazine) and from women's groups at Spelman College. However, it is worth noting that he would not concede that making the video was a mistake—thereby solidifying his rank as public enemy number one among prominent feminist groups. Despite heated questioning and accusations from various panelists including Michael Eric Dyson, Kim Osorio, Diane Weathers, and the host, Jeff Johnson, Nelly staunchly defended his role in the making of the video which features several other notable rappers, including Jermaine Dupree. This conversation about the portrayal of women in rap music and videos spans across too many media narratives to delineate here (Bill O'Reilly, Don Imus, and C. Delores Tucker/ Bill Bennett just to name just a few), but suffice it to say that there is (and has been) an engaging discourse within Hip-Hop culture that challenges, critiques, and combats the exploitation and hatred of women in music, videos, and magazines.

If we compare the lewd images in the "Tip Drill" video to the definitive standards for pornography articulated by early proponents of the anti-pornography movement, Cynthia MacKinnon and Andrea Dworkin, revealing connections emerge. For MacKinnon and Dworkin, pornography is formally defined as "the graphic sexually explicit subordination of women through pictures and/or words that also include one or more of the following: (i) women are presented dehumanized as sexual objects, things, or *commodities*; … (vi) women's body parts—including but not limited to vaginas, breasts, or buttocks—are exhibited such that women are *reduced to those parts*; …"[25] "Tip Drill" inspires a prurient sexual gaze, cinematically limited to a Black woman's buttocks. Nearly every scene of the video re-inscribes this gaze. At best, these images are simply deemed as sexist. At their worst, they are pornographic. Regardless of their categorization, however, a line/boundary was crossed with the infamous credit card swipe. Music videos that reduce women of color to their body parts have unfortunately become commonplace on mainstream music video channels such as MTV and BET. This corporeal reduction harkens directly back to the sordid, exploitative history of the Hottentot Venus.[26] Still, the racial and racist implications of this buttocks-centric imagery are subtle given the counter-hegemonic narratives of beauty and body image in the African American community. The credit card swipe, however, does not enjoy the duplicitous nature of the Big Beautiful Woman (BBW) narrative. On the contrary, the swipe blatantly symbolizes the crass commodification of women based on historical narratives of anatomical inspection that are undeniable derivatives from the institution of slavery.

Immortalized in the slave experiences of Sethe, Toni Morrison's protagonist in the classic novel, *Beloved,* exploring the trauma and the traumatic memory of slavery, this dehumanizing behavior cannot circumvent its historical context.[27] When Nelly suggests (as he did on Hip Hop vs. America) that the swipe was the video model's idea or that she may not have interpreted the event in a historical context similar to the one that I have outlined above, he is silencing this young woman (who is only eighteen at the time of video shoot) again and—quite literally—stripping her of all agency and autonomy.[28] The fact that he would speak for her on this subject is doubly disturbing, but his insistence of his own innocence is only complicated by his insistence of her ignorance. We ultimately do not know what she knows. Our only experience with her is to see her butt—never to see her face and certainly never to hear her voice.

"Tip Drill" was released in 2003 and the public response was vehement. Some argue that Nelly was made an example of by Essence Magazine and by the women of Spelman because he is one of the most popular and successful rap artists to date. This may be true, but I maintain that Nelly overstepped his creative boundaries with the credit card swipe. The line to which I am referring to here is the line between what was only reluctantly acceptable by a viewing audience and what was patently offensive. The credit card swipe might appear to be an arbitrary distinction to make considering the overall objectification of women present in the "Tip Drill" video and in other music videos of similar ilk, but that is actually the point. Public tolerance for these kinds of images changes over time, place/region, religion, ethnic background, gender, and so on.

Amy Adler shares a similar sentiment in her *California Law Review* article, "What's Left?: Hate Speech, Pornography, and the Problem for Artistic Expression."[29] According to Adler, there can be no censorship without a well-developed theory of interpretation. This theory of interpretation must first and foremost account for the presence of deconstructive practices in postmodern art forms: "Out of the deconstructive vision of language has sprung a postmodern art that depends on co-opting, reversing, and destabilizing words and images. Rather than attempting to create new, 'original' work, many contemporary artists rely on the appropriation of pre-existing images and words."[30] What logically follows from the postmodern approach to First Amendment discourses is a fluid engagement with speech preferences and public tolerance for obscenity and exploitation.

In Byron Hurt's award-winning documentary, *Beyond Beats and Rhymes*, a candid exploration of Black masculine images and standards in mainstream rap music unveils rampant violence and misogyny in the lyrics and in the music videos. Once again, Nelly's "Tip Drill" is the poster-example here (among many, many others). In fact, Hurt's documentary relies heavily on the images in videos like "Tip Drill" in order to corroborate several key insights about Black masculinity and its severe limitations. In *Beyond Beats and Rhymes*, Byron Hurt embarks on an introspective journey to evaluate his own sense of Black masculinity in the context of paradigmatic content shifts in the music and culture of the Hip-Hop generation. He was a star football player in high school and college, and was also a prominent member of a historically Black Greek-letter organization—Omega Psi Phi Fraternity, Inc. He admits his own chauvinistic development and rejects it on film by divulging his personal narrative and clearly depicting the misogynistic tendencies in some of the most popular rap lyrics and videos.

The film also deals with violence and other negative reflections in music as well as the history of these images and ideas in American art. The most prominent example is D.W. Griffith's *The Birth of a Nation* and various cinematic clips from American Westerns.[31] However, the dialogues that ensue from screenings of the film seem to favor gender issues. As a community, members of the Hip-Hop generation (many born between 1965 and 1984, as well as some older and younger) are challenging the negativity in Hip-Hop music with an expressed emphasis on the portrayal of women. Clearly this is a vital discussion for members within the Hip-Hop Nation to have.[32] Misogynistic music can unduly influence the minds of some people. Indeed, especially younger, impressionable individuals who are without proactive and/or counter-influences in their lives.

Since violence against women, corporate/economic inequality, and sexual exploitation plague the communities out of which Hip Hop emerges, we must continue to discuss and deconstruct certain femiphobic and oppressive ideologies that are deeply engrained in both the media and the culture.[33] The documentary film and the program on BET correspondingly contribute to a discourse in the Black public sphere specifically intended to educate listeners about the music they are consuming. Per Adler's intimations, the postmodern approach (in the documentary especially) generates important discourse and dialogue in the public sphere. To censor the likes of Nelly would unfortunately also preclude some of the most enlightened discussions occurring within Hip-Hop culture about violence, misogyny, and language. Even if some argue that we might not need these discussions of certain videos, lyrical language, and other Hip-Hop images and standards did not exist, this argument cannot hold true in the face of the misogyny that exists in popular culture proper. Similarly, these arguments cannot hold if we consider the violence and language that emanates from Hollywood sans Hip-Hop culture. According to Adler, "a theory of political censorship must recognize that words and images are arbitrary and that the conditions of interpretation, themselves unpredictable, are all that gives words and images meaning."[34]

III

"But there are bitches, niggers, and ho's that live in America. And as long as that fact exists, I think rappers deserve the right to talk about it."[35]

The three words that were under consideration for being banned in the lyrics of rap music made available to the public are nigger, bitch, and ho. "Expressing concern about the 'growing public outrage' over the use of such words in rap lyrics, Simmons said the words ... should be considered 'extreme curse words'" (AP—"Ban on Hip Hop Epithets Endorsed").[36] In the public sphere, it seems as if the pressure from appearing on *The Oprah Winfrey Show* and her clear disdain for misogyny in Hip Hop (or quite possibly for Hip Hop itself) functioned as a persuading factor in Mr. Simmons' decision to endorse a ban on these three words. Prior to his appearance on Oprah, Mr. Simmons repeatedly responded to criticism about the offensive language in rap music (including its continuous misogyny) by employing his self-contrived mirror-metaphor (i.e., rap music is often a reflection of the community from which it is derived). With the mirror-metaphor, Simmons is suggesting that if we are invested in changing the music, then we must likewise be invested in changing the communities from which Hip-Hop artists emerge.

Notwithstanding the fact that some rappers come from middle-class, and even suburban communities, Mr. Simmons' mirror-metaphor leaves the boundaries of Free Speech wholly intact. This position is dually designed to safeguard the First Amendment as well as Mr. Simmons' interests and investments in the multi-billion dollar commodification of Hip-Hop culture. In a revealing scene in the documentary, *Beyond Beats and Rhymes*, Simmons affirms his conviction to this ideal. Interesting to consider what could have prompted this response. It certainly was not Imus' comments themselves as he was quoted as employing the mirror-metaphor in the immediate aftermath of the Imus controversy. Only after his appearance on *The Oprah Winfrey Show*, did Simmons so radically reverse his stance and call for the universal ban of these three words.

The Oprah Winfrey Show, which has been publicly accused of harboring bias against rap music, hosted a panel that consisted of Russell Simmons, Ben Chavis, CEO Kevin Liles, and rapper, Common, as well as the group of women from Spelman College who were responsible for championing the movement against misogyny based upon the spark that "Tip Drill" ignited. Simmons and company were mercilessly criticized and directly challenged for the social ills of Hip Hop.[37] In many ways, Simmons and his co-panelists were in no position to answer to the women of Spelman, or to Oprah, or to her audience. Not only are they not the culprits (either as executives or as artists) of the most misogynistic or violent elements of rap music, they are also not cultural critics, scholars, or public intellectuals. Their weak positionality on *The Oprah Winfrey Show* was a powerful metaphor for the role of women in rap music videos. They were not exactly silent, but certainly their voices were occasionally drowned out by the cacophony/chorus of women speaking against them and, by extension, speaking against the hatred of how women are represented in Hip-Hop culture. Subsequently and consequently, Simmons endorsed the ban on nigger, bitch, and ho after his appearance on Oprah's show.

First, there is a significant difference between Russell Simmons calling for censorship of rap music and Bob Dole, Bill Bennett, Newt Gingrich, and/or the late C. Delores Tucker promoting the censorship of rap music. There are some political considerations and distinctions to note since Russell Simmons has aligned himself with democratic candidates and issues/platforms in the past. Most important here, is that Simmons is a part of Hip-Hop culture, and by most accounts, a central figure in that culture's economic and global development: "Even as hip hop struggles to define what it is politically, it has always professed to know what it is not—the civil rights movement. Like most youth-based cultures, generation hip hop believed that previous generations simply did not understand the world it inherited or why the movement was so important to them."[38] Russell Simmons' call for a ban on words, therefore, is separate from calls from the Right or calls for censorship from those who are clearly outside of the culture. Should rappers heed his call because of this fact?

That question, at least publicly, remains unanswered. Certainly, his positionality with respect to the culture renders him a more authentic voice from this side of the debate, but I would argue that his endorsement faces the same critique that all censorship efforts will face in Hip-Hop culture. To wit, the dialogue and activist appropriation of misogynistic images and lyrics warrants First Amendment legal protections so that the real issues of misogyny and violence (as opposed to just the lyrics or music videos reflecting these unfortunate themes) can be addressed in sui generis fashion from within the culture itself.

Several rappers have implicitly and explicitly addressed Imus' comments as well as the discursive storm that ensued in response to those comments and rap music's role in the discourse. In a single entitled "Hi-Definition" from his 2007 album, *The Cool*, Lupe Fiasco quips: "Oprah put it on my culture now that ain't wrong/Imus got it from the rhymers now if that ain't blown …"[39] Ironically, the song features Snoop Dogg, an interesting and relatively unexpected collaboration since many critics of rap music would categorize Lupe as conscious and Snoop as gangster.[40] Lupe's lines directly position him in the Imus controversy, but his stance is nuanced. He welcomes Oprah Winfrey's suggestion (and criticism) that Hip-Hop culture itself must be responsible for its misogyny and hate speech in general. At the same time (and in the next line) he blasts Imus for suggesting that he somehow borrowed his ideas from rhymers.

Jay-Z is more explicit but similarly nuanced in his lyrical response to the controversy in a classic song entitled "Ignorant Shit" from his *American Gangster* album.[41] "I missed the part when it start being about Imus/ What do my lyrics got to do with this shit?! *Scarface* the movie did more than Scarface the rapper to me/So that ain't to blame for all the shit that's happened to me."[42] Here, Jay-Z disavows any connection between himself and Imus, thus underscoring the absurdity of the assertion that Don Imus is influenced by rappers. Moreover, he directs attention to violence in film via the juxtaposition of Scarface, the popular gangsta rapper from Houston, Texas and the film from which he borrows his name, Brian DePalma's 1983 remake, *Scarface*.[43] For Jay-Z, the film was far more influential on his former life as a crack dealer in Brooklyn than the lyrics of one of the most authentic street rhymers in the history of Hip-Hop culture. The general theme of the song is to expose the problems of censorship in rap music through the art of exaggeration. The hook/refrain of the song is as follows: "This is that ignorant shit you like, nigger, fuck, shit ass, bitch, trick plus ice ... ." While critiquing the public impulse to censor rap music, "Ignorant Shit" exposes the ignorant inclinations in rap music and challenges listeners to be critical of the same.

A few additional examples will help to elucidate the possibilities for public discourse and protected speech. When I was invited to appear on CNN for Anderson Cooper's program *AC360*, I was pitted against Jason Whitlock, sports writer, on the occasion of the NAACP's public and generally symbolic burial of the N-word. During the segment on AC360, cultural critic, Michaela Angela Davis, explained it as follows: "I think that a symbolic burial of the N-word is misdirected energy, particularly from a trusted organization like the NAACP today. I think that energy should be spent more [on] resurrecting their image with young people than with burying words."[44] Mr. Whitlock's counterposition was that although he had been critical of the NAACP in the past, this particular move was a solid first step in the right direction to try and save Black youth from the clutches of self-hate reflected in the rampant and currently normalized use of the N-word in rap music. Many scholars (Randall Kennedy, Cornel West, Jabari Asim, and Michael Eric Dyson, to name a few) have engaged in the public debate about the use, meaning, and racist/racial implications of the term.

Many of these debates center around three formulated conditions/criteria: (1) The multilayered meaning of the term, (2) The various sociolinguistic incarnations of it (nigga vs. nigger, niggaz, nigguhs, etc.), and/or (3) The ability of changing the semantics of the term by shifting its contexts chronologically, racially, and discursively. My response was simple. There must be a public/private division with respect to how we attempt to regulate the word or not. In the public realm, it is extremely difficult to divorce the word from its historical origins. Thus, whenever a member of the Klan or the Aryan nation scrawls this racial epithet in a public place or uses the word in public to refer to people of African descent, then the term automatically engenders the "hate speech" designation so problematically protected by the First Amendment.[45] This public/private distinction also applies to any rapper who uses the term in public or records the term on a record that will be publicly released. I am not suggesting that we censor these uses, only that we recognize that the deconstructive readings or listenings of the word cannot be guaranteed in the public sphere.

That said, censoring the term will not in and of itself negate the history and awful legacy of racism in America. What it will do, however, is preclude the use of the term in some liberating and politically challenging ways. The Last Poets' tune, "Niggers Are Scared of Revolution"[46] comes immediately to mind here, but for a more recent example of artistically and socially significant uses of the so-called N-word please refer to Chris Rock's HBO special, *Bring the Pain*, where he eloquently and comically makes a distinction between Black folk and niggers.[47] "I love Black people, but I hate niggas!" These variations in usage also exist within Hip Hop itself. Many times when artists use the term, they are in some ways maintaining and perpetuating its negative, historic, and dictionary definitions. Other times, however, the term can engender a feeling of community or camaraderie among the African population. In short, censoring its usage will not serve to address or eradicate racism or self-hate in the African American community. The point here, is that much of this dialogue around the use of the N-word helps to elevate the level of critical literacy about nigger, its etymology, and its integral epithetic role in white supremacy.

Censoring the N-word proves problematic for a number of reasons. The narratives of the N-word are conflicted and complex, and much of this tension came to a head when the well-known MC/rapper, Nas (ne Nasir Jones) decided to entitle his album—*Nigger*. By deliberately employing the term's traditional spelling rather than the dialectal or vernacular orthography (e.g., "nigga") Nas incited a firestorm of controversy that resulted in him being censored.

Unfortunately, the prevailing narrative at work here is that rappers and the youth of the Hip-Hop generation are unaware of the terms abhorrent history. Thus, they believe that by tweaking the pronunciation and social context of the term, they can readily deconstruct its meaning and in some ways put into play the semantic effects of white supremacy attached to the term throughout history.

In these narratives, regardless of how much status an African American man may garner either through degrees or, in this case, a fancy suit, he is still "a nigger."[48] This is the narrative inherent in Nas' cover art. There is not enough space to fully explicate this here, but the songs and lyrics on the now *Untitled* album bear out this complex narratological entanglement. Not to be outdone by arbitrary market forces or his censors, Nas erased the N-word from his title and replaced the cover art of him wearing a suit with his back exposed to us and his initial, "N" emblazoned on his back in the images of scars reminiscent of those left on the backs of African America's enslaved ancestors. This produces a provocative visual narrative that rivals the former, and unveils the powerful imprint of Nas' initial and his initial title. Although Nas was forced to censor the original title of his album, he was able to at once debunk the notion that the Hip-Hop generation uses the N-word ahistorically and prove that the potential to wrestle with the history of the term lies within the culture and music often accused for being ignorant of that history.

The term "bitch" follows closely and in parallel fashion with my discussion of the N-word and its presence and use in the public sphere. Banning the word does not directly address the issue of misogyny in our communities nor does the censorship of it necessarily change the hearts and minds of those men (and women) who are most susceptible to ideologies of misogyny. Bitch is nearly ubiquitous in the lyrics of rap music by both men and women. Jeffrey Ogbar explores many of these issues in his article, "Slouching toward Bork: The Culture Wars and Self-Criticism in Hip Hop Music."[49] In this essay, Ogbar suggests that "without doubt, the misogyny, debauchery, and antisocial hedonism of some lyrics deserve to be attacked. But what may appear to be a sincere concern for the well-being of America's youth is often a guise of a more sordid and insidious attack on Black youth culture and its ability to critique, analyze, and provide commentary on society."[50] One example of this is Queen

Latifah's golden-aged single "U.N.I.T.Y" where she periodically interrogates the misogynistic lyrics of Hip Hop by employing the term bitch in rhetorical fashion[51] asking "Who you callin' a bitch?!"[52] Of course, her lyrics here serve to press these issues in the actual public not just on a record. For me, protecting this speech is far more important than censoring the sordid language of chauvinistic rappers, some of whom are pandering to their seventy percent white buying audience.

The term "ho," a Black vernacular version of the Standard English word, whore, does not fit so neatly into this discussion of the benefits of free speech for artists of the Hip-Hop generation. While there may be some female rappers who employ the term and some male rappers who use the term to refer to other men, the negative connotations of prostitution among poor women cohere to even its vernacular usage. Nonetheless, the desire to ban these three words is most peculiar when one considers the absence of the term "pimp" from this list. After all, pimp has been deliberately rehabilitated in the vernacular by rappers, the Hip-Hop generation, and even some scholars.[53] Stanley Crouch presciently highlights the glaring absence of 'pimp' from the proposed ban in a January 2005 column in the Daily News: "The elevation of pimps and pimp attitudes creates a sadomasochistic relationship with female fans. They support a popular idiom that consistently showers them with contempt."[54]

The absence of pimp from the proposed ban on the three words in Hip Hop puts into bold relief the misogyny inherent in the actual discourse designed to challenge misogyny in rap music and Hip-Hop culture. Since pimps (or the term itself) have/has been recuperated in the artistic and cinematic fabric of imagination (consider the Oscar award bestowed upon Three Six Mafia for the single "It's Hard Out Here for a Pimp" featured in the pimp narrative, *Hustle and Flow*) and because the term implicitly re-inscribes men's relationships to women, as well as men's relationship to capital, it is (and has been) protected.[55] It will never engender the anathema distinction proposed for the three words in question here. It is protected because male supremacy tends to be protected. It is invisible because the institution of prostitution tends to be associated solely with women and not the men who are bound to them in oppressive fashion.

Finally though, all of this energy leveled at censoring rap music is somewhat misdirected when one considers the social issues that must be addressed first in order to directly affect change in our communities and in the public sphere. If the desire to censor rap music persists (and there are many indications that it will), certain theories of interpretation must emerge as corollaries to the discussion. First, the deconstruction and its attendant theories and philosophies must be brought to bear on any censorship efforts. The multiplicity of meaning in the private and the public sphere is a critical fact of our post (post) modern existence. Second, any interpretive theory for censorship in rap music and Hip-Hop culture must also account for the primary predicament of oppressed, socially invisible young people who are empowered by the forms of rap music to talk Black and talk back to the powers that be. Censoring what is worst about rap music will simultaneously stunt and censor what is best about it. The logical answer, then, is to protect artistic speech and follow closely with the powerful dialogic exchanges that ensue.

Corner Boy Masculinity

Corner-boy masculinity: Intersections of inner-city manhood

In *Blues, Ideology, and Afro-American Literature,* Dr. Houston Baker analyzes the intersecting matrices of lack and desire for the enigmatic bluesman.[1] These crossroads of lack and desire, according to Baker, became a foundational intersection for the formulation of the African American identity. Fast forward to the postindustrial economic conditions of the twenty-first-century inner city and this foundational intersection finds an extraordinary consistency with the lack of economic opportunity available to generations of inner-city youth who are exposed to many of the most desirable outposts of a capitalist society. The unfortunate corollary to this desire-producing exposure is an utter absence of the structural and civic resources necessary to transcend abject poverty. The spectacle of this society notwithstanding, various verbal and visual discourses generated in popular media seek to construct original models of masculinity for these generational constituents.

In this chapter, I engage emerging theoretical conceptions of Black masculinity (a'la Mark Anthony Neal and others) and juxtapose these ideas with several specific constructions of Black masculinity performed by and through the characters of *The Wire*.[2] Of significance to this discussion is rapper, Common, and his brilliant musical collaboration with The Last Poets, aptly entitled, "The Corner."[3] In this critically acclaimed single, Common brilliantly exemplifies the urban corner as a master site for the production of Black masculinity. For the purposes of this chapter, I focus on the proliferation of various complex representations of urban Black masculinity detailed in the critically acclaimed HBO series, *The Wire*.

The Wire reveals a dramatically realistic Baltimore where corner boys inaugurate an inner-city "juvenacracy" based on the unchecked drug trade.[4] Yet even within this hyper-violent world of criminalized man-children, extraordinary models of Black masculinity emerge. According to Davis, "Masculinity is a social fact produced through a set of both educational and social practices that function to regulate and circumscribe the lives of young men, as well as reinforce dominant social norms at a time of transition and uncertainty."[5] The models of masculinity in *The Wire* (most notably in Seasons 4 and 5) converge on the proverbial corners of the inner-city experience. Preston "Bodie" Broadus is raised, comes of age, thrives, and dies on the corner. Omar Little makes his name in the street by terrorizing those same corners even though his sexual identity and privately tender nature should preclude him from the legendary street status he attains. The various types of masculinity performed in *The Wire* provide incisive depictions of a wide range of Black being. The corner is merely the nexus through which this profusion of Black manhood is enacted.

The opening quote for the "Corner Boys" episode of *The Wire* cites Zenobia as saying: "We got our thing, but it's just part of the big thing."[6] Corner boys are the youngest initiates and/or liaisons into the illicit drug game. From Avon Barksdale to Marlo Stanfield, bosses or drug kingpins on *The Wire* exploit their allure with the youngest and most vulnerable denizens of inner-city neighborhoods in order to compel them to work the corners. The drug lord thereby accomplishes (at least) two objectives: (1) Since the majority of the corner boys are younger than the age of legal responsibility, they automatically circumvent the criminal justice system. (2) By recruiting the youngest of the youth, the drug organization indoctrinates them into the central "code of the street." In his ethnographic research conducted in inner-city Philadelphia, Elijah Anderson draws the following incisive conclusions:

> It must be continually underscored that much of this violence and drug activity is a reflection of the dislocations brought about by economic transformations, shifts that are occurring in the context of the new global economy. … Where the wider economy is not receptive to these dislocated people, the underground economy is. … The facts of race relations, unemployment, dislocation, and destitution create alienation, and alienation

allows for certain receptivity to overtures made by people seeking youthful new recruits for the drug trade.[7]

Zenobia's quote assumes powerful connotations in the context of the classroom scenario in which she makes this claim. Although Zenobia is an African American girl, she is, in the context of this episode and from the viewpoint of her alternative educators, a corner boy.[8] Her corner-boy status is marked by her posture, attitude, and vocal outbursts in class. She, like several other junior high school students, is forced into an alternative curricular program where they are studied and in some ways further alienated from their classmates and traditional classrooms. As a group, they face extraordinary challenges including neglect, abuse, violence, and the resultant psychosocial trauma. Over the course of the "Corner Boys" episode, the researchers, mostly led by Howard "Bunny" Colvin, formerly of the police, make an experimental breakthrough. They had been trying for weeks to foster a genuine connection with the students in this recently isolated "research project." Their work eventually falls under the scrutiny of various political interests, but in this episode they are still relatively free to explore the possibilities of an educational experiment that removes the most troubled and troublesome youth from the traditional classroom.

The consequent breakthrough occurs in the latter part of this episode when Bunny intercedes during one of the other researcher's exercises. He has become somewhat flustered with their efforts to have an authentic interaction with the corner-boy students when it dawns on him that even in this nontraditional school setting, the corner-boy students are consistently trying to outsmart and undermine their teachers and the researchers. Immediately, Bunny confronts the class on this fact. He unveils their in-school "hustle" as a mere training ground for the streets, where they are the corner boys and the teachers, administrators, and researchers are the police. Here Zenobia (through obvious and subversive body language, visage, and subtle commentary) underscores the fact that this is true in less metaphorical ways since Bunny actually was a police officer. Ultimately, Bunny gives them various opportunities to reflect on, discuss, and write about their lives as corner boys. He even invites them to develop a code for corner-boy life—a survival guide, of sorts, comprising the "do's" and "don'ts" of the street.

These scenes are powerful moments for educators who watch *The Wire* and know the challenges, possibilities, and failures, and frustrations of inner-city classrooms overrun by children of the drug trade. According to James E. Davis, a professor and researcher in the Department of Educational Leadership and Policy Studies at Temple University, "The interaction of school context and masculine identities and socialization is important to consider. I see masculinity as a way that young men 'perform' to enact some personal power given their limited social and learning positions in school. These performances of masculinity are not necessarily linked to troublemaking but to how teachers and other adults interpret these performances."[9] Professor Davis' insight sheds (instructive) light on the interaction that ensues in the corner-boy classroom after Bunny radically reinterprets the educational proceedings.[10]

Once the corner-boy students accept the interpretation of their classroom as a training ground for their involvement in the illegal drug trade—as well as their own limited life experiences and truncated opportunities on the mean streets of Baltimore—they become willing participants in the educational process. The idea that masculinity is inextricably linked to economic prowess (and possibility) is especially relevant and particularly compelling to dispossessed African American youth.[11] The corner-boy students no longer rebel against this marginalized curriculum, but instead, participate in discussions, work together in groups to construct the code of streets from the corner-boy perspective, and even talk about their learning outside of the classroom among their peers.

Zenobia's quote, "We got our thing, but it's just a part of the big thing," is delivered in the midst of one of these engaging dialogues. She situates the drug trade within the context of the dislocating power of the global economy. From the corner-boy perspective, at the crossroads of lack and desire, selling drugs is no different from selling cigarettes or alcohol except that some trades are arbitrarily deemed legal and others are not. This suggestion (duly noted and quoted) and these scenes unveil an abiding intersectionality with respect to how Black masculinity is conceptualized and operationalized (but likewise racialized and criminalized) on *The Wire*. That girls can be corner boys is important to recognize here, but the youths' acknowledgment of the interdisciplinary relationships between aspirational masculinity, global capital, arbitrary illegality and the possibility of public education as a means to overcome socioeconomic challenges are also powerful intersecting messages in this popular TV narrative.

Alcyee J. Jane states that "intersectionality calls into question the construction of monolithic identities and forces one to consider how one is positioned by the intersecting and multiple hegemonies that structure American culture."[12] If Black masculinity was or is in anyway monolithic, the corner-as-metaphor in *The Wire* represents numerous attempts to deconstruct the monolithic notion of Black manhood. Since the corner is literarily an urban intersection, it is a befitting metaphor for the deconstructive work necessary to unpack and reformulate stereotypical notions of Black masculinity in the twenty-first century and reformulate and represent them indiscriminately. Some of the hegemonic forces that rigidly construct Black masculinity are the economic lack and ad-induced desires that collude to produce the collective willingness to engage in the underground economy. Poor public education, decaying postindustrial residential neighborhoods, and the inherently violent communities that result from these structural challenges all work to obscure the full range of Black masculine possibilities. It follows that the literature, film, and music that represents Black masculine behavior inclines toward these monolithic depictions. *The Wire* departs from this monolithic morass and dwells comfortably within the spaces of intersectionality that the real life geography of an urban corner subtly reflects.

The quintessential corner boy of the entire series is Preston "Bodie" Broadus. Bodie worked corners for the Barksdale cartel as well as for Marlo Stanfield's cartel. He even attempted a brief stint on his own as the power struggle within the drug trade shifted from Barksdale to Stanfield, but throughout most of *The Wire* he was the most loyal, dedicated, and maybe the hardest working hustler on the corner. Technically speaking, he had younger corner boys working for him, but the preponderance of Bodie's scenes in *The Wire* are on a corner or at some intersection hustling illegal substances. Bodie's fierce determination and steadfast dedication allowed him to thrive within the Barksdale drug organization. But after the cartel crumbles, he is quickly absorbed by Marlo's organization. Bodie's work ethic is indefatigable over several seasons and thus, even in that one sense, he debunks stereotypes about Black male laziness.

Moreover, Bodie challenges the Horatio Alger narrative of drug dealing and hustling. His tenacious morality and kindhearted nature do not allow him to achieve the economic spoils of his bosses. In fact, Bodie seems to live a fairly modest—if not meager—working-class existence. He usually eats in bodegas or cheap corner store shops. He never wears expensive clothes or jewelry (Season 4), and he never flashes or flosses his cash. Bodie lives at the intersections of working-class intellectual/hustler but unfortunately, he is not permitted to live through the conclusion of *The Wire*. In one of his final dialogues (with Officer McNulty as he analyzes his years in "the game" and concludes that the "game is rigged"),[13] he recognizes that he is and has been a pawn. McNulty is ultimately able to convince Bodie to consider providing some information. Through a series of somewhat arbitrary and inconceivable events, Marlo is made aware of the possibility that Bodie will become a police informant: "Ofc. Mcnulty talks him (Bodie) into informing on Marlo, but Marlo has him killed before he can do any damage."[14] Consequently, Bodie is murdered by Marlo's ruthless assassins Chris and Snoop. He may have had a chance to escape their well-calculated plot, but he refused to abandon his corner.

More than any other character on *The Wire*, Bodie reflects the cacophony of voices in one of Common's most popular singles, "The Corner." As the lead single off of Common's 2005 critically acclaimed album, *Be*, "The Corner" features appearances/contributions by Kanye West and The Last Poets. Lyrically, "The Corner" has three vocal performances and conceptual perspectives. Common, Kanye, and The Last Poets articulate three trajectories that observe the concept of the urban corner as a critical site for the construction of Black masculinity with attendant imagery intersecting through the vocal performances of the artists. In Common's lyrics, he verbalizes the hopelessness of urban environments centered on the street life that corners have come to represent.

> Corners leave souls opened and closed hoping for more
> With nowhere to go niggas rolling in droves
> They shoot the wrong way cause they ain't knowing they goal
> The streets ain't safe cause they ain't knowing the code
>   (Common, "The Corner")

In addition to the internal rhyme schemes of these lines, Common reveals himself as a skillful practitioners of enjambment—a technique in which rappers/MCs break poetic lines in the midst of a sentence. The poetic effect of Common's repeated use of enjambment throughout his verses is to sound as if he rhymes around corners. Thus, the fluidity of Common's lyrical delivery reflects the culturally intersecting space of the song's subject while the content of the lyrics reveals the working-class aesthetics inherent in Bodie's characterization as the quintessential corner boy on *The Wire*.

Kanye West and The Last Poets represent two distinct but likewise intersecting trajectories of "The Corner." West's hook "I wish I could give you this feeling: On the corners, niggas robbing, killing, dying/Just to make a living, huh?" can be interpreted as a subtle glorification of the violent ways and means of the underground economy. He "wishes" that he could somehow give his listeners the feeling of the corner. In fact by "wishing it" he likely does provide his listeners (many of whom do not live in inner-city neighborhoods) with some visceral sense of the allure that the drug trade procures at the crossroads/intersections of lack and desire. West's voice and conceptual trajectory is limited to the refrain of the song, but it clearly intersects with and confronts the general thematics of Common's more somber, less glorified verses.

The Last Poets also proffer a distinct but intersecting trajectory into this song. They are relegated to the ad-lib portion of the song, but their presence is remarkable for at least two reasons: (1) The Last Poets are the artistic progenitors of all rappers/MCs (though they are rarely recognized as such). (2) Their verses engender a completely new conceptualization of the corner as a nostalgic historical monument of inner-city existence. "The corner was our Rock of Gibraltar, our Stonehenge/Our Taj Mahal, our monument, Our testimonial to freedom, to peace and to love/Down on the corner ..." (Last Poets, The Corner). By positioning the corner as a historical monument, The Last Poets have further fleshed out an intersecting discourse on the point of urban existence. The corner depicted in Common's lyrics, Kanye West's refrain, and The Last Poets' ad-libs is the bedrock of Bodie's demographic identity. He says as much in his last extended dialogue on the series (with McNulty). He represents the underground economy's working-class aesthetics depicted by Common's verses; he lives and dies on the corners gently glorified in West's refrain, and he spends much of his life paying homage to a historicized version of those corners that at the time of his murder cease to exist.

Corner boy masculinity conceptually thrives at the intersections represented by several pairings or groupings of characters in *The Wire*. Like Bodie's brilliant reflection of Common's lyrics and/or Zenobia's complex encapsulation of the coglike existence of the corner-boy figure, corner-boy masculinity is enmeshed in the public sphere through lived experiences, artistic production, and various social theories. In his groundbreaking work, *New Black Man*, Mark Anthony Neal traces some of these intersecting theories and experiences and suggests that a "NewBlackMan" exists "for those willing to embrace the fuzzy edges of Black masculinity that in reality is still under construction."[15] According to Neal, our uncritical allegiance to the "Strong Black Man," forged in the crucible of racial hatred and historical oppression, obscures the multifaceted range of Black masculine expression in reality, in the media, and in artistic production. My argument here is that *The Wire* (almost by default) challenges the rigid conceptualizations of the "Strong Black Man" and offers the broader range reflected by Neal's sense of the "NewBlackMan":

> NewBlackMan is about resisting being inscribed by a wide range of forces and finding a comfort with a complex and progressive existence as a black man in America. As such NewBlackMan is not so much about conceiving of a more positive version of black masculinity … but rather a concept that acknowledges the many complex aspects, often contradictory, that make up a progressive and meaningful black masculinity.[16]

Corner boy masculinity is merely one of many socially intertextual models for better understanding how Black masculinity is fleshed out through the various characters depicted in *The Wire*.

Over the course of Season 4, Namond Brice becomes a corner boy/drug runner under Bodie. Namond's parents overdetermine his identity, and through his character, audiences bear honest witness to the struggles that young men must face with the brutality of urban inner-city life and nothing less than their existential sense of self hanging in the balance. Namond's father Wee-Bay Brice was an enforcer for the Barksdale drug cartel who will spend the rest of his life in jail for his crimes. Namond is thus blessed with the credibility of his father's name, but also the crushing weight of his violent legacy. These challenges are only exacerbated by his mother, DeLonda, who after enjoying the spoils of Wee-Bay's affiliation with the Barksdales, fully expects her son to carry on in his father's footsteps. DeLonda is an easy-to-demonize maternal figure that seems to have stepped right out of the Moynihan Report. Sociologist, S. Craig Watkins summarizes the report as follows:

> The report concluded that the structure of family life in the black community constituted a "tangle of pathology ... capable of perpetuating itself without assistance from the white world," and that "at the heart of the deterioration of the fabric of Negro society is the deterioration of the Negro family. It is the fundamental source of the weakness of the Negro community at the present time." Further, the report argued that the matriarchal structure of black culture weakened the ability of black men to function as authority figures. This particular notion of black familial life has become a widespread, if not dominant, paradigm for comprehending the social and economic disintegration of late twentieth-century black urban life.[17]

DeLonda is certainly a powerful, and at times, punitive and physically imposing, matriarch. At one point during the season, she slaps Namond when he makes yet another attempt to express his unwillingness to be the man that she wants him to be.[18] Namond's mother does all that she can to instill him with a materialistic set of values. In fact, among the four young men around whom Season 4 centers (Namond, Duquan, Michael, and Randy), Namond is always the best dressed. He also lives in the most economically sound household, a middle class byproduct of his father's work with the Barksdales. Even though he appears to be the most economically comfortable, his mother's inexorable coercion ultimately pushes him to sell drugs with Bodie. In this sense, the Moynihanian notion of pathology in the Black family is not a default byproduct of fatherlessness. Instead, for the Brice family, Namond's pathological behavior is the desired result.

DeLonda's influence on Namond utterly shapes his sense of himself as a man. Although he is ultimately saved from her by his father's decision to relinquish custody to Bunny Colvin, DeLonda represents the signal role that mothers play in the construction of Black masculinity.[19] By focusing so effortlessly on the deleterious effects of her materialism and general affinity for the trappings of the drug trade, *The Wire* puts into bold relief the awesome potential of the single parent household to negatively impact the young Black male. Through Namond, the audience of *The Wire* experiences the resultant emotional trauma of becoming a Black man in a nihilistic material environment. We are often invited to critique his emotional responses in certain brutal scenes (i.e., his confrontations with Kenard, Michael, and his mother), but ultimately viewers pity Namond and appreciate the fact that at least he will have an opportunity to live. The potential opportunities of his new life with Bunny Colvin and his wife are powerfully reflected in the closing scenes of Season 4.[20] As Namond finishes his homework on the porch, one of his homie's from his corner-boy days drives by in a stolen vehicle. Both of the boys appear visibly older than at the outset of the season. As the boy in the stolen car speeds through the intersection, he nearly causes an accident. Namond stares thoughtfully at the intersection and the corners. The camera view lingers on the intersection, intentionally emphasizing the difference in this neighborhood. Namond also notices this difference—as reflected by the haunting absence of corner boys on these corners.

Opposite of Namond's emotional character is Michael Lee's stoic, brooding demeanor and budding violent nature. Unlike Namond, Michael does not have any parents to coerce him into being a corner boy. Although his mother is an addict who regularly sells their groceries and otherwise makes life impossible for him and his little brother, Michael distinguishes himself from his peers by not accepting free money from Marlo at the beginning of the school year.[21] Marlo takes an instant interest in Michael and soon Chris Partlow (Marlo's Lieutenant and all around enforcer) begins to court him. For the most part Michael refuses these advances. He does not have any contrived or coerced affinity for the underworld. However, Chris makes it clear to him that if ever he needs their services they will be there for him. Of the four boys in Season 4, Michael most represents the traditional "Strong Black Man" characterization. He is the natural leader of the four corner boys; he is fathering his younger brother; he protects Dukie, Randy, and Namond at different points throughout the season; and he at least attempts to be his own man by initially resisting the offers from Marlo and his crew.

Eventually and unfortunately, Michael does seek the help of Chris and Snoop—two of the most ruthless murderers in television history. When his brother Bug's father returns home from prison, Michael is immediately agitated and upset. He blames his mother for Bug's father's return, and after only one interaction it is clear that Michael has been sexually abused by him.[22] In an episode titled "Misgivings," Michael walks with Chris and Snoop in order to scope out and identify Bug's father for the hit.[23] They mark him coming up to a corner to buy drugs for Michael's mother. Snoop questions, "What the fuck did he do to you?" to which Michael offers no reply. However, Chris gives him a knowing look. When Chris and Snoop return to that same corner to escort Bug's father to his death, Chris asks him questions about sexual assault along the way. Throughout the season, Chris and Snoop have murdered multiple people with guns, usually a gunshot to the head. But in the ultimate scene of "Misgivings," Chris brutally beats Bug's father to death. He punches and kicks him repeatedly and then spits on him to punctuate his hate for this man he does not know. Snoop can only look on in surprise, but a plausible interpretation of this brutal slaying is that Chris identifies with Michael based on a shared past of sexual assault and rape. That two men bond over being rape survivors/victims is a singular achievement accomplished by this series. Yet, this bond is formulated over the series' most brutal murder and it will require Michael's wholesale capitulation to the Marlo Stanfield organization.

One final example to consider here is the extraordinary character, Omar Little. Technically speaking, Omar is not a corner boy. That is, he does not sell drugs and he is older than any of the corner boys already exemplified in this chapter. He is much closer in age to the drug bosses, detectives, and politicos that populate the world of *The Wire*. However, Omar is the most feared and respected figure in this world. After crippling the Barksdale organization, most notably by assassinating Stringer Bell,[24] he spends much of Seasons 4 and 5 robbing the drug "co-op" and hunting members of Marlo's organization who he holds responsible for torturing and murdering his friend, Butchie. Omar is an urban Robin Hood of sorts whose sartorial presentation reflects the aesthetics of the Wild West. The duster, vest, and shotguns and pistols notwithstanding, Omar is gay. This fact remains somewhat unremarkable throughout his reign on *The Wire*, but the creators write Omar's character in such a way that his love for Brandon (Season 3) and for Reynaldo (Seasons 4 and 5) is tender and genuine. Omar is not the first gay character or Black gay character to appear on film or television. He is, however, the first Black gay character to so readily and regularly empower himself through the phallic symbolism of the gun.

And finally, Omar's sexual identity only becomes notable as it intersects with his character's persona as one of the most violent vigilantes in Baltimore's history. His character is then a repository of what Mark Anthony Neal refers to as "black meta-identities," various and varied identities that exist beneath the surface of the American public sphere.[25] In order to better appreciate the multiplicity of identities—vigilante, gay man, most feared, and respected underworld figure—the corner-boy masculinity model becomes wholly applicable here. When Omar emerges from any of his hideouts during the day, corner boys spot him from a distance and warn all of the dealers and people in the vicinity that "Omar is coming! Omar is coming!"[26] In a silk pink bathrobe and armed with an enormous silver-plated pistol Omar walks and stalks the corners, embodying the intersectional nature of corner-boy masculinity—with his reputation for violence utterly obscuring homophobic perspectives of Black manhood. *The Wire's* Omar is a clarion call for viewers of the program to listen critically to the powerful statements constructed through original characterizations of Black intersectional identities.

Rewriting the Remix

College composition and the educational elements of Hip Hop

Composition courses at universities tend to employ a wide range of thematic content that is often contingent upon the interests of the individuals teaching them. As scholars of Hip-Hop culture continue to enter and thrive within the academy, the advent of composition courses that reflect the scholarly curiosities of this growing group of composition pedagogues continues steadily. In this context, the emergence of Hip Hop–themed composition courses has been inevitable. Hip-Hop composition is not, at least in this chapter, about crafting or performing rap lyrics as a means of learning how to compose descriptive, argumentative, analytical, persuasive, or research-based papers. Instead, Hip-Hop composition explores various aspects of Hip-Hop culture in order to engage the learning processes involved in cultivating strong(er) writers and continuous critical thinkers.

This chapter establishes pedagogical and theoretical foundations for the thematic utility of Hip-Hop culture in composition courses. Accordingly, these pedagogical foundations rest upon the aesthetic utility of specific elements of Hip-Hop culture (such as MC-ing and DJ-ing), and the intuitive relationships that these elements have with education as well as with certain writing/composition techniques specifically (e.g., brainstorming or authorship itself). Hip-Hop culture's pedagogical potential in the composition classroom relies heavily on rap music's obsession with language, wordplay, and various linguistic interactions. Some scholars (including Schuaib Meachum and Elaine Richardson) employ the West African term *nommo* to capture this emphasis on the power of the word.[1] The crux of the pedagogical argument is that

Hip-Hop culture presents numerous opportunities for teachers to leverage popular culture in order to make instructive interventions in the composition classroom.

The power of education cannot be overstated here, as one of the culture's founding figures, Afrika Bambaataa, argues that the "fifth element" of Hip-Hop culture is knowledge. This assertion is predicated on a range of epistemic considerations that are generated through Hip-Hop discourses. These discourses aptly articulate the artistry and aesthetics in the foundational elements, as well as the knowledge that underpins our best comprehension of the culture's history, its relationship to politics, and its emergence in certain socioeconomic circumstances. In this chapter, the fifth element is situated atop the list of what I am referring to as Hip Hop's educational elements: knowledge, consciousness, search and discovery, and participation.

The educational elements of Hip-Hop culture

Although there is an inherent educational capacity in the literal elements of Hip Hop, less attention has been devoted to how education is implicitly framed through Hip-Hop culture, or what I call the educational elements of Hip Hop. These four educational elements are as follows: (1) Knowledge, (2) Consciousness, (3) Search and Discovery, and (4) Participation. Together with the foundational elements of Hip Hop, the educational elements underwrite many initiatives that bring Hip-Hop culture into classrooms at different levels of schooling and across various disciplines. Importantly, these educational elements are not disconnected from the traditional four elements of Hip Hop. Rather, the educational elements derive from the sensibilities, mindsets, and approaches imbedded in the four expressive Hip-Hop elements, or what Petchauer (2009) calls "Hip Hop aesthetic forms."[2]

Knowledge

Knowledge of (or about) Hip Hop is one of the authenticating principles of the culture's constituents. Much like jazz or other forms of Black musical culture, the denizens of Hip Hop pride their selves on an unmatched ability to reproduce the facts, information, and/or what is otherwise lesser known about the culture. This practice has been buttressed by an array of other cultural/ social practices such as Hip Hop's overall competitiveness, an infusion of influences from certain philosophical entities such as the 5 percent Nation of Gods and Earths, and an abiding protectiveness of the culture from exploitation and external appropriation. The knowledge element of Hip-Hop culture also assumes its traditional meaning of skills and information cultivated through education and experience. Thus, the concept of mastery, as exemplified via monikers such as "Grand Master," pervades each of the foundational elements. The artisans and organic historians of the culture demonstrate the wealth of knowledge generated through the practice of any of the foundational elements as well as the history that shapes the development of the culture overall. This elemental-based knowledge is complemented by the experiential content that Hip-Hop music proffers to its constituents.

One of the most widely known verbal purveyors of experiential content-based knowledge in Hip-Hop culture, Charles Ridenhour (Chuck D) of Public Enemy, famously quipped that rap music was Black folk's CNN. This oft quoted analogy between rap music and the first twenty-four-hour cable news network suggests a number of important parallels about the kind of knowledge particular to Hip Hop. First, it suggests the infinite transfer of information among enclaves of Hip-Hop culture around the world. Chuck D was implying that the multimedia developments of the information age, in conjunction with Hip-Hop culture's explosive popularity, were establishing an international network of informational exchange through various media platforms (e.g., internet, TV, radio, CDs, and DVDs). Second, a central aspect of Chuck D's equation of Hip Hop with a Black CNN is that Hip Hop was (and in some ways still is) an information source for Black folk. Golden era Hip-Hop narratives of power relationships, inner-city poverty, gang violence, and police brutality provided intricate insights into the lived experiences of Black folk across the United States. Still today, the music of the culture is a source of information about the experiences of Black folk around the world in the late twentieth and early twenty-first centuries. Within this parallel lies the vital truth that knowledge within Hip Hop is most frequently a counter-narrative to the mainstream news media. That is, Hip Hop is not simply a rich news/information source but one that often challenges and contests the dominant and hegemonic narratives that circulate in society.

This educational element has implications for classrooms generally, but it also has precise implications for composition classrooms. One of the ways we cultivate critical thinking in the composition classroom is through substantive discussions about current events. Twenty-first-century college students can often be encouraged to engage in continuous critical thinking when they are challenged to interrogate the various media with which they regularly interface. Music is one such form (among many others) and Hip-Hop music proffers a litany of examples to work with in terms of experiential content that invites critical thinking about relevant and/or important issues. For almost any topical issue that affects the communities from which Hip-Hop culture derives, an artist will craft lyrics that address, critique, and/or inform the listeners about the issue (e.g., Hurricane Katrina's impact on New Orleans and Jay-Z's "Minority Report"[3] or Lil Wayne's "Georgia Bush,"[4] or Mos Def/Yasin Bey's "Dollar Day"[5]).

One can only imagine how often the Trayvon Martin case came up in college classrooms during the Spring 2012 semester. Or how the litany of hashtags, civic actions organized by the Movement 4 Black Lives (#BlackLivesMatter), and the long list of victims of state-sanctioned police violence continue to shape the current event discourses of the twenty-first-century classroom. Issues/cases such as these are important opportunities to bring Hip Hop directly into the composition classroom in order to facilitate critical discussions on relevant issues. In my own Hip-Hop culture and composition courses, I regularly incorporate lyrics, play songs, or show music videos as points of entry into complex discussions. Although there are too many songs/tributes made specifically to address the Martin case to list here, one powerful selection that I used was Reef's "The Prey," a bleak reimagining of the final minutes of Trayvon Martin's life.[6]

Reef the Lost Cauze is an "underground" Philadelphian rapper whose music often chronicles, local inner-city struggles. While his rap moniker alone is enough consideration for an engaging discussion around Hip-Hop culture, nihilism, and urban life, his lyrics in "The Prey" recount a version of the events leading up to Trayvon Martin's death, make incisive allusions to historical racism, and outline the practices of institutional racism and police brutality. The epilogue to the song quotes (i.e., samples or excerpts) comments made by Charles Dutton's character in the now classic Hughes brothers' film *Menace II Society*. In a cautionary conversation with several of the film's protagonists, young Black men who are inherently seen as society's menace, Dutton's character states the following: "The hunt is on. And you're the prey." The use of this quote in "The Prey" is an important opportunity for composition students to appreciate the value of a well-researched and well-placed quote in terms of developing (or in this case, introducing) their arguments or compositional discussions. It also serves as an essential springboard for the initiation of candid discussions about the vilification of inner-city youth and the institutional challenges that continue to afflict young Black men in America.

Some of the most common counter narratives that Hip Hop offers deal with the reporting of violence in urban communities, and in reference to the case above, a gated middle-class community. These counter narratives matter because too often, the most prevalent reports of violence in urban communities focus on various pathologies and deficit explanations for people of color. The knowledge conveyed through Hip Hop often renders a more sophisticated view of violence, including an acknowledgment of social inequalities, an engagement with historical racial violence, and the environmental toxins that work to sustain violence in the present. This type of knowledge from Hip Hop ultimately results in (and resides with) knowledge of the self. That is, exposure to the counter narratives and testimonials from Hip Hop (regardless of one's racial identification) feed and shape how one understands their self with relationship to systems of power and oppression in the world.

Consciousness

Directly related to knowledge is consciousness. Consciousness is knowledge of the self, knowledge of one's surroundings, and knowledge of the social and/or historical forces at play in one's existence. For Hip Hop, a fundamental aspect of the educational element of consciousness resides at the heart of the ongoing debates about the content of the music. The rampant misogyny, consumerism, and violence in most popular manifestations of the culture are often critiqued based upon the assumption that a certain level of consciousness about social conditions is central to Hip-Hop culture. This old school era (1970s to mid-1980s) or golden era (mid-1980s to mid-1990s) bias occasionally obscures the rich corpus of underground/ grassroots Hip Hop not readily available on mainstream platforms for the music industry.[7] That said, consciousness is an important element for educators interested in employing Hip Hop in the classroom because it flies so forcefully in the face of the anti-intellectual nature of popular culture and mainstream representations of Hip Hop.

A tremendous amount of Hip-Hop artistry is dedicated to articulating place and space. Murray Forman's *The 'Hood Comes First* is a scholarly monograph dedicated to this phenomenon in the music.[8] At its core, the consciousness element of Hip-Hop culture necessitates one's awareness of his/her immediate surroundings. However, consciousness also features other relevant issues and valuable composition classroom learning opportunities beyond the space/place awareness factor. This element, more than any other educational element, demands a commitment to social justice. In fact, consciousness in most Hip-Hop "circles" suggests knowledge of institutional and historical forms of oppression as well as a dedicated interest in addressing and reforming the societies that continue to support forms of oppression. One of the more lighthearted means of tapping into the potential in this particular educational element comes from Aaron McGruder's "The Boondocks."[9]

"The Boondocks" is an animated series and a serialized, nationally syndi-cated comic strip. The strip and the series are equal parts urban humor and sociopolitical commentary via satire. More often than not, it directs attacks on and against some of the more egregious purveyors of Black pathology in the eyes of McGruder—like R. Kelly or Black Entertainment Television (BET). However, the series offers some productive opportunities for the composi-tion classroom, student writing, and critical thinking. The title of the strip and series gestures toward the consciousness of place so prevalent in Hip-Hop discourses—artistic and otherwise. The "boondocks" refers to a place far away from the "'hood" or inner-city existence. The distance is geopolitical in the sense that the "boondocks" is further away from the urban world in class or station than it is in plain geography. The main characters of "The Boon-docks," Huey and Riley are brothers who reflect a twenty-first-century Hip-Hop double consciousness. Riley exudes a thug mentality. He is anti-society, and devises violent means to steal the material items so often lauded in Hip-Hop music. Huey (like his founding Black Panther party member namesake) is sociopolitically conscious. Both brothers are voiced by actress, Regina King, and their repartee forms the substance of the strip and the animated series. "The Boondocks" is exceptional subject matter for comparative analysis com-position assignments. It can function as the workshop/in-class example or as the subject for the assignment itself, but it features a wide range of comparative-analytical possibilities: the boondocks and the 'hood; Huey and Riley; and/or DuBoisian double consciousness and that proffered by McGruder through his characters. Ultimately, the consciousness element of Hip-Hop culture does not require Hip-Hop texts to make the point or to shape the lesson. Young people who consider themselves constituents of a Hip-Hop generation will likely be invested in the sociopolitical issues of the day, especially as they are chronicled by and through the music of the culture. The ultimate question for educators is are we prepared to seek these chronicles out in order to better discover the educational potential of youth culture in the composition classroom.

Search and discovery

Search and discovery is that rarely realized educational element of Hip-Hop culture that beckons young people to situate themselves in the music/experiences of Hip Hop that speak directly to their own experiences. Neate speaks to this element and its central role throughout Hip Hop:

> When people say that Hip Hop is dead it just shows they're not in touch. People talk about the elements of Hip Hop culture but ... in any period of Hip Hop, the best stuff had to be searched for. That's why ... *search and discovery* is the most neglected element of Hip Hop.[10] (58)

Search and discovery encourages students influenced by Hip-Hop culture to pursue knowledge and prepare themselves for the ongoing benefits of intellectual discovery. The strongest sense of search extends beyond simply comprehending the lyrics of Hip-Hop music. The traditional methods of Hip

Hop composition use "samples" from previously recorded music to create new music[11] (Schloss 2004). One representative example is Jay-Z's "Hard Knock Life" which samples "The Hard Knock Life" from the Broadway classic, *Annie*.[12] Often misunderstood as simply plagiarizing previous music, the practice of sampling is so sophisticated that cultural outsiders cannot recognize when or why it is taking place. People deeply familiar with Hip Hop and its norms cannot only easily identify sample-based music, but they are in tune with the aesthetic and expect it. This sensibility can simultaneously instigate and perpetuate the listener's search for its historic musicological origins.

This kind of search, however, is not limited to musical sources and origins. In local Hip-Hop communities, for example, this kind of search can be a central component of autonomous educational pursuit (Schloss 2009). In higher education, students who understand and abode by this sensibility can use it as a means to search and discover information sources relevant to their learning experiences (Petchauer 2011). One way to situate this element within the composition framework requires students to visit the library and familiarize themselves with the various databases and research resources available to them. The spirit of search and discovery is an important element to introduce to students of the Hip-Hop composition classroom. Many of these students will already be conversant with a wide array of search engines and internet-based search tools. The real challenge is to impress upon them the true meaning of discovery that challenges students to view writing and writing courses/assignments as something other than an academic requirement. One way of defining discovery in a way that matters to students is through autobiographical writing. Autobiographical writing and assignments or discussions that allow for personal testimony resonate with students (pedagogically).

Participation

Perhaps most significant among the educational elements is the mandate to participate in Hip-Hop culture. For those teachers and scholars who wonder how Hip-Hop culture transformed from an inner-city phenomenon into an international mainstay of popular youth culture, the origins of the b-boy/girl are instructive (see Schloss 2009). The b-boy's role as a dancer quickly developed into one of the earliest points of entry for a generation of young people who were invited to participate in the frustrated, angst-ridden, and brazenly responsive culture of the era. Participation is the central impulse that the various initiatives to implement Hip-Hop culture into the classroom will employ. According to KRS-One, the legendary artist and self-professed Teacher of Hip Hop, the culture is driven by being: "Hiphop is the mental activity of oppressed creativity. Hiphop is not a theory and you cannot do Hiphop. Oppressed urban youth living in the ghettos of America are Hiphop. Rap is something you do; Hiphop is something you live."[13]

From this perspective, Hip Hop is principally a participatory culture. There is no such thing as being part of Hip Hop but not actively participating in some way—they are, according to KRS-One, confluent states of being. Even those who watch, applaud, and cheer for those b-girl's whose kinesthetic abilities inspire awe, are fundamentally participating in the culture (Schloss 2009). This mandate of participation extends beyond the specific element of b-boying and b-girling too. The cipher, the key unit of participation in Hip-Hop activities, is itself a form of participation[14] (Johnson 2009). Given the centrality of participation, this educational element inspires teachers and scholars to re-conceptualize the ways that participation can function in different classroom contexts (see, e.g., Emdin, in Petchaeur and Hill 2012). In the composition classroom, participation is required in each aspect of the course, but it is most important during classroom discussions. The Hip-Hop culture composition classroom (like any composition classroom) thrives on the day-to-day, in-class discussions that allow students to hone their critical thinking skills and develop their knowledge of composition vis-à-vis a range of topical considerations—current and historical. All humanities classrooms can thrive off of robust intellectual discourse. The Hip-Hop composition classroom simply requires active participation in the conversations that serve as catalysts for Hip-Hop intellectualism.

Remixing is rewriting

While the four educational elements of Hip Hop have specific implications for classrooms and composition classrooms specifically, there is an undeniable connection between the notion of remix in Hip Hop and composition classrooms. The theoretical underpinnings of this discussion stem from a synthesis of Lawrence Lessig's (2008) *Remix: Making Art and Commerce Thrive in the Hybrid Economy*[15] with ideas detailed in Joseph Harris's (2006) composition primer, *Rewriting: How to do Things with Text.*[16] Each of these scholars negligibly acknowledges the importance of Hip-Hop culture in the development of their own scholarly work on composition, mostly because neither is a scholar of Hip-Hop culture. Thus, Lessig and Harris tend to skirt the issue of Hip-Hop culture's emergence and its inherent capacity to formally embrace the rewriting and/or remixing of music, culture, history, and politics.

The theoretical synthesis of Lessig and Harris's work concerns the areas of read only (RO) and read/write (RW) cultures, which are two opposing concepts in composition that deal with artistic and commercial engagement with media. According to Lessig (2008), advancements in technology, especially the internet, and the exponential growth in memory/space capacity of computers has facilitated the emergence of a RW culture that uses "tokens" of RO culture in order to produce novel artistic texts. Lessig's formulation considers how countless computer users excerpt, sample, or quote from previously produced images, films, or music (content easily found online) in order to revise, remake, or remix these RO tokens into completely different artistic texts. Although Lessig is primarily concerned with the limitations of current copyright laws to account for the potential creativity inherent in twenty-first-century RW culture, he also provides a solid, operational definition of remix worth repeating here: "Remix is collage; it comes from combining elements of Read Only culture; it succeeds by leveraging the meaning created by the reference to build something new."[17]

Hip-Hop culture has been engaged in RW culture (e.g., sampling tokens of RO culture) since its inception in the mid-1970s. With a long and storied presence in Hip-Hop culture, the musical remix provides one of the clearest examples of this engagement. The remix is a retooled or revised version of a song. Per Hip-Hop history, remixes have assumed various forms. They can feature additional artists/lyricists, new or distinct lyrics, new sample-based productions, and/or extended versions of the original. Often times in contemporary Hip-Hop music, the most popular or successful rap songs are revisited and remixed by adding other lyricists to the production. Remixing in Hip-Hop culture further underscores the extent to which the culture itself relies on collage and the reuse and/or reimagining of other texts, especially previously recorded sounds in order to produce new texts, new records, and new styles. Here again, Hip-Hop culture is a heuristic device. For all of Lessig's astute theorization of the relationship between RW and RO cultures, Hip Hop is historically and in current practice already there. Remix is a fundamental component of the compositional aspects of Hip-Hop culture, thus it materially models Lessig's sophisticated discussion of Remix culture.

This sense of the remix also lends itself directly to Harris's thesis in *Rewriting* and my own sense of the interstitial relationships between Hip-Hop culture, Harris's approach to composition, and Lessig's conceptualization of RO/RW cultures. For Harris, the kind of intellectual writing most often exercised in composition classrooms is "bound up inextricably with the books we are reading, the movies we are watching, the music we are listening to, and the ideas of the people we are talking with. Our creativity thus has its roots in the work of others—in response, reuse, and rewriting."[18] Harris continues to define rewriting as a "social practice," so that he can develop his emphasis on the "how" of composition in the twenty-first century. He hopes to respond to this "how" promptly by delineating key moves that rewriters make. At issue here is rewriting as social practice, a concept with direct ties to the aesthetic forms of remix and revision within Hip-Hop culture. His book's subtitle, *How To Do Things With Texts,* is a not so subtle remix of John L. Austin's (1965) book title *How To Do Things With Words.*[19] Harris insists that this remix is his way of transforming the dialogue about composition from something that is generally static into something much more dynamic.

Throughout *Rewriting*, Harris (2008) develops five rewriting progressions: (1) *coming to terms*, which he defines as "re-presenting the work of others in ways that are both fair and useful" in your own writing; (2) *forwarding*, which is the practice by which writers forward other texts and concepts with their own framework or commentary; (3) *countering*, which is the process by which the "rewriter" rethinks or qualifies a position or argument; (4) *taking an approach*, which is drawing upon a distinctive style or mode; and (5) *revising*, which is combining the previous four moves in efforts to revisit and rework your own writing. These five techniques create valuable writing templates for the Hip-Hop culture and composition classroom. Here again, the aesthetic forms of Hip-Hop culture function heuristically as a means to attain the learning outcomes of the traditional composition course. Each element of Hip-Hop culture relies on various rewriting moves. Moreover, writing about Hip-Hop culture invites students to assess the rewriting and remixing elements of Hip Hop's aesthetic forms utilizing the tools of rewriting and remixing in their own compositional efforts. For example, quoting another scholar or writer in order to develop an argument is both a rewriting move (either forwarding, countering, and/or taking an approach) as well as an implementation of the aesthetic form in Hip Hop most commonly referred to as sampling (Schloss 2004).

Each of the rewriting moves have their advantages (and resultant disadvantages), but the notion of *forwarding*, because it relies on an email analogy and because it specifically requires the reuse of other texts and concepts, bears a striking parallel with Lessig's ideas about RW culture and challenges us to rethink this particular move as a model for composition students. Over the last ten years, email forwarding has degenerated into an endless succession of prayer chains, banking scams, and the occasionally inappropriate attempt at humor. As an analogy for a move that students might make/take in the processes of writing or composition, forwarding will ring stale among current students as many of them automatically delete any and all forwards.

Forwarding, then, is probably not the best metaphor for Harris's attempt to explicate an evolution that is essential to the Hip-Hop culture and composition classrooms. He clarifies that "a writer forwards the views of another when he or she takes terms and concepts from one text and applies them to a reading of other texts or situations."[20] Here is where the confluence of Lessig's (2006) and Harris's concepts is especially instructive and productive. While Harris signals the import of considering newer technologies and media in the composition classroom, Lessig is ready and willing to minimize traditional notions of composition and enhance the concept with the kind of democratized, participatory processes that result in the proliferation of sample-based digital compositions found on various media sites.

Harris's (2008) *Rewriting* and Lessig's (2006) *Remix* are certainly not either/or propositions for the Hip-Hop composition classroom. Instead they offer distinct, sometimes overlapping, sometimes contested approaches to crafting compositions that are formally and aesthetically consistent with various aspects of Hip-Hop culture. Note well here that Hip-Hop culture developed parallel to the information age. The Hip-Hop generation, those born between 1964 and 1985, have born witness to an extraordinarily fast pace technological advancement.[21] Likewise, consider the marked shift in musical platforms from the eight-track, to vinyl, to the cassette, to CDs, to digital formats such as MP3s. Harris argues that the reuse of texts in this moment or climate is completely natural and should be cultivated in the composition classroom; while Lessig strongly suggests that technology now allows us to engage other texts to create original compositions—something that the artisans of Hip Hop have been doing since the mid-1970s. Although these theories or pedagogical approaches put into bold relief the formal aesthetic potential of Hip Hop in the classroom, many in the academy (and beyond) remain unconvinced or unreceptive to the idea that Hip Hop should even be in a classroom.

According to Kermit Campbell (2005), "Instead of reaching out to youth in communities and schools by drawing on their potential for critical consciousness through rap and Hip Hop, politicians, parents, and media pundits censure such creative expression, turning a deaf ear to a generation increasingly shaped by the digitally mixed and sampled rhetoric of Hip Hop."[22] The best of Hip-Hop scholarship seeks to reverse the trajectory of this quote. What follows are brief sketches of the Hip-Hop culture and composition courses that I have proffered in this effort to leverage the intellectual interests of "a generation increasingly shaped by the digitally mixed and sampled rhetoric of Hip Hop."[23]

Teaching Hip-Hop Composition

The first Hip Hop and composition course that I taught was entitled "Writing about Hip Hop Culture." I offered this course as part of the Writing Across the University program at the University of Pennsylvania during the spring of 1997. Arguably one of the earliest attempts to connect Hip Hop and composition at the post-secondary level, this course reached capacity immediately and was one of the most diverse groups of students that I had ever had while teaching at the University of Pennsylvania. As this course took place in 1997, most of these students were born in the late 1970s and fit squarely within Kitwana's (2002) Hip-Hop generation framework. At this time, much of the scholarship on Hip-Hop culture, remix culture, and the shifting sense of revision and rewriting in the information age did not yet exist or was otherwise unavailable to me at this early stage of my career as an instructor. There were very few critical texts centered on Hip-Hop studies, so this early iteration of the Hip Hop and composition course was very much grounded in the aesthetic sensibilities of Hip Hop.

Students in this course were particularly concerned with the aesthetic forms of Hip Hop and how they connected to composition. Their commitment to these specific cultural and/or aesthetic principles challenged them to engage in practices related to the classroom but indicative of their own relationships to Hip-Hop culture. The students in this class, for example, generated a bevy of cultural products and compositions that underscored their critical engagement with Hip-Hop culture beyond the classroom. Several students organized a journalistic publication entitled H2O that focused on the local Hip-Hop scene and the artistry of the students in the course. Other students initiated a weekly open mic performance event in Philadelphia called "The Gathering" open to all artisans of Hip-Hop culture. Since its inception, the event has been maintained by many different community members in Philadelphia and still operates as one of the longest running all-ages Hip-Hop community events in the United States. Some of the students in this course have gone on to film school, the fashion industry, the academy, and the music industry. In each of these cases, Hip-Hop culture has been a common presence in the subsequent careers of these former students.

For many reasons, this initial composition course does not present a replicable model. In fact, most of my Hip-Hop composition courses after this initial one were essentially different in both form and function. Yet, there are still important points about course design and classroom practice from this first course that I continue to employ in a variety of Hip-Hop courses. These points serve as the basis for practical applications in Hip-Hop composition courses.

The design of Hip-Hop composition

In over fifteen years of teaching various incarnations/iterations of the Hip-Hop culture and composition course, I often distill the educational elements within the mix of the traditional composition course and its requisite "outcome" expectations. The ways that I have done this, however, have changed over the years. These changes illustrate some of the quintessential characteristics of Hip-Hop composition courses. An introduction to one of my early course syllabi is an important starting point to illustrate such changes:

> This course is designed to enhance and develop your writing skills for the challenges, experiences and assignments that you will face and/or be required to execute as an Undergraduate. In general this course uses various aspects and/or artistic manifestations of Hip Hop culture as the impetus to think critically, articulate accurately, and to write clear and compelling prose. The goal of English 15 is to enhance students' writing by sensitizing them to their composing processes and familiarizing them with the features of effective and persuasive prose. Students will learn to think critically, observe closely, and assess rhetorical situations accurately in order to respond confidently and flexibly to various audiences, aims, subjects, and forms.

In this course overview, Hip-Hop culture is the catalyst for capable writing. Students are asked to engage the culture more as observers than as actual participants, participant-observers, or constituents of the culture. Thus, in this initial iteration of the course, the educational element of participation is less than salient. Of course, students were expected to participate in the class in various ways as they are in every course, but the types of participation that are central to Hip Hop were not infused in the class.

Note also that in this first course, the aesthetic forms of the culture are not necessarily held as exemplars for composition or engagement. The initial course description implies that Hip Hop is an object about which students will write, respond, articulate, and think critically. What the description largely ignores is that Hip Hop operates according to sensibilities, habits, mindsets, etc. It is important to keep in mind that during this early period, there were few documented connections between Hip Hop and formal school settings. Without a doubt, this was a burgeoning time for Hip-Hop scholarship more

broadly with the seminal publications of Rose's *Black Noise* in 1994 and
Perkin's *Droppin' Science* in 1996. Additionally, Hip-Hop educational activities
were taking place undocumented by scholarly disciplines during this time.
However, specific educational and pedagogical connections in scholarly
communities were yet to develop.

A more recent introduction to one of these course syllabi showcases
some important changes that reflect the developments within Hip Hop and
education since my first composition course in 1997. Attention is still given
to the traditional aims of the composition classroom, but my approach
shifts generally to engaging/understanding Hip Hop as a discursive and
compositional model. This shift is based upon a tacit recognition that Hip Hop
is not simply an object but a culture with aesthetic forms. The description that
guided the course reads as follows:

> This course is designed to explore the numerous ways in which Hip Hop
> culture functions as a discourse in the public sphere, including but not
> limited to the study of: poetry, cultural criticism, journalism, literature,
> drama, film, and socio-political movements. These various exploratory
> approaches to Hip Hop reveal the complexities of a culture, once labeled a
> "fad" that has since become ubiquitous on the American popular landscape.
> The course uses film, literature, music, music video and scholarly-cultural
> criticism to investigate Hip Hop and the various discourses that attend
> it. We will explore the origins and various eras (Old School, Golden Age,
> and Current) of Hip Hop and we will compare and contrast the critical
> and creative literature that derives from rap music and Hip Hop culture.
> We will embrace the debates of authenticity and identity and through close
> readings, hearings, and viewings of the texts of Hip Hop, we will construct
> well-informed positions on how writers, rappers, and regular folks use texts
> and contexts to achieve "authentic" identities. A key goal of the course is to
> explore and develop scholarly ways of engaging Hip Hop culture.

Subtle changes in the second course overview shape the compositional focus
in a few key ways. First, there is a strategic shift away from Hip Hop as a
distant objective and toward Hip Hop as a discursive model. In this way, the
course centers on the notion that various manifestations of Hip Hop possess
argumentation, debate, persuasive logic, and emic ways of making truthful

claims. These manifestations then become useful tools for the composition student when they are the subject of rigorous study.

A second key change is a shift in participation. Students study the critical discourses on Hip-Hop culture, debates of authenticity and identity, and other discursive aspects of Hip Hop, but are also invited to participate in this very discourse. Unlike in the earlier iteration of the course, students are not simply writing *about* Hip Hop. By studying the ways that Hip Hop makes claims and then using those same modes to make claims about Hip Hop, composition students are engaging a deeper type of participation unique to Hip Hop. Forman (2002) makes the important point that scholarly, journalistic, and social commentary literature that engages Hip Hop is actually a critical part of Hip-Hop culture. This is evidenced by the long-standing tradition within Hip Hop of independently collecting cultural documents such as flyers, tapes, records, video and television footage, newspaper clippings, personalized and time-period clothes, interviews, and more into personal archives. From this perspective, writing about Hip Hop through studying the discursive models of Hip Hop is a form of participation in the culture.

Hip-Hop composition in practice

Not to be overlooked are the scholarly ways of engaging Hip Hop in the composition classroom that assume a variety of forms. With each of these approaches, the general aesthetics of Hip Hop serve as the bases for classroom composition techniques.

(1) *Creative revision.* Creative revision is an unparalleled approach to writing in the composition classroom. Of course, students have to document all of their sources accurately, but in the spirited sense with which Harris positions rewriting, I have encouraged my students by helping them to understand that their work is in collaboration with hundreds of other scholars who have spoken and written before them. Thus, "saying something new" is a matter of "how" rather than "what." From the perspectives of Lessig's remix theory and Harris's rewriting approaches, we have only begun to institute the means of

defamiliarizing texts and manipulating them in compositional environments (paper, online, audiovisual, etc.). Much of the language about compositional citation focuses too intently on the consequences of poor documentation or mis-documentation, rather than acknowledging the central problem in first year composition courses: How do students write something refreshing, insightful, and interesting to themselves and their intended audience? The answer has, and continues to be defamiliarization: representing a text in such a way that it appears in a new light to your audience. Defamiliarization indulges various aspects of Harris's rewriting moves, including coming to terms, forwarding, and countering. At its best, defamiliarization also allows students to incorporate multimedia resources into their research as well as their actual compositions. A pragmatic assignment for the application of creative revision is the album review assignment. This assignment requires students to choose a popular album and research the reviews written about the album. When composing their review they must cite and otherwise situate themselves within the published discourse on the album. However, as part of their argument/ discussion they must establish a reading/listening of the album that cuts against the grain of the conventional reviews. Students will almost always rely on the texts of the album itself or music videos made from specific songs in order to present a less familiar take on the album under consideration.

(2) **Cutting and quoting.** *Cutting and quoting* is a viable way of defamiliarizing a text aesthetically/formally consistent with Hip-Hop culture. The cut defamiliarizes the text from that which it is borrowed. According to late literary critic, James A. Snead, "James Brown is an example of a brilliant American practitioner of the cut whose skill is readily admired by African as well as American musicians."[24] Snead suggests that in Brown's performance, the ruptures (i.e., cuts) strengthen the rhythm rather than weaken it. Furthermore, Snead argues, "black music sets up expectations and disturbs them at irregular intervals: that it will do this, however, is itself an expectation."[25]

Two important pedagogical opportunities emerge from this segment of Snead's discussion. First, current, practical examples of cut and repetition are located in Hip-Hop culture. Using Brown as the example, the rap group EPMD samples (i.e., cuts from and repeats) James Brown's song "The Payback."[26] One

EPMD song entitled "I'm Mad" from their 1990 album, *Business as Usual* uses the line "I'm Mad" from Brown's "The Payback" as the refrain or quote.[27] Their use of the James Brown cut demonstrates their own acknowledgment of Brown's authenticity and the respect that he garners in African and American communities. In some ways, a James Brown cut supports and authenticates a rap lyric while it reinscribes the musical genius of Brown. If his lines are quotable in rap music, then he is "down with" the Hip-Hop generation. If his lines are quoted in rap music, then rap music is connected to the success, social acceptance, and cultural iconography of James Brown. In EPMD's "The Big Payback," (from their 1989 album entitled *Unfinished Business*), the group signified off of Brown's "The Payback" again.[28] This time they sample the line/refrain, "the payback" and modify the title of the original (The *Big* Payback) so that at the same time that they are referencing Brown's musical authenticity, they are submitting their own virtuosity in relation to his.

This kind of cutting in Hip Hop functions as a heuristic device for the composition classroom. Through a fairly common practice of sampling and cutting, EPMD demonstrates the value of the principles of Harris's rewriting and the formal properties of Lessig's notion of remix culture. EPMD quotes/samples James Brown and in doing so, they defamiliarize Brown's text, authenticate their own, and in the process, also craft an original composition. This is a classic model for the work that writers strive to do in the composition classroom. The musical interactions between EPMD, Brown, and the cut reflect the reciprocal connections between composition writers, texts, and the quote. Intertextual quotes should not only authenticate and/or exemplify the composition, but they should, by virtue of being a part of the text in some new and interesting way, posit the original text in an unconventional and/or unfamiliar light. The relationship between the quote and the essay should be similar to the recursive relationship between EPMD's "I'm Mad" and "The Big Payback," and James Brown's "The Payback."

(3) *Freestyling and brainstorming.* As another example, brainstorming is a vital component in all composition processes and of special import in the Hip-Hop culture and composition classroom. Brainstorming remains one of the most effective prewriting strategies available to students who are learning how

to write. Regardless of what form it takes, listing, clustering, and/or tree-diagrams, the brainstorm is an integral part of the preliminary composition process. For the Hip-Hop composition classroom, the ritualistic pastime known popularly as freestyling is an important cultural counterpart to brainstorming. When explored and employed as a writing strategy, freestyling sparks student creativity and other important writing tools such as structural and spatial order, chronology, and improvisation. Freestyling or freestyle sessions are when groups of MCs/rappers form a cipher and improvise rhymes/lyrics in turns. In many cases, a freestyle rhyme functions similarly to an improvised jazz riff in that it spontaneously derives from the author/MC/musician but crystallizes in the performance.

The freestyle prewriting exercise is designed to function in much the same way. Groups of students are challenged to freestyle (not necessarily in verse) their ideas, theses, or topics in small groups. They each have a turn to verbally freestyle while another person within the group takes notes on their content. In the best case scenario, each student-writer can freestyle their ideas and take notes on someone else's. Students then share/compare results. Usually students realize that freestyle is actually not that free at all, but that it is an opportunity to verbalize ideas in a setting conducive to creativity. This freestyle exercise actually adds a subtle competitive aspect to traditional brainstorming activities. The objective of this verbal freestyling exercise is twofold: (1) For students to learn more about a type of brainstorming that is characteristic of Hip Hop, and (2) To appreciate the competitive nature of on-the-spot composition. By positing brainstorming as a form of freestyling or freestyling as a form of brainstorming, students are invited to approach this prewriting exercise via an aesthetic form particular to Hip-Hop culture and valuable to those developing writers for whom traditional structures might seem limiting or impertinent to their own creative processes.

Conclusions: Resisting Prescriptions

Alongside the guidelines and strategies in this chapter, my intention has not been to prescribe rigid ways of implementing Hip-Hop culture and/or rap music into composition courses. Instead, my intention has been to share some themes, approaches, examples, successes, and challenges that I have encountered on my journey to integrate my own culture into specific academic and pedagogical practices. In full disclosure, I have to acknowledge that although I tend to argue for a constructivist, culturally pertinent appeal of Hip-Hop culture in a wide variety of classrooms (high school and college); there are clear limitations to integrating Hip-Hop music and lyrics into the composition classroom. The central limitation bares revelation here. The *nommo* or word power of rap music and Hip-Hop culture derive primarily from the African American oral and folk traditions. As such, rap music, much like the blues or a Black Baptist sermon, tends to thrive in oral-aural contexts and can appear to be flat and/or stale on the printed page. Any of the examples described herein will certainly bare this out pale in comparison when compared to listening or viewing the recorded performances of Hip Hop. This particular challenge is one with which Hip-Hop scholars and teachers are regularly confronted.

Despite these challenges, the composition classroom generates a lesson that can be drawn from this problem of context. That is, every composition has a particular and appropriate context. This particular oral-literal dichotomy only serves to underscore this fact and in turn, provide Hip-Hop composition instructors with an inaugural lesson about writing. The situation (i.e., the assignment, the audience, and the platform) shapes the reception of the composition: "The purpose and audience for each text define writing tasks. Because tasks are not uniform, students need to have the ability to write in multiple genres, formats, and styles."[1] If as scholars and teachers we can come to appreciate and understand the Hip-Hop generation's preference for technological composition and Hip Hop as a viable economy of expression, then the potential of our composition classrooms increases exponentially. "This thing called Hip Hop, this inner city, youth-driven artistic and cultural movement has accomplished in our society what embattled multiculturalism has been powerless to accomplish—that is to make the inhabitants of America's inner cities relatable and indeed lovable."[2]

Epilogue: B-Boy Rules for Hip-Hop Scholars

I love shouting out the fact that I am from Newark, New Jersey. Growing up in "Brick City," just as Hip Hop germinated in postindustrial America, was an acculturating and intellectually developmental experience. Through this project, I hope that I have revealed that my aesthetic sensibilities developed through Hip Hop's fundamental components, including DJ-ing, MC-ing, breaking, and Graf art. Early on, I was cognizant of the intellectualizing forces at work in my lived experiences with the culture. It gradually crept up on me in Newark; and at a certain point in my adolescence, Hip-Hop culture shaped the aesthetic tapestry of my existence. I remember, quite vividly, that after the success of "Rappers Delight" a chain reaction of radio acceptable singles exploded from the culture into the mainstream sound waves. Indeed, I can remember when Kurtis Blow's "The Breaks" was a hit.[1] Black/Urban radio stations in New York City played "The Breaks" at most once or twice a day, but it was always at the same time and my brothers, sisters, and cousins would all gather together in the kitchen—where the loudest radio in our house was—and party around that one song. The ritualistic fervor with which we approached these listenings, memorized the words, and talked about the songs and the artists merely hinted at the signifying force of these moments.

This epilogue is a point of entry for a discussion about scholars/intellectuals of Hip-Hop culture because I hope that *Hip-Hop Headphones* thrives at the intersections between popular culture, academic theory, social critique, and community that are necessary for most of the intellectual work detailed in these pages. Consider the work on this subject produced by scholars as wide-ranging as Houston Baker, Harold Cruse, Amiri Baraka, Tricia Rose, Michael Eric Dyson, and Mark Anthony Neal on the subjects related to Black public intellectuals. And in that vein, I want to point to some sense through which the "B-Boy rules for Hip Hop Scholars" might emerge. B-boys or B-girls are those infinitely talented performers from foundational moments of Hip-Hop culture who danced to the manually looped breaks of old soul and disco records. Breakin (or break dancing) along with poppin/pop locking were early forms of dance from the culture itself. Break dancing derives its name from the breakbeats that drove the music and culture at the outset. But b-boying and b-girling came to adopt more meaning and significance within the culture of Hip Hop beyond the singular signification attached to those early performers who drove the kinesthetic energy of early Hip-Hop jams. B-boys (in the twenty-first century) are still known as guardians of the culture. They have earned this distinction over the decades because of the ascribed rules of b-boy-dom. B-boys had to be proficient in at least two elements of the culture, although authentic b-boys were participants in many aspects of the culture. A b-boy would not only break dance, but would also write graffiti and/or MC or DJ as well. Many embodied combinations of two or three elements concurrently. These rules were simple and only loosely patrolled, but the ideology that produced them demanded, and continues to demand, multilevel engagement with the culture across elemental comfort zones. I want to extend the properties of these rules (through an intellectual transformation) to those figures who would/could be considered Hip-Hop scholars.

First, some clarification of the b-boy rules is necessary. By most conventional definitions, b-boys are break dancers who embody the cultural roots of Hip Hop: they dress a certain way, usually harkening back to Hip-Hop style circa 1980, and they dance to the breaks recreating settings that reflect the original impulses of the culture. The only rule for b-boys is that they must "live the lifestyle of b-boying."[2] When asked to define himself, Virginian b-boy Tazk narrated the following:

> You can spot a bboy from a mile away. A bboy for me is someone who doesn't wear a spin jacket for looks, but to actually spin, or a mesh hat. Yo there have been times I roll up to jams looking busted, people are probably like, wtf is that nigga wearing, but you know why I wear what I wear cause das ma gear that I can perform ma best at. Bboyin is deep man, its not just on the outside. The definition of a bboy is someone who lives the lifestyle of bboying. There are breakers and then there are bboys, a real bboy knows the difference[3] (www.bboy.com).

The idea of multiple levels of engagement with respect to the fundamental elements of Hip-Hop culture derives organically from the culture through various b-boys and artists—most notably, KRS-One who also likens b-boying to a particular lifestyle. Note Tazk's oblique reference to his ability to identify an authentic b-boy on sight, but more importantly, how he claims to be able to distinguish authentic b-boys from breakers who, by implication, are charlatans who dwell in the margins of the b-boy world.

This discourse on the authenticity of b-boys yields the b-boy rules requiring the multiple levels of engagement with the fundamental elements of Hip-Hop culture. These rules, which necessitate multiple levels of comprehension and engagement, may be seen by b-boys as being artificial and exaggerated. For my purposes, though, they serve to augment the significance of authenticity for Hip-Hop culture and the discursive content of the culture that lends itself to multifaceted notions and interpretations of an authentic existence. These socially constructed notions of authenticity—which are simultaneously contingent upon, and constituted by, the participants' multilevel engagement with the foundational elements of the culture—underwrite my thesis concerning the applicability and reflexivity of b-boy rules for Hip-Hop intellectuals.

Defining the intellectualism of, for, and around Hip-Hop culture has been the subject matter of several journalistic articles and performing it has been a great part of my academic work over the last decade. The effort that most comprehensively articulates the definition of Hip-Hop scholars and intellectuals is Adam Mansbach's article which is aptly titled, "Hip Hop Intellectuals" and originally published in the *San Frisco Gate* on June 25, 2003, and later collected in The DeCapo *Best Music Writing* 2004.[4] Mansbach defines Hip-Hop intellectuals as "folks who derive their basic artistic, intellectual, and political strategies from the tenets of the musical form itself—collage, reclamation of public space, [and] the re-purposing of technology—even if they are not kicking rhymes and scratching records".[5] What Mansbach deftly delineates here are the aesthetics of Hip-Hop intellectualism vis-à-vis the structural expressions of collaging, reclaiming public spaces, and repurposing technology. His coalition of intellectuals ranges from Jeff Chang, Touré, and William Upski Wimsatt to artists like novelist, Paul Beatty, and actor, Danny Hoch.

In addition to these structural aesthetics of Hip-Hop intellectualism, the historical ruminations on Black intellectuals in Harold Cruse's *The Crisis of the Negro Intellectual*, seem readily applicable to this discourse in a number of ways.[6] What follows is a simplified paraphrasing of Cruse's outlining of the key duties for African American intellectuals. His prescriptions should be thought of, at least initially here, as applying directly to Hip-Hop culture. For our purposes, substitute Afro-American, Black, or Negro with Hip Hop. The key duties of the African American/Hip-Hop intellectuals are as follows:

(1)   To be knowledgeable of their intellectual predecessors, and intellectually familiar with historical, political, and cultural movements.

(2)   To analyze explanations for the "pendulum swings between the two poles of integration and black nationalism," combine and theorize these explanations.

(3)   To distill and discern the behaviors, cultural traits, and conditions that will advance Black culture. This process requires a more critical relationship with Afro-American culture and American capitalism, where "group culture either flourishes or atrophies."[7]

(4)   To continually acknowledge the uniqueness of the African American experience.

Mansbach's selection of Hip-Hop intellectuals focuses on a radical generation that comes of age. This generation was comprised of individuals who were the primary constituents of the culture through its zeitgeist era—what I have repeatedly referred to here as the golden age. If we follow Dr. Cruse's first directive, configured for Hip Hop, Mark Anthony Neal exemplifies and writes about the generation of intellectuals that immediately precede Mansbach's radical generation. Neal writes extensively about the Post-Soul generation while simultaneously reflecting on the positionality of a Civil Rights/Hip-Hop "tweener" generation—that is, those scholars and thinkers who are of the same age as the founding figures of Hip-Hop culture. He includes Todd Boyd and Michael Eric Dyson on this list of emerging Black scholars with a distinctly Hip-Hop attitude. For Neal, his stance as a member of the Post-Soul generation is in dialogic opposition with the traditional academic network as well as the more conservative Black academic guard. This intellectual sentiment is ideologically rooted in a psyche that is cultivated within the milieu of the early founders of Hip-Hop culture.

Neal himself hails from the birth borough of Hip-Hop culture, the South Bronx. Yet the intellectuals discussed in Neal's narrative are not part of the same set to which Mansbach attributes the nerve system of Hip-Hop intellectual energy. Neal's intellectual energy precedes my list of Hip-Hop intellectuals (in age and in entrance into the academy proper) by about ten years. An amended inventory of these early Hip-Hop intellectuals includes David Toop, Houston Baker, Tricia Rose, Marcyliena Morgan, and Cheryl Keyes as well as Neal, Todd Boyd, Dyson, and a plethora of others cited by Neal. Toop is responsible for the earliest and most comprehensive journalistic chronology of Hip Hop, *Rap Attack*(s) 1, 2 and 3.[8] Houston Baker introduced the notions of reclaiming public space via boom boxes, breakdancing, and "wilding" in his critical essay entitled *Black Studies, Rap, and the Academy.*[9] Not least, Tricia Rose solidified the field of Hip-Hop studies with *Black Noise.*[10] Nearly every scholarly text that immediately followed *Black Noise* had to pay homage to its insuperable brilliance. These scholar-intellectuals have generally moved on to other disciplines of inquiry, but their early impact profoundly influenced the intellectual exchange that followed.

Neither Mansbach, Neal, nor any of the other writers who directly addressed notions of Hip-Hop intellectualism take considerable time to confront the cultural or political movements of the past that tend to influence the Hip-Hop intellectuals of the present. However, now that we can better distinguish the sociopolitical history of the early Hip-Hop intellectuals from a newer crop, the political and cultural movements in common with the early set readily reveal themselves. The political movements are the Nation of Islam, The 5 percent Nation of Gods and Earths, The Black Panther Party for self-defense, and various "Stop the Violence"/"Cease Fire" campaigns. The corroborative cultural movements include blues, bebop, rock, soul, funk, disco, the digital age, and various forms of hustling.

Dr. Cruse's second directive is even more compellingly complex in its anticipation of challenges for Hip Hop's intellectuals. The aforementioned "pendulum swings" phenomenon refers to an intellectual history charted laboriously in the work of Cruse, which suggests a bipolar model of intellectual thought alternating between Nationalist and integrationist ideologies.[11] Consider Malcolm X's Black Nationalist stance and fierce rhetoric vis-à-vis Dr. King's Civil Rights agendas and peaceful protests. The same pendulum also swings in Hip-Hop culture, manifesting this bipolarity in successive eras. Mark Harris, in an online Popmatters piece, entitled "Edutainment: the Rise and Fall of the Hip Hop Intelligentsia," wrestles with the intellectual pedagogues of Hip Hop who assumed responsibility of edutaining, rapping, and teaching.[12] Harris does an expert job of chronicling the internecine relationships between the music of these conscious, political edutainers and the music of their "keepin' it real" gangsta counterparts in the west. Harris suggests that the verbal virtuosity of movements like the Nation of Gods and Earths enjoyed extensive valence and cultural resonance with inner-city Hip Hoppers (especially those on the East Coast) who knew and understood some of the cryptic and encoded lyrics of edutainment artists.

Cruse's third directive suggests that intellectuals organize and unite. Among the Hip-Hop generation, however, this has been a glaring absence. This may be, in part, because younger constituents of the Hip-Hop generation are unsure of what it means to be an "organizer" or what unified organization looks like or entails. Yvonne Bynoe says as much in her critical tract, *Stand and Deliver: Political Activism, Leadership, and Hip Hop Culture*.[13] Bynoe's central thesis postulates that due to the extraordinary popularity of rap music, the media has effectively appointed the artisans of Hip-Hop culture as the Post-Civil Rights leaders of Black America. For Bynoe, political involvement is an essential requirement for Hip-Hop intellectuals. She contends, "Continuing this farce called Hip-Hop politics does a disservice to the important work labored by our elders and ancestors, and obscures the real work that this generation needs to take on and move forward."[14] Most Hip-Hop intellectuals would probably agree that being a full-time rapper/entertainer and a full-time political activist is a near impossibility. However, there are artists who directly contribute to the political discourses via savvy distillations of socioeconomic, racial, spiritual, and political challenges in our society. These artists include Public Enemy and KRS-One, as well as the more recent work of Paris, Nas, Dead Prez, the Flobots and MF Doom. This is not to mention the more contemporary crop of artist-activists engaged in the Movement 4 Black Lives—including Talib Kweli, Rebel Diaz, Janelle Monae, and Tef Poe.

One of the more interesting examples of artistry acting in service of some political or social justice motive is Nas' 2008 song entitled "Sly Fox."[15] In the lyrics of "Sly Fox," Nas challenges his listeners to be media literate critical thinkers. He also organized a protest to petition against the undertones of racism in Fox News' coverage of social and political issues. Some will demur at my suggestion that this reflects genuine political activism on behalf of Nas (Nasir Jones). However, Nas is the only popular artist of note (and on record) as directly contesting the racist comments of Fox News' major political pundits, Bill O'Reilly and Sean Hannity. He worked collaboratively with a grassroots organization to deliver the petitions signed by hundreds of thousands of likeminded activists, and he spoke publicly (albeit apprehensively) at the community rally at which the petition was delivered. Of course, one act does not a political activist make, but surely this instance paves the way for future endeavors of activism.

A lesser known group based in Denver, Colorado, the Flobots, reflected another bright spot pre-#BlackLivesMatter with respect to rap music. The powerful video for their debut album's lead single, "Handlebars" quickly shifts from a pop-folksy tune into an apocalyptic vision of the world ruled by despots and war-mongering leaders.[16] The album, *Fight With Tools*, presents much more of the same critical engagement with various political and historical issues.[17] Its theme and title song suggests that young people have all of the requisite and necessary tools at their disposal to empower themselves to change the world. The music is not what is most political here though, as the Flobots have used their magnetic live performances and political candor to organize and inspire their fan base across the country. Through street teams directed and delegated via their website, the Flobots are registering voters, organizing food drives, and championing various volunteer efforts among their fans.

Harold Cruse's final directive comprehensively buttresses the first three since its principal focus is on centralizing the unique qualities of the African American experience. For Hip-Hop culture, this directive requires (at least for intellectuals) a working knowledge of the history of Hip-Hop, a wholesome understanding of Hip Hop's fundamental aspects, as well as the culture's overall impact on American society and the rest of the world that has come to claim Hip Hop as a signal component of various youth cultures. With a basic understanding of Harold Cruse's classic instructions/requirements for Black intellectuals and their parallel valence with would-be intellectuals/scholars of Hip-Hop culture, I invite readers of this text to come up with the lists of Hip-Hop scholars who might satisfy these b-boy/b-girl rules.

Ultimately, there really is no sufficient way to conclude a collection such as this. My hope (again) is that the readings, writings, and critical listenings documented and collected here might be helpful to educators invested in deploying and leveraging aspects of Hip-Hop culture in the classroom. I am also earnestly interested in pushing critical listening as an important strategic technique for students and scholars who are learning in the new media environs of the twenty-first century.

Appendix: A Collection of Hip-Hop Syllabi

James Peterson
English 002
Spring 1997
Office Hours: M 2:00 pm–3:00 pm, H 2:00 pm–3:00 pm
Bennett Hall, Room A6
jamesp@dept.english.upenn.edu
First-Year Composition

Keepin' it real: writing in and about Hip-Hop culture

In this course, we will explore, compare, and contrast the critical and creative literature that derives from rap music and Hip-Hop culture. We will take up the debates of authenticity and Blackness, and through close readings, hearings, and viewings of the texts of Hip Hop, we will construct well-informed positions on how writers, rappers, and regular folks use texts and contexts to achieve authenticity. The main goal of the course is to explore and develop various ways of writing in and about Hip-Hop culture.

Texts:
Black Noise
Black Studies, Rap, and the Academy
Droppin' Science
Twisted Tales in the Hip Hop Streets of Philly
Between God and Gangsta Rap (Selections)

Monster
No Disrespect
Philadelphia Fire
The 2Pac Bulkpack
Films:
The Show
Menace II Society
Fear of a Black Hat
Dead Presidents

January 13	Introduction
January 15	BN Introduction and Chapter 1
January 20	BN Chapters 2 and 3 (MLK's B-Day)
January 22	BN Chapter 4
January 27	BN Chapter 5
January 29	Finish *Black Noise* (First Review Is Due)
February 3	BSR Chapters 1 and 2
February 5	Finish *Black Studies, Rap, and the Academy*
February 10	Read up to p. 200 of TT
February 12	Read up to p. 247 of TT
February 17	Finish TT
February 19	Film Screening: The Show
February 24	DS Introduction and Section I
February 26	DS Section II
March 3	DS Section III
March 5	Midterm Paper Is Due
March 10	Spring Break (Watch Menace II if You Haven't)
March 12	Spring Break
March 17	Possible Panel Day/Possible Workshop Day
March 19	Possible Panel Day/Possible Workshop Day

March 24	BG & G Selections
March 26	2Pac Readings
March 31	Begin Monster (first 200 pages)
April 2	Finish Monster
April 7	Begin No Disrespect (first 200 pages)
April 9	Continue ND (Second Review Is Due)
April 14	Finish ND
April 16	Begin Philadelphia Fire
April 21	Finish Philadelphia Fire
April 23	Movie Screening: Fear of a Black Hat
April 28	Conclusions, Q&A
April 30	Last Day of Classes (Final Papers Are Due May 5)

This is a large seminar, but I expect each student to always be prepared. I expect everyone to participate in class discussion on a regular basis. I will monitor your participation since it is 10 percent of your final grade. I reserve the right to administer pop quizzes on any day that readings are assigned. Attendance is mandatory.

Including all emergencies, I will allow only two absences without penalty to your grade.

You have four writing assignments. Two of these assignments are music or movie reviews that should be no longer than 3 pages. We will read several examples of reviews. The mid-term project will be an essay or proposal of 4–6 pages and the final paper (which must be approved by me) will be 6–8 pages in length.

Your grade breaks down as follows:
- 10% Attendance and Participation
- 10% Pop Quizzes
- 20% Two Reviews
- 25% Mid-Term Paper
- 35% Final Paper

"The Literature of Hip Hop Culture" English 409, Sec. 10 Washington College, Tuesday 4 pm–6:30 pm

Professor:	Dr. James Peterson
Office:	104 Daly
Office Hours:	By Appointment
Email Address:	jpeterson2@washcoll.edu

Course description

This course is designed to demonstrate the numerous ways in which Hip-Hop culture (particularly rap music) functions as, produces, and inspires literature in both traditional and innovative cultural products, including but not limited to poetry, cultural criticism, journalism, literature, animation, film, and sociopolitical discourses. The various literary approaches to Hip-Hop culture reveal the complexities of a culture, once labeled a "fad" that has since become ubiquitous on the American popular landscape.

Hip Hop is the most pervasive youth-driven cultural movement of our time. The literary approaches in this course take for granted the fact that Hip-Hop culture has produced numerous works of art that potentially satisfy the qualitative connotations of canonized literature. We will therefore engage the work of those poetic and literary artisans who specifically emerge from the cultural milieu of Hip Hop.

Course objectives

The main goal of this course is to assess an emerging body of literature, poetry, film, and music that is generated by and through Hip-Hop culture. Students will be challenged to discern the qualitative literary elements of these various pieces of literature in order to academically frame a Hip-Hop tradition in the literature.

Course format

This course will be conducted as an advanced seminar. Students are expected to come to present on the readings regularly, write short response papers and generally examine the materials of the course through a combination of critique, insight, and analysis.

Reading for class is essential. Our classroom discussions will be built around assigned texts, and each student is expected to contribute to the intellectual community of the classroom. Even when you are not writing a response or giving a presentation, preparing for class should involve reflecting upon the reading that is due.

Course texts

The following texts can be purchased in the Washington College Bookstore. Please bring the necessary book to class when assigned.

The Coldest Winter Ever by Sister Souljah

Gunshots in My Cook-Up by Selwyn Seyfu Hinds

The Portable Promised Land by Toure

Know What I Mean by Michael Eric Dyson

Angry Black White Boy by Adam Mansbach

Course requirements

Final Paper	30%
Participation/Presentations	30%
Attendance	10%
Quizzes	30%
Final Grade Total	**100%**

Class **Attendance** and regular **Participation** are key requirements in this course. Students are expected to attend classes (one or more unexcused absences will result in a lowering of your grade); participate in all class discussions, which will be based on the readings, presentations, and listening assignments, as well as any film screenings and other materials assigned for that week.

Students must prepare five- to seven-minute **Presentations** on the dates selected by them on the syllabus. Each student must present twice (there are numerous opportunities to do so). You should also work together to prevent info overlap. For each presentation you will submit a typed "one-sheet" that outlines your presentation. Although most presentations have a specific topic the presenter should be mindful of the text/topic/film/album of that week and make incisive connections between their research findings and the text under study.

The **Final Paper** is a research assignment where students are expected to explore in great detail how to discern a "tradition" of literature that emerges out of Hip-Hop culture. All research papers (pp. 12–15) must be written in MLA-format and should have at least seven sources (scholarly articles and/or critical monographs). Research papers must include a fifteen- to twenty-entry annotated literary bibliography of Hip-Hop culture—this course's texts can be included. They will be due during finals week.

Attendance, participation, and quizzes: Attendance is expected. Excessive absence (more than three absences) will significantly lower your grade. Participation is a significant component of this course and will benefit your understanding of the material. You will be quizzed weekly on the reading.

Course schedule

Week of August 27	Course Introduction—What Is Hip Hop? What Is Literature; What Is the Literature of Hip Hop?
Week of September 3	*Know What I Mean: Reflections on Hip Hop*
Week of September 10	*The Global Cipha*
Week of September 17	*Slam* Starring Saul Williams (Screened in Class) Post Responses on Blackboard
Week of September 24	*Gunshots in My Cook-Up* Discography Assignment (12–15 entries)
Week of October 1	*Beyond Beats and Rhymes* (Screened in Class) Feminism and Hip Hop Culture (Presentations)
Week of October 8	*The Coldest Winter Ever* (First ½) Drug Culture (Presentations)
Week of October 15	*The Coldest Winter Ever*
Week of October 22	Selected Readings Dr. Imani Perry Free Speech/Censorship (Presentations)

Week of October 29	*Angry Black White Boy* (Books 1 and 2)
	The LA Riots (Presentations)
Week of November 5	*Angry Black White Boy* (Completed)
	Whiteness Studies (Presentations)
Week of November 12	*Hip Hop Is Dead*
	Best Rap Lyric EVER (Presentations)
	Album Review Paper Due (3–5 pages)
Week of November 19	In-Class Music Video Screenings—"Jesus Walks"
	In-Class Exegesis (Biblical and Literary)
THANKSGIVING	
Week of November 26	Selected Readings from Toure
	Post-Modern Narrative (Presentations)
Week of December 3	In-Class Screening/Listening: *Letter to the President*
	Individual Conferences on Final Project

"Critical Approaches to Hip Hop Culture" English 397, Sec. 01 Bucknell University, Wednesdays 7:00 pm–9:52 pm

Professor:	Dr. James Peterson
Office:	Vaughn Lit. 209A
Office Hours:	Tuesday/Thursday 10:00 am–11:00 am and by appointment
Email Address:	james.peterson@bucknell.edu

Course description

Over the last thirty years, Hip-Hop culture has developed from a relatively unknown and largely ignored inner-city culture into a global phenomenon. The foundational elements of Hip-Hop culture (DJ-ing, MC-ing, breakdance, and graffiti/graf) are manifest in youth culture across the globe, including Japan, France, Germany, South Africa, Cuba, and the UK. Considering its humble beginnings in the South and West Bronx, the global development of Hip Hop is an amazing cultural feat. Its current popularity suggests and reflects its culturally rich origins. Moreover, the presence of rap music and other elements of the culture in television, film, marketing, and advertising signal American mainstream acceptance. In fact, its dominance in popular culture often obscures the negative and at times malicious treatment of Hip Hop (and its youthful constituents) in the public sphere. With all of its attendant complexities and apparent contradictions, Hip-Hop culture is dense subject matter for critical inquiry.

Course objectives

This course examines Hip-Hop culture through the lyrics of the music, one to two films, and several of the scholarly texts that have been written about Hip-Hop Culture in recent years. The objective of the course is enhance students critical engagement with popular cultural forms such as music, TV, and film by reading some of the most sophisticated scholarship on Hip-Hop culture that has been published since the late 1990s.

Textual analysis and interpretation

Students will interpret texts with awareness of the texts' basic orientation in the world (historical, philosophical, religious, linguistic, etc.).

Students will be able to construct arguments and evaluate canons using the evidence and tools of critical analysis appropriate to the object of inquiry.

Students will develop an appreciation of the fundamental ambiguities and complexities involved in all human attempts to answer questions about knowledge, values, and life.

Course format

This course will be conducted as an advanced seminar. Class **Attendance** and regular **Participation** are key requirements. Students are expected to attend all classes. Any more than one excused/unexcused absence will result in a lowering of your final grade. All students are expected to participate in all class discussions, which will be based on the readings, the presentations, as well as any film screenings and other materials assigned for that week. Students are expected to come to class fully prepared to engage the course texts. This includes bringing in (typed) insightful discussion questions each week and examining the materials of the course through a combination of critique, insight, and analysis.

Reading for class is essential. Our classroom discussions will be built around assigned texts, and each student is expected to contribute to these discussions on a regularly basis. A significant percentage of your final grade will be based on your overall contribution to in-class discussions.

Course texts

Pimp's Up Ho's Down	Tracey Sharpley Whiting
Let's Get Free	Paul Butler
The Dead Emcee Scrolls	Saul Williams
Book of Rhymes	Adam Bradley
Making Beats	Joseph Schloss
Hip Hop Wars	Tricia Rose
Know What I Mean	Michael Eric Dyson
Born to Use Mics	Edited by Michael Dyson and Sohail Doulhatzie

Wake-Up Everybody John Legend and the Roots
Illmatic—Nas
Yes We Can—African Hip-Hop Compilation

Course requirements

Mid-Term Exam	30%
Final Project	30%
Quizzes and Discussion Questions	30%
Participation and Attendance	10%

The **Mid-Term** examination is an in-class short answer exercise that will cover the subject matter of the course up to that point (twenty to twenty-five questions). You are expected to answer exam questions in complete sentences and with as much specific detail as time and space will allow. The exam is not scheduled for the middle of the term, but the early part of the latter half (most likely after spring break). Makeup exams will only be administered if absolutely necessary.

There will be unannounced **Quizzes** given intermittently throughout the term. These quizzes will be simple unless you have not done the reading/ listening/viewing. They usually consist of one or two questions and they tend to be good models of exam questions.

Each week students are required to do the reading and to bring to class two typed **Discussion Questions**. Discussion questions are in-depth reflective questions that are usually four to six lines (i.e., several sentences/queries) each. Please consult with the TA/instructor if you have any questions about format. These will be collected at the beginning of each class and used to facilitate class discussions. NO LATE/EMAILED DISCUSSION QUESTIONS WILL BE ACCEPTED.

Each student will be required to give one twenty to twenty-five minutes **Presentation** over the course of the term. Presentation topics are connected to the readings each week and require significant preparation and at least some consultation with the instructor. In most cases, presenters should select several songs that are referenced and/or alluded to in the text. The presentations should reflect extensive research into the subject area(s); they should be interactive (using PowerPoint, handouts, or both); and they should raise questions for the class to reflect upon and answer during and after the presentation. Presenters can (and should) consult with the professor prior to presenting.

For the final project you are required to compile/produce a "mixtape" (i.e., a compilation of musical selections). You may generate this compilation as you see fit but you must vary your artists—no more than two selections from any one artist and your project must have at least fifteen selections. The compilation should have a cohesive theme and you must write an 8–10 pages rationale that explains your theme, the reasons behind your choices, and the significance and/or import of the selections that you have made. Finally, each final project should have well thought-out and well-designed packaging that is also in concert with the project's theme. Thus, if you produce your compilation on a CD it should have an originally designed CD jacket. If you produce your compilation on a zip/jump drive, that drive should be placed in a well-designed package. If you opt for a purely digital production then that compilation should be located on a website or some well-designed virtual location. This is a final project that will require you to start EARLY. Due date TBA.

Attendance and Participation: Attendance is expected. Excessive absence (more than one absence) will significantly lower your final grade. **Please note:** you have a total of one excused/unexcused absence—one week of class. This includes any emergencies, health issues, early departures for fall break or winter vacation. Participation is a significant component of this course and will benefit your understanding of the material.

Please turn off all cell phones, pagers, and anything else that beeps/ rings/sings before you come to class. No computer use is allowed during class unless express permission is granted by the professor. Anyone caught using a cell phone or computer during class will be penalized by lowering the final grade for the course (at least ½ a letter grade).

Academic integrity

From Bucknell's policy on academic responsibility—"Bucknell students are responsible to the academic community for the preparation and presentation of work representing their own individual efforts. Acceptance of this responsibility is essential to the educational process and must be considered as an expression of mutual trust, the foundation upon which creative scholarship rests. Students are directed to use great care when preparing all written work and to acknowledge fully the source of all ideas and language other than their own."

Cheating, fabrication, plagiarism, academic misconduct, or misuse of computing facilities will not be tolerated. All incidents of which will be reported to the appropriate associate dean to be vigorously pursued in accordance with Bucknell's academic responsibility policy.

Please review the new Bucknell web resources on academic responsibility at http://www.bucknell.edu/AcademicResponsibility/

Course schedule

	Date	Reading Due	Assignment Due
Wed	25-Aug	Course Introduction "The Narrative Arcs of Hip Hop Culture"	
Wed	1-Sep	*The Dead Emcee Scrolls: The Lost Teachings of Hip Hop*	Discussion Questions (D/Q)
Wed	8-Sep	*Know What I Mean: Reflections on Hip Hop*	D/Q
Wed	15-Sep	Book of Rhymes: The Poetics of Hip Hop (Part I)	
Wed	22-Sep	*Book of Rhymes: The Poetics of Hip Hop* (Part II) Listening and Discussion: *Wake Up* by The Roots and John Legend	D/Q
Wed	29-Sep	*Making Beats: The Art of Sample Based Hip Hop* (Introduction—Chap. 4)	
Wed	6-Oct	*Making Beats: The Art of Sample Based Hip Hop* (Chap. 5—Conclusion and Epilogue)	D/Q
Wed	13-Oct	*Let's Get Free: A Hip Hop Theory of Justice* In-Class Screening—Clips from *Letter to the President*	D/Q
Wed	20-Oct	*Pimps Up, Ho's Down: Hip Hop's hold on Young Black Women*	D/Q
Wed	27-Oct	Selections from *Born to Use Mics: Reading Nas's Illmatic* Exam Review	
Wed	3-Nov	EXAM	
Wed	10-Nov	*The Hip Hop Wars: What We Talk About When We Talk About Hip Hop—And Why It Matters.* (Chaps 1–8)	D/Q
Wed	17-Nov	*The Hip Hop Wars* (Chaps 9–13)	
Wed	1-Dec	Discussion of Final Projects	

"Hip Hop Culture and Composition" English 101, Sec. 07 Bucknell University, Monday, Wednesday and Friday, 9:00 am–9:52 am

Professor:	Dr. James Peterson
Office:	Vaughn Lit. 209A
Office Hours:	Wednesday 10:00 am–12:00 pm and by appointment
Email Address:	james.peterson@bucknell.edu

Course description

This course uses scholarly and cultural criticism, film, music, music video, and the internet to engage the global phenomenon known as Hip-Hop culture. In this course, we will explore, compare, and contrast the critical and creative literature that derives from rap music and Hip-Hop culture. We will take up the debates of politics, authenticity, and identity through close readings, hearings, and viewings of the texts of Hip Hop, and we will construct well-informed positions on how writers, rappers, and regular folks use texts and contexts to achieve "authentic" identities. The main goal of the course is to explore and develop various ways of writing in and about Hip-Hop culture. You should leave this class with a working knowledge of Hip-Hop culture, its history, and the various critical ways in which we can think and write about popular culture in general.

In the last thirty years, Hip-Hop culture has developed from a relatively unknown and largely ignored inner-city culture into a global phenomenon. The foundational elements of Hip-Hop culture (DJ-ing, MC-ing, breakdance, and graffiti/graf) are manifest in youth culture across the globe, including Japan, France, Germany, South Africa, Cuba, and the UK. Considering its humble beginnings in the South and West Bronx, the global development of Hip Hop is an amazing cultural feat. Its current popularity suggests and reflects its culturally rich origins. Moreover, the presence of rap music and other elements of the culture in television, film, marketing and advertising signal American mainstream acceptance. In fact, its dominance in popular culture often obscures the negative and at times malicious treatment of Hip Hop (and its youthful constituents) in the public sphere. With all of its attendant complexities and apparent contradictions, Hip-Hop culture is dense subject matter for critical inquiry.

Course objectives

The goals of this course include challenging students to engage popular culture, analyze it and critique it. Class discussions, assignments, quizzes, and papers are all geared toward developing writing and critical thinking skills. Some additional goals are:

- To thoroughly exercise close reading skills (all text-types).
- To continue to develop and hone critical thinking skills by participating in class discussions and completing writing assignments.
- To learn sophisticated reader-response writing skills.
- To develop research and research paper-writing skills through the development of an annotated (MLA-style) discography and bibliography in addition to the final research paper.

Course format

This course will be conducted as a first-year seminar course. As such students are expected to come to class prepared to discuss the readings or texts assigned for that day. We will regularly spend some class time discussing and work-shopping papers and/or paper topics. There will also be video screenings, pop quizzes and in-class writing exercises.

Reading for class is essential. Our classroom discussions will be built around assigned texts, and each student is expected to contribute to the intellectual community of the classroom. Preparing for class should involve reflecting upon the reading that is due.

Course texts

The following texts can be purchased in the Bucknell Bookstore. Please bring the necessary book to class when assigned.

The Hip Hop Reader edited by Tim Strode and Tim Wood
Where You're At by Patrick Neate
The Message: 100 Life Lessons from Hip Hop's Greatest Songs
When Chickenheads Come Home to Roost by Joan Morgan

Course requirements

Music Review	10%
Two Papers	40% (20% each)
Research Paper	30% (2 drafts)
Participation and Quizzes	20%

Each of the first **Two Papers** (due dates on syllabus) will be 20 percent of your final grade. Paper One is a lyrical analysis paper. For this assignment you will select the rap lyric of your choice and write a detailed analysis of it. The analytical paper dissects its subject matter and explicates the relationships between the parts or sections. Paper Two is an argumentative essay. The argumentative essay is "in media res" with respect to some ongoing debate, dialogue, or discourse connected to or manifested in Hip-Hop culture. These papers are 4–6 pages each. They both require at least three sources not including your primary source (the lyric for P1).

The **Research Paper** is your opportunity to demonstrate your ability to develop an in-depth analysis of a research problem related to Hip-Hop culture or specific to the Hip-Hop generation. The research paper has a page requirement of 8–10 pages and must incorporate seven traditional academic sources (a combination of journals and academic monographs), three non-traditional sources (websites), and a minimum ten-entry discography. Your citations must be annotated.

Attendance, participation, and quizzes: Attendance is expected. Excessive absence (more than three absences) will significantly lower your grade. Participation is a significant component of this course and will benefit your understanding of the material. Occasionally, you may be quizzed on the reading.

Academic integrity

From Bucknell's policy on academic responsibility—"Bucknell students are responsible to the academic community for the preparation and presentation of work representing their own individual efforts. Acceptance of this responsibility is essential to the educational process and must be considered as an expression of mutual trust, the foundation upon which creative scholarship rests. Students are directed to use great care when preparing all written work and to acknowledge fully the source of all ideas and language other than their own."

Cheating, fabrication, plagiarism, academic misconduct, or misuse of computing facilities will not be tolerated. All incidents of which will be reported to the appropriate associate dean to be vigorously pursued in accordance with Bucknell's academic responsibility policy.

Please review the new Bucknell web resources on academic responsibility at http://www.bucknell.edu/AcademicResponsibility/

Course schedule

Week of January 16	Course Introduction—Defining Hip Hop
Week of January 21	*The Hip Hop Reader*—Chapter I
Week of January 28	*The Hip Hop Reader*—Chapter II
	In-Class Lyrical Analysis Exercises
Week of February 4	*The Message* (the First Twenty-Five Songs)
	New Music Reviews Due (Friday)
Week of February 11	*The Hip Hop Reader*—Chapter III
Week of February 18	HHR—Chapter IV
	[PAPER 1 Lyrical Analysis Is Due on Friday]
Week of March 3	Finish the *Hip Hop Reader*
Week of March 17	In-Class screening: Dave Chapelle's *Block Party*
	Continue *The Message* (25–50)
Week of March 24	Finish *The Message*
	Hip Hop Playlists Are Due
Week of March 31	*When Chicken Heads Come Home to Roost*
	Argumentative Essay Workshops
Week of April 7	*When Chicken Heads Come Home to Roost*
	PAPER 2 (Argumentative Essay Is Due on Friday)
Week of April 14	*Where Ya At*—NYC, Tokyo, and Jo-Berg
	Research Paper Possibilities
Week of April 21	Research Topics, Theses, and/or Investigative Questions
	Where You're At—Capetown, Rio, and the Outro
Week of April 28	ROUGH DRAFTS of Research Paper Are Due

Hip-Hop Culture and Composition Grading Standards

	A Outstanding	B Above Average	C Average	D Below Average	F Unacceptable
Content	A significant central idea clearly defined and supported with concrete, substantial, and relevant detail. Audience awareness apparent. Tone consistent and appropriate. Writer establishes a consistent and authoritative voice. The assignment is fulfilled.	Significant central idea ambitious and generally well supported, but occasionally details missing. Shows some complexity of thought. Tone reasonably well maintained, but there is a lapse in consistency or appropriateness. Some audience awareness evident. Developed in accordance with purpose.	Central idea apparent but unoriginal, trivial, or too general; supported with detail, but it is occasionally obvious, repetitious, irrelevant, or sketchy. Some attention paid to tone. Some audience awareness. Assignment is followed, but not fulfilled.	Central idea confused or unsupported by concrete and relevant detail. Little, if any, awareness of audience or attempt at creating a tone.	The essay has no central idea; no audience awareness, and the paper is quite short. Writer has no concept of tone and little, if any, control over the thoughts presented. It goes off in several different directions. Assignment not fulfilled.
Organization	Logical and clearly developed paragraphs. Transitions effective. Proportion and emphasis consistent. The writer is in control of the material.	Clear, logical, and easy to follow. Paragraphs coherent, unified, and developed. Most transitions effective.	Plan and purpose apparent but not consistently fulfilled. Paragraphs adequately developed, divided, unified, and coherent with only occasional disproportion or inappropriate emphasis. Many transitions between paragraphs abrupt and repetitious.	Plan and purpose not apparent. Paragraphs not well developed, well divided, or appropriately arranged. Characterized by irrelevancy, redundancy, or inconsistency. Transitions between paragraphs either missing, unclear, or ineffective.	Lacks a purpose or plan.
Sentence Structure	Sentences skillfully constructed (unified, coherent, forceful, effectively varied with attention to style, and rhythm). Structures fluent and suited to the meaning of the paper.	Sentences have some variety and are generally unified and coherent. Sentences vary in length. Some structures unclear or wordy.	Sentence structure correct, but lacks distinction. Little or no variation in structure. Phrases often awkwardly placed.	Sentences not unified, coherent, complete, or varied. Too many simple (not complex) sentences.	Sentences incoherent. Lack of logical connections between sentences.

(Continued)

(Continued)

	A Outstanding	B Above Average	C Average	D Below Average	F Unacceptable
Diction	Distinctive: fresh, precise, economical, and idiomatic. Sensitive to connotative and denotative meanings. An absence of "clutter" or hackneyed expressions.	Word choice workable and clear, but words (especially verbs) may lack freshness or strength. General absence of clutter and clichés. Vocabulary precise and varied.	Word choice clear and idiomatic, but the paper is characterized by wordiness and clichés. Vocabulary limited.	Inappropriate: vague, unidiomatic, or sub-standard.	
Grammar Punctuation Spelling	Virtually no errors.	Some errors in internal punctuation (commas, semicolons). A few spelling errors.	Clarity and effectiveness of expression weakened by occasional deviations from standard grammar, punctuation, and spelling.	Comprehension and communication obscured by frequent deviations from standard grammar, punctuation, and spelling.	Comprehension and communication obscured by frequent deviations from standard grammar, punctuation, and spelling. Multiple errors in subject/verb, noun/pronoun agreement, tense shifts, modification, or parallel structure. Misuse of common words such as *their*, *there, they're, its, it's, your, you're* makes the writing substandard.
Use of Sources (MLA = Humanities; APA = Social Sciences)	Source material incorporated logically and insightfully. Sources properly documented.	Source material incorporated logically. Sources properly documented.	Source material incorporated adequately. Sources properly documented.	Source material incorporated, but sometimes inappropriately or unclearly. Some sources not properly documented.	Plagiarized work.

"ME, MYSELF, and I: AUTOBIOGRAPHY IN HIP HOP CULTURE"[1] AAS 396/ENGL 396, Section 010 ENGL 496 Section 011 Lehigh University, Tuesdays and Thursdays 9:20 am–10:35 am

Professor:	Dr. James Peterson
Office:	302A Drown Hall
Office Hours:	Tuesdays 11:00 am—Noon and by appointment
Email Address:	jbp211@lehigh.edu

Course description

This course is designed to explore the genre of autobiography within Hip-Hop culture, including the lyrics of rap music; literature published by Hip-Hop generational artists, thinkers, writers, and poets; and the films that attempt to capture the Hip-Hop generation's autobiographical narratives. This course is an upper level/graduate seminar that will require students to make formal in-class presentations, take quizzes regularly, and develop substantial final research projects. With all of its attendant complexities and apparent contradictions, Hip-Hop culture is dense subject matter for critical inquiry.

Course objectives

This course examines Hip-Hop culture through the genre of autobiography. The objective of the course is to enhance students' critical engagement with autobiographical narratives crafted by writers of the Hip-Hop generation.

Autobiography is a formative literary genre within the literature of Africana Studies with roots in first-person narratives depicting the experiences of enslaved Africans in the "New World." Students will learn to construct arguments, facilitate discourse, and participate in critical discussions about this literary genre and Hip-Hop culture more broadly.

Course format

This course will be conducted as an advanced seminar. Class **Attendance** and regular **Participation** are key requirements. Students are expected to attend all classes. Any more than two excused/unexcused absences will result in a lowering of your final grade. All students are expected to participate in all class discussions, which will be based on the readings, the presentations, as well as any film/album screenings and other materials assigned for that week. Students are expected to come to class fully prepared to engage the course texts. This includes bringing in (typed) insightful discussion questions regularly and examining the materials of the course through a combination of critique, insight and analysis.

    Reading for class is essential. Our classroom discussions will be built around assigned texts, and each student is expected to contribute to these discussions on a regularly basis. A significant percentage of your final grade will be based on your overall contribution to in-class discussions.

Course texts

- Breis, *Brilliant Rappers Educate Intelligent Students* (9780956850409)
- Geoffrey Canada, *Fist, Stick, Knife, Gun* (0807004235)
- Jay-Z, *Decoded* (9781400068920)
- Karrine Steffans, *Confessions of a Video Vixen* (9780060892487)
- Sister Souljah, *No Disrespect* (9780679767084)
- Suheir Hammad, *Breaking Poems* (9780981913124)
- Thomas Chatterton Williams, *Losing My Cool: How A Father's Love and 15,000 Books Beat Hip Hop Culture* (9781594202636)
- Ta-Nehisi Coates' *The Beautiful Struggle* (9780385527460)

We will also be reading excerpts from several autobiographical texts including selections from Joan Morgan's *When Chickenheads Come Home to Roost*, Afeni Shakur's *Evolution of a Revolutionary*, Sanyika Shakur's *Monster*, Angela Nissel's *The Broke Diaries*, and William Jelani Cobb's *To The Break of Dawn*.

Course requirements

Mid-Term Exam	30%
Final Project	30%
Quizzes and Discussion Questions	15%
In-Class Presentations	15%
Participation and Attendance	10%

The **Mid-Term** examination is an in-class short answer exercise that will cover the subject matter of the course up to that point (twenty to twenty-five questions). You are expected to answer exam questions in complete sentences and with as much specific detail as time and space will allow. The exam is not scheduled for the middle of the term, but the early part of the latter half (most likely after the semester break). Make up exams will only be administered if absolutely necessary.

There will be unannounced **Quizzes** given intermittently throughout the term. These quizzes will be simple unless you have not done the reading/listening/viewing. They usually consist of one or two questions, and they tend to be good models of exam questions.

Each week students are required to do the reading and to bring to class two typed **Discussion Questions**. Discussion questions are in-depth reflective questions that are usually 3–5 lines (i.e., several sentences/queries) each. Please consult with the Professor if you have any questions about format. These will be collected at the beginning of each class and used to facilitate class discussions. NO LATE/EMAILED DISCUSSION QUESTIONS WILL BE ACCEPTED.

Each student will be required to give two to three, ten to fifteen minutes **Presentations** over the course of the term. Presentation topics are chosen at the discretion of the student and can be connected to the readings. These presentations will require significant preparation and at least some consultation with the instructor. Students should select a Hip-Hop artist and present on his/her autobiographical song and/or video. The presentations should reflect extensive research into the subject area(s); they should be interactive (using PowerPoint, handouts, or both); and they should raise questions for the class to reflect upon and answer during and after the presentation. Presenters can (and should) consult with the professor prior to presenting.

For the final project you are required to compile/produce a "mixtape" (i.e., a compilation of musical selections). You may generate this compilation as you see fit but you must vary your artists—no more than two selections from any one artist and your project must have at least ten selections. The compilation should have an autobiographical theme and you must write an 8–10 pages rationale that explains your theme, the reasons behind your choices, and the significance and/or import of the selections that you have made. Finally, each final project should have well thought-out and well-designed packaging that is also in concert with the project's theme. Thus, if you produce your compilation on a CD it should have an originally designed CD jacket. If you produce your compilation on a zip/jump drive, that drive should be placed in a well-designed package. If you opt for a purely digital production then that compilation should be located on a website or some well-designed virtual location. This is a final project that will require you to start EARLY. Due date TBA.

Attendance and Participation: Attendance is expected. Excessive absence (more than two absences) will significantly lower your final grade. **Please note:** you have a total of two excused/unexcused absences—one week of class. This includes any emergencies, health issues, early departures for fall break or winter vacation. Participation is a significant component of this course and will benefit your understanding of the material.

Please turn off all cell phones, pagers, and anything else that beeps/ rings/sings before you come to class. No computer use is allowed during class unless express permission is granted by the professor. Anyone caught using a cell phone or computer during class will be penalized by lowering the final grade for the course (at least ½ a letter grade).

Academic integrity

From Lehigh's policy on academic responsibility—"We, the Lehigh University Student Senate, as the standing representative body of all undergraduates, reaffirm the duty and obligation of students to meet and uphold the highest principles and values of personal, moral and ethical conduct. As partners in our educational community, both students and faculty share the responsibility for promoting and helping to ensure an environment of academic integrity. As such, each student is expected to complete all academic course work in accordance to the standards set forth by the faculty and in compliance with the University's Code of Conduct."

Cheating, fabrication, plagiarism, academic misconduct, or misuse of computing facilities will not be tolerated. All incidents of which will be reported to the appropriate associate dean to be vigorously pursued in accordance with Lehigh's academic responsibility policy.

Please review Lehigh's web resources on academic responsibility at: http://www.lehigh.edu/~indost/conduct/aireporting.shtml

Accommodations for students with disabilities

If you have a disability for which you are or may be requesting accommodations, please contact both your instructor and the Office of Academic Support Services, University Center 212 (610.758.4152) as early as possible in the semester. You must have documentation from the Office of Academic Support Services before accommodations can be granted.

Take responsibility for your learning. Use the Writing Center in Drown [www.lehigh.edu/~incent/incent] if you need writing help of any kind, from brainstorming to drafting to revising.

Course schedule

	Date	Reading Due	Assignment Due
Tues	30-Aug	Course Introduction	
Thurs	1-Sep	*To the Break of Dawn* (Excerpt) "The Subject and Power" (Excerpt)	Autobiography Definitions
Tues	6-Sep	"Hip Hop Stole My Black Boy" (pdf on Course Site)	DQ
Thurs	8-Sep	*The Broke Diaries* (Excerpt)	DQ
Tues	13-Sep	*Monster* (Excerpt)	DQ
Thurs	15-Sep	Begin *Fist, Stick Knife, Gun* (Part I)	Begin Student Presentations
Tues	20-Sep	Complete *Fist, Stick Knife, Gun*	DQ
Thurs	22-Sep	*Brilliant Rappers Educate Intelligent …*	DQ and Student Presentations
Tues	27-Sep	*When Chickenheads Come Home to Roost* (Excerpt)	DQ
Thurs	29-Sep	*No Disrespect* (pp. 1–117)	Student Presentations
Tues	4-Oct	*No Disrespect* (pp. 118–226)	DQ
Thurs	6-Oct	Complete *No Disrespect*	Student Presentations
Tues	11-Oct	Pacing Break-No Class	
Thurs	13-Oct	*Evolution of a Revolutionary* (Excerpt)	
Tues	18-Oct	*Breaking Poems*	DQ
Thurs	20-Oct	Catch up and Mid-Term Review	
Tues	25-Oct	Mid-Term Examination	
Thurs	27-Oct	Film Screening (TBA) Begin *Confessions of a Video Vixen*	
Tues	1-Nov	Film Screening cont'd Complete *Confessions*	
Thurs	3-Nov	Begin *Losing My Cool*	
Tues	8-Nov	Complete *Losing My Cool*	DQ
Thurs	10-Nov	Complete *Losing My Cool* Begin Jay-Z's *Decoded*	Student Presentations
Tues	15-Nov	Continue Jay-Z's *Decoded*	
Thurs	17-Nov	Complete *Decoded*	DQ/Student Presentations

	Date	Reading Due	Assignment Due
Tues	22-Nov	Film Screening: *Tupac: Resurrection*	
Thurs	24-Nov	Thanksgiving Break	
Tues	29-Nov	Begin *The Beautiful Struggle*	
Thurs	1-Dec	Continue *The Beautiful Struggle*	DQ
Tues	6-Dec	Student Presentations (Makeup) Graduate Students: Conference Presentations	
Thurs	8-Dec	Discuss Final Projects Course Evaluations	

Africana Studies 295: Spring/Summer Term 2015 "Concepts of the Underground in Black Literature and Culture"

Professor James B. Peterson
Payne 108, x8924, jbp211@lehigh.edu

Course Concept/Course Description: This course is designed to explore the concept of the underground through various examples of underground literature, underground cultural, and social movements as well as various films and music that configure the underground symbolically or literally with its main characters, settings, plots, and themes. An "underground" text can be about the Underground Railroad (e.g., Lorene Cary's *Price of a Child*), the psychological descent into madness (Dyostoyevsky's *Notes from Underground*), or the surreal effects of racism in America (Ralph Ellison's *Invisible Man*). One of the goals of this course is to develop a working definition of the underground as a sociopolitical concept and as a social construct. We will also be concerned with establishing a theoretical link across various ways in which the underground is employed throughout literary history. The chronological range of this project roughly extends from the nineteenth century (slavery and the underground railroad) to the twenty-first century (including underground moments in Black literature, film, and the underground constitutions of Hip-Hop culture). The subject of the "underground" is the consistent theme/thread throughout the course. Whether it appears in literature, film, music, political movements, philosophy, or cultural theory, the underground signals one of the most complex formulations of human identity.

Course format and requirements: This course will be conducted as an advanced seminar. Students are expected to come to class fully prepared to engage the course texts. This includes bringing (typed) insightful discussion questions each week and examining the materials of the course through a combination of critique, insight, and analysis.

Participation in and reading for class is essential: Our classroom discussions will be built around assigned texts, and each student is expected to contribute to the intellectual community of the classroom. Even when you are not giving a presentation, preparing for class should involve reflecting upon the reading that is due. If you do not contribute to class discussions consistently throughout the semester your final grade will be adversely affected.

There will be four short-answer **Quizzes** given over the course of the term. Each quiz, worth twenty-five points, will pose questions on the readings for that week and previous in-class discussions. These quizzes will be administered on each Thursday of the term.

Each week students are required to do the reading and to bring to class two typed **Discussion Questions.** These will be collected at the beginning of class on Wednesdays and used to facilitate class discussions.

Each student will be required to give two ten to fifteen minutes **Presentation** over the course of the term. Presentation topics are connected to the readings each week and the presentations must be followed up by a brief statement summarizing the presentation in writing (1–2 pages). The presentation should reflect extensive research into the subject area; it should be interactive (using PowerPoint, handouts, or both); and it should raise questions for the class to reflect upon and answer during and after the presentation. Presenters can (and should) consult with the professor prior to presenting.

Response Papers are due at 5:00 pm on Friday during throughout the course. Responses should be 2–3 pages in length (typed, double-spaced, 12-point font) and they require that you reflect upon the most compelling scene, image, concept, or insight derived from the exercise/prompt or film related to that week's Response Paper assignment. LATE RESPONSE PAPERS ARE NOT ACCEPTED—NO EXCEPTIONS.

Grades will be determined as follows: 20 percent for quizzes; 30 percent for response papers; 30 percent for presentations, presentation write-ups, and discussion questions; and 20 percent for participation, including all class discussions.

Week One: The Philosophical Underground

Plato, "The Parable of the Cave"
Fyodor Doystoyevsky, *Notes from Underground*
Project #1: A visual/artistic project rendering "The Parable of the Cave"
Response Paper #1: A Combined Definition of Plato and Dostoyevsky's Underground(s)

Monday: Read "The Parable of the Cave" and Google-Image search the reading. Begin to plot and conceptualize your own visual interpretation of the parable for your presentation during Thursday's class.
Tuesday, 9:05 am–12:10 pm, seminar discussion of "The Parable of the Cave" and Introduction of the "Hip Hop Underground Playlist" (three hours of listening per week through the course—list attached).
Wednesday, 9:05 am–12:10 pm: seminar discussion of *Notes from Underground*
Thursday, 9:05 am–12:10 pm: 1st Weekly Quiz on the Readings and Student presentations of Project #1
Friday, 5:00 pm: Response Paper #1 is due. Please submit via email in MS Word (docx) file.

Week Two: The Underground Railroad

Lorene Cary, *The Price of a Child*
Kyle Baker, *Nat Turner* (graphic novel)
Project #2: Web/internet search and research for VA sites on the Underground Railroad and Listening to and decoding the "Negro Spiritual"—selections TBD
Film #1: *Underground Railroad*

Monday: screening the History Channel's *Underground Railroad* documentary (narrated by Alfre Woodard. 7:00 pm–9:30 pm.

Tuesday, 9:05 am–12:10 pm: seminar discussion—understanding the Underground Railroad and the encoded "Negro Spirituals."
Wednesday, 9:05 am–12:10 pm: seminar discussion of *The Price of a Child*
Thursday, 9:05 am–12:10 pm: seminar discussion of *Nat Turner*, 2nd Quiz and short student presentations on VA sites of the Underground Railroad.
Friday, 5:00 pm: Response Paper #2 is due. Please submit via email in MS Word (docx) file.

Week Three: The Cipher of the Underground in Black Culture

Thelonius Monk, *Underground* (1968)
Richard Wright, *The Man Who Lived Underground*
Ralph Ellison, *Invisible Man* (selections)
Amiri Baraka, *Dutchman and The Slave*
Film #2: *Dark Days*
Response Paper #3: "Who are the Mole People?"

Monday: Listening hours (2) for TheloniusMonk's Underground. Reading hours (4) and researching this week's authors/artists—Wright, Ellison, Monk and Baraka
Tuesday, 9:05 am–12:10 pm, seminar discussion of *The Man Who Lived Underground and IM*
Wednesday, 9:05 am–12:10 pm: seminar discussion of Thelonius Monk's *Underground*
Thursday, 9:05 am–12:10 pm: seminar discussion of *Dutchman and The Slave*, Quiz #3 and introduction of *Dark Days* documentary
Friday: Screening *Dark Days*, 9:00 am–10:30 am
Friday, 5:00 pm: Response Paper #3 is due. Please submit via email in MS Word (docx) file.

Week Four: The Hip Hop Underground and African American Culture

James Peterson, *The Hip Hop Underground and African American Culture*
Project #2: "Expanding the Hip Hop Underground Playlist"

Film #3: *This is the Life: How the West Was Won*
Response Paper #4: "The Most Significant Underground Hip Hop lyric(s) of All Time"

Monday, 7:30 pm–9:30 pm: Screening Ava DuVernay's *This is the Life* documentary and Listening to the Hip Hop Underground playlist.
Tuesday, 9:05 am–12:10 pm, seminar discussion of *This is the Life* and selections from the Hip Hop Underground playlist
Wednesday, 9:05 am–12:10 pm: seminar discussion of The Hip Hop Underground and African American Culture (part 1)
Thursday, 9:05 am–12:10 pm: seminar discussion of The Hip Hop Underground (part 2), Quiz #4 and final student presentations
Friday, 5:00 pm: Response Paper #4 is due. Please submit via email in MS Word (docx) file.

TEXTS: Plato, "The Parable of the Cave," Fyodor Dostoyevsky, *Notes from Underground*, Lorene Carey, The Price of a Child, Kyle Baker, Nat Turner, Richard Wright, The Man Who Lived Underground, Ralph Ellison, Invisible Man, Amiri Baraka, Dutchman and The Slave, and James Braxton Peterson, The Hip-Hop Underground and African American Culture.

Course Objectives for a 200-level English class: Students will learn how to …

1. Write clear, persuasive analytical essays driven by arguments about texts. (Assessment: professor's evaluation of response papers and presentation write-ups)
2. Read closely, recognizing subtle and complex differences in language use. (Assessment: professor's evaluation of response papers and class discussion)
3. Seek out further knowledge about literary works, authors, and contexts, and document research appropriately, adhering to the highest standards of intellectual honesty. (Assessment: professor's evaluation of seminar discussion, discussion questions, class presentations, and write-ups)
4. Broaden the range of literary texts and performances from which they can derive pleasure and edification. (Assessment: course evaluations, as well as seminar discussion, class presentations, and film screenings)

Foundation requirements for literature objectives: Literary study aims to understand the human condition and experience as expressed by the individual imagination through language. Through such study, students acquire an aesthetic interest to pursue throughout their lifetime. Courses may focus on literature written in English, in a foreign language, or in translation. In literature courses, students

- acquire knowledge about the cultural and historical context of literature;
- learn to analyze various literary forms and complex and difficult language;
- learn to read with imagination; and
- respond critically to literature orally and in writing.

Assessment of these objectives occurs mainly in professor's evaluation of students' written work (including formal essays and exams), class discussions, and formal oral presentations, augmented by the end-of-term student evaluations, and the senior exit survey.

Standards and expectations: A major part of this class depends upon active and thoughtful participation by all members. To clarify what I regard as "active and thoughtful participation," and how I will grade and evaluate student participation, I offer the following descriptions:

- Outstanding ("A" grade participation): Contributions or questions reflect exceptional preparation prior to class. Ideas are substantive and provide major insights. Questions reflect prior intellectual engagement with the material, they make linkages to other relevant material, and they often contribute to the learning of others. If this person were not a member of the class, the quality of discussion would be diminished markedly.
- Good ("B" grade participation): Contributions reflect thorough preparation. Ideas offered are usually substantive and provide good insights. Questions are thoughtful and serve to clarify important issues. If this person were not a member of the class, the quality of discussion would be diminished.
- Adequate ("C" grade participation): Contributions in class reflect satisfactory preparation. Ideas offered are sometimes substantive and provide generally useful insights. Questions help to clarify material. If this

person were not a member of the class, the quality of discussion would be somewhat diminished.

- Non-participant ("D" grade participation): Person says little or nothing in class. Hence, there is not an adequate basis for evaluation. If this person were not a member of the class, the quality of discussion would not be changed.

- Unsatisfactory ("F" grade participation): Contributions in class reflect inadequate preparation. Ideas offered are seldom substantive; provide few, if any, insights and never a constructive direction for the class. Questions clearly indicate a lack of preparation for the class. Student often talks much, but says little. If this person were not a member of the class, class discussion would actually be better.

Table 4.1 A Hip-Hop underground playlist

Song Title	Artist/Speaker	Year	CS	CM	SOS
"You Can't Hate the Roots…	Malcolm X	1962	X	X	X
"Go Underground"	B.B. King	1970	X		
"Underground"	EPMD	1990	X		
"Funky Child"	Lords of the Underground	1993	X		
"Hold"/hole/whole	KRSONE	1995	X	X	
"Underground Lockdown"	Hurricane G	1997	X	X	
"M.U.G."—Money Underground	O.C. fca. Freddie Foxxx	1997	X	X	
"In(Scnsc)"/*Beneath the Surface*	Onomatopoeia	1998		X	
"Nathaniel"	Outkast	1998			
"Liberation"	Cee-Lo/Outkast	1998		X	X
"Underground"	Thcma Simonc Bryant	1999	X	X	X
"Mathematics"	Mos Dcf	1999			
"Harriet Thugman"/*Djrfy Harriet*	Rah Digga	2000			X
"Liberty"/*Underground Railroad*	Mastermind	2000	X	X	
"Africa Dream"	Talib Kwcli	2000			X
"Something's Gotta Give"	V.I.Kings	2003		X	
"Still Ain't Good Enough"	Random	2006			

(Continued)

(Continued)

"Underground Kingz"	UGK-Underground Kingz	2007		X	
"Keep It Keal"/*African Underground-Depths of Dakar*	Pato	2007	X		
"Bboy Underground"	Digikid84	2008	X		
"Underground"	Eminem	2009			
"The Grand Illusion (Circa 1973)"	Pharoahe Monch feat. Citizen Cope	2011	X	X	X
"Praying Man"/*Lwefrom the Underground*	Big K.R.I.T. feat. B.B. King	2012	X	X	X

Appendix: The Play List Pedagogy

All Black everything playlist

ARTIST	YEAR	TRACK	ALBUM
Spade Gang	2010	"All Black Everything"	*Spade Gang***
Jellytoofly	2011	"All Black Everything"†	
Derrick Mitchell, Five82Six & Rob	2009	"All Black Everything"	*The Prequel Day One*
Jay-Z Feat. Rihanna & Kanye West	2009	"Run This Town"	*The Blueprint 3*
Shiest Bubz	2010	"A.B.E. (All Black Everything)"	*Everydaze My Birthday*
Baylock-n-Deload	2009	"All Black Everything"	*Back 4 More*
Kanye West & JAY Z	2011	"Murder To Excellence"	*Watch the Throne* (Deluxe Version)
Lupe Fiasco	2011	"All Black Everything"	*Lasers*
Rapsody	2011	"All Black Everythng"	*For Everything*
Profit Ft. Donsai & Tyler Durand	2012	"All Black Everything"	*Takeover*

* Single
† Single

Black prison narratives playlist

ARTIST	YEAR	TRACK	ALBUM
The Geto Boys	1996	"Ghetto Prisoner"	*The Resurrection*
Angela Davis	2000	"Race, Class And Incarceration"	*The Prison Industrial Complex*‡
Angela Davis	2000	"Young Black Men And Prison"	The Prison Industrial Complex§
Nas	1999	"Ghetto Prisoners"	*I Am...*
Sean Price	2005	"Jail Shit Featuring Rock"	*Monkey Barz*
Angela Davis	2000	"The Prison Industrial Complex"	*The Prison Industrial Complex***

‡ Books and spoken word
§ Books and spoken word
** Books and spoken word

Education policy playlist

ARTIST	YEAR	TRACK	ALBUM
Excerpt from HH in the Classroom Ft. Shuaib Meachum S. Meachum	Act 48 2004 Part II††		
KRS-One	1988	"My Philosophy"	*By All Means Necessary*
Boogie Down Productions	1987	"poetry"	*Criminal Minded*
James Braxton Peterson	DATE	"The Deficit"	*Here We Go Again*
Blue Scholars	2004	"Blue School"	*Blue Scholars*
Big L	2000	"Ebonics"	*The Big Picture*
Common	1994	"I Used To Love H.E.R."	*Resurrection*
Jay-Z	2002	"Meet The Parents"	*The Blueprint 2: The Curse*
Dead Prez	2000	"'They' Schools"	*Let's Get Free*
Funkamentals	DATE?	"I want your elements"	*One Time for the Mind*
Saul Williams	1997	"Twice the First Time"	*Eargasms‡‡*
Chris Rock	2005	"Rap Standup"	*Never Scared§§*
Random	2006	"Still Ain't Good Enough"	*The Call*
KRS-One	2003??	"The Elements"	*Ruminations***
KRS-One	2004	"A Call To Order: Spoken by Afrika Bambaataa"	*Keep Right*
Nas	2002	"I Can"	*God's Son*
Boogie Down Productions	1989	"You Must Learn"	*Ghetto Music: The Blueprint Of Hip Hop*
Foreign Exchange	2004	"Brave New World"	*Connected*
Ty	2001	"Hercules"	*Awkward*
KRS-One	2001	"HipHop Knowledge"	*The Sneak Attack*
Blackalicious	2002	"Brain Washers"	*Blazing Arrow*
Pharoahe Monch Ft. Erykah Badu	2007	"Hold On"	*Desire*
2Pac	1995	"Old School"	*Me Against The World*

ARTIST	YEAR	TRACK	ALBUM
Jay-Z Ft. Ne-Yo	2006	"Minority Report"	*Kingdom Come*
Nas	1999	"Nas Is Like"	*I Am…*
Kanye West	2007	"Interviews"	*Can't Tell Me Nothing Mixtape*
Lauryn Hill	1998	"Miseducation Of Lauryn Hill"	*The Miseducation Of Lauryn Hill*
OutKast Ft. Cee-Lo & Erykah Badu	1998	"Liberation"	*Aquemini*
Das EFX	1998	"Rap Scholar"	*Generation EFX*
Mos Def	1999	"Mathematics"	*Black On Both Sides*
KRS-One	2004	"Rap History"	*Keep Right*
Eminem Ft. Jay-Z, Dr. Dre, Stat Quo, 50 Cent & Cahi	2010		"Syllables"[†††]
Martin Smith and James Peterson (jbp)	2008	"The Deficit"	*Dr. Hip Hop Vol. 1*

[††] Workshop
[‡‡] Spoken word
[§§] Comedy
[***] Books and spoken word
[†††] Single

Allusions to Emmett Till in Hip Hop

ARTIST	YEAR	TRACK	ALBUM
Labetkwon	2007	"Arise Lazarus 2007"	*Emmett Till's Revenge*
Labtekwon	2007	"The Foundation"	*Emmett Till's Revenge*
Labtekwon & Supreme	2007	"Black Iz Back"	*Emmett Till's Revenge*
Chinchilla	2007	"410 Block Boss"	*Emmett Till's Revenge*
Jeff Busch	2006	"?We're fighting still for Emmett Till"	*Colors in Between*
Ice Cube	1993	"Cave Bitch"	*Lethal Injection*
Supreme	2007	"Secret Weapon"	*Emmett Till's Revenge*
Kanye West	2007	"Can't Tell Me Nothing"	*Graduation*
Chinchilla	2007	"Cruz 2007"	*Emmett Till's Revenge*
Labtekwon	2007	"B Boy Radio"	*Emmett Till's Revenge*
Hypnotic Brass Ensemble	2005	"Emmett Till"	*Jupiter*

ARTIST	YEAR	TRACK	ALBUM
Labtekwon	2007	"When Emcees Attack"	*Emmett Till's Revenge*
Bristol Pomeroy	2007	"The Emmett Till Story"	*Bedtime Stories*
Emmett Till	2007	"Emmett Till Poem Snippet"	*True 2 Life: The Mixtape, Vol. 2*
Blind Boy Grunt (Bob Dylan)	1972	"The Ballad of Emmett Till"	*Broadside Ballads, Volume 6: Broadside Reunion*
Kanye West	2004	"Through The Wire"	*The College Dropout*
Naledge	DATE?	"EmittTil (Never Forget)"	UNRELEASED

Conceptualizations of flight in Hip Hop

ARTIST	YEAR	TRACK	ALBUM
Slim Ft. Yung Joc	2008	"So Fly"	*Love's Crazy*
James Earl Jones & Virginia Hamilton	1993	*The People Could Fly: American Black Folktales*‡‡‡	
Nas	2001	"The Flyest"	*Stillmatic*
R. Kelly	1998	"I Believe I Can Fly"	*R.*
Lenny Kravitz	1998	"Fly Away"	*5*
Steve Miller Band	2006	"Fly Like an Eagle"	*Fly Like an Eagle*
Three 6 Mafia	2005	"Stay Fly"	*Most Known Unknown*
Sugar Ray	1997	"Fly"	*Floored*
Murs Feat. Will.I.Am	2008	"Lookin' Fly"	*Murs For President*
M.I.A. Ft. Bun B & Rich Boy	2008	"Paper Planes"	*Paper Planes (Homeland Security Remixes)*
Big Tymers	2002	"Still Fly"	*Hood Rich*
M.I.A.	2007	"Paper Planes" [Dembo's Mix]	*Kala*
Kanye West	2004	"I'll Fly Away"	*The College Dropout*
Queen Latifah	1991	"Fly Girl"	*Nature Of A Sista'*
Etta James	2006	"I Believe I Can Fly"	*All the Way*
DMX	1998	"Let Me Fly"	*It's Dark And Hell Is Hot*

ARTIST	YEAR	TRACK	ALBUM
Jim Jones	2006	"We Fly High"	*Hustler's P.O.M.E. (Product of My Environment)*
Familiars Unseen	2007	"Fly Girl"	*Grown and Fresh*
Will.I.Am	2007	"Fly Girl"	*Songs About Girls*
Nikki Giovanni	2004	"Ego Tripping"	*My House*§§§
Three 6 Mafia	2006	"Stay Fly (Still Fly Remix)"	*Most Known Unknown*

‡‡‡ Audiobook
§§§ Spoken word

The Hip Hop "Tellability" playlist

ARTIST	YEAR	TRACK	ALBUM
Nas	2004	"Sekou Story"	Street's Disciple
The Notorious B.I.G.	1997	"I Got A Story To Tell"	*Life After Death*
The Game	2005	"Westside Story"	*Westside Story*
Slick Rick	1995	"Children's Story"	*The Great Adventures of Slick Rick*
2Pac	1992	"Soulja's Story"	*2Pacalypse Now*
Jean Grae	2008	"My Story"	*Jeanius*
Scarface & Z-Ro	2008	"Soldier Story The Product"	*Emeritus*
Outkast	1998	"Da Art of Storytellin' (Pt. 1)"	*Aquemini*
Outkast	1998	"Da Art of Storytellin' (Pt. 2)"	*Aquemini*
DMX	1998	"Crime Story"	*It's Dark and Hell is Hot*
The Notorious B.I.G. Ft. Scarface, Akon & Bee Gee	2005	"Hustler's Story"	*Duets: The Final Chapter*
Immortal Technique	2001	"Dance With The Devil"	*Revolutionary Vol.1*
Lupe Fiasco	2007	"Ghetto Story"	*It was written*

A language and race playlist

ARTIST	YEAR	TRACK	ALBUM
Paul Robeson	1991	"Go Down, Moses"	*The Power and The Glory*
Gil Scott-Heron	1970	"The Revolution Will Not Be Televised"	*Small Talk at 125th and Lenox*
Rev. C.L. Franklin	1999	"Two Fish and Five Loaves of Bread, Pt. 1"	*Legendary Sermons*****
Big L	2000	"Ebonics"	*The Big Picture 1977–1999*
James Brown	1974	"Funky President (People It's Bad)"	*Reality*
Dead Prez	2000	"They" Schools"	*Let's Get Free*
Das EFX	1992	"They Want EFX"	*Dead Serious*
Saul Williams	1997	"Twice the First Time"	*Eargasms*
Bernice Johnson Reagon	1965	"Steal Away To Jesus"	*Various Artists*
Malcom X	1992	"I'm A Field Negro"	*Words From The Frontlines: Excerpts From The Great Speeches††††*
Mahalia Jackson	1988	"Trouble Of The World"	*Gospels, Spirituals, & Hymns*
KRS-One	1995	"Hold"	*KRS-One*
Boogie Down Productions	1988	"Part Time Suckers"	*By All Means Necessary*
Brownie McGhee And Sonny Terry	1958	"John Henry"	*Brownie McGhee And Sonny Terry*
Nappy Roots Feat. Anthony Hamilton	2002	"Po' Folks"	*Watermelon, Chicken & Gritz*
Ghostface Killah	1996	"Motherless Child"	*Ironman*
Zora Neale Hurston	2006	"How Do You Learn Most Of Your Songs?"	*Harlem Speaks‡‡‡‡*
Nikki Giovanni	1972	"Ego Tripping (there may be a reason why)"	*My House§§§§*
Nas & DJ Green Lantern	2008	"Outro Ft. Richard Pryor"	*The Nigger Mixtape*

ARTIST	YEAR	TRACK	ALBUM
Zora Neale Hurston	2006	"Uncle Bud"	*Harlem Speaks******
Louis Armstrong	1955	"(What Did I Do To Be So) Black And Blue?"	*Satch Plays Fats*
Alain Locke	1940	"The Negro Spiritual"	*Harlem Speaks*†††††

**** Sermon
†††† Speeches, spoken word
‡‡‡‡ Spoken word
§§§§ Spoken word
***** Spoken word
††††† Spoken word

The Odes of/to Hip-Hop culture

ARTIST	YEAR	TRACK	ALBUM
Rakim	2008	"Hip Hop"	*The Archive: Live, Lost & Found*
Redman	1998	"Welcome 2 Da Bricks"	*Doc's Da Name 2000*
Lords Of The Underground	1993	"From Da Bricks"	*Here Come The Lords*
Guerilla Black	2004	"Guerilla City"	*Guerrilla City*
KRS-One & Marley Marl	2007	"Hip Hop Lives"	*Hip Hop Lives*
Mos Def	1999	"Hip Hop"	*Black On Both Sides*
Nas	1994	"N.Y. State Of Mind"	*Illmatic*
Nas	1999	"NY State Of Mind, Pt. II"	*I Am...*
Boogie Down Productions	1987	"South Bronx"	*Criminal Minded*
Nelly	2000	"St. Louie"	*Country Grammar*
Erykah Badu	2008	"The Healer/Hip Hop"	*New Amerykah: Part One (4th World War)*
M.O.P.	2000	"Welcome To Brownsville"	*Warriorz*
The Game	2005	"Westside Story"	*Westside Story*
2Pac Ft. Dr. Dre	1998	"California Love"	*2Pac Greatest Hits*
Nyoil	2007	"Hip Hop Ya Don't Stop"	*Hood TREASON: The Warm Up Album*
Lil' Kim	2005	"Lighters Up"	*The Naked Truth*

ARTIST	YEAR	TRACK	ALBUM
Pharoahe Monch	1999	"Queens"	*Internal Affairs*
Digable Planets	1993	"Where I'm from"	*Reachin' (A New Refutation Of Time And Space)*
Foxy Brown	2001	"B.K. Anthem"	*Broken Silence*
Ol' Dirty Bastard	1995	"Brooklyn Zoo"	*Return To The 36 Chambers*
Jay-Z Ft. Lil Wayne	2007	"Hello Brooklyn 2.0"	*American Gangster*
Busta Rhymes Ft. Swizz Beatz	2006	"New York shit"	*The Big Bang*
2Pac	1996	"To Live & Die In L.A."	*Don Killuminati: The 7 Day Theory*
Nas	2006	"Where Are They Now"	*Hip Hop Is Dead*
De La Soul	1996	"Wonce Again Long Island"	*Stakes Is High*
Jay-Z Ft. Alicia Keys	2009	"Empire State of Mind"	*The Blueprint 3*
Nas Ft. Will.I.am	2006	"Hip Hop Is Dead"	*Hip Hop Is Dead*
The Roots	2006	"In The Music"	*Game Theory*
Scarface	2002	"On My Block"	*The Fix*
Eve Ft. Beanie Sigel	1999	"Philly, Philly"	*Let There Be Eve: Ruff Ryders' First Lady*
Common & Kanye West	2007	"Southside"	*Finding Forever*
MC Shan	1987	"The Bridge"	*Down By Law*
Nas	2006	"Who Killed It?"	*Hip Hop Is Dead*
Common	2005	"Chi City"	*Be*
-Murs	2006	"L.A."	*Murray's Revenge*
K'naan	2009	"Somalia"	*Troubadour*
Jay-Z Ft. J. Cole	2009	"A Star is Born"	*The Blueprint 3*
Naughty by Nature	1993	"Hip Hop Hooray"	*19 Naughty III*
Lupe Fiasco	2007	"Hip Hop Saved My Life"	*Lupe Fiasco's The Cool*
Lauryn Hill	1998	"I Used To Love Him"	*The Miseducation Of Lauryn Hill*
De La Soul	1996	"Long Island Degrees"	*Stakes Is High*
Blu & Exile	2007	"No Greater Love"	*Below The Heavens*
Rakim	1997	"New York (Ya Out There)"	*The 18th Letter*
Fabolous Ft. Jay-Z & Uncle Murda	2007	"Brooklyn"	*From Nothin To Somethin*

ARTIST	YEAR	TRACK	ALBUM
Dujeous	2004	"City Limits"	*City Limits*
Little Brother Ft. Big Daddy Kane	2005	"Welcome to Durham"	*The Chitlin Circuit 1.5*
2Pac	1995	"Old School"	*Me Against The World*
Mos Def	1999	"Brooklyn"	*Black On Both Sides*
Ludacris Ft. Nas & Jay-Z	2008	"I Do It For Hip Hop"	*Theater Of The Mind*
Jay-Z	1997	"Where I'm From"	*In My Lifetime, Vol. 1*
Arrested Development	1992	"Tennessee"	*3 Years, 5 Months And 2 Days In The Life Of …*
Redman	2001	"Bricks Two"	*Malpractice*
Capone-n-Noreaga	1997	"L.a., L.a." (Kuwait Mix by Marley Marl)	*The War Report*
Onyx	1995	"Walk In New York"	All We Got Iz Us
KRS-One	2003	"Hip Hop Vs. Rap"	*D.I.G.I.T.A.L.*
Common	1994	"I Used To Love H.E.R."	*Resurrection*
Alicia Keys ft. Nas & Rakim	2003	"Streets Of N.Y."	*The Diary of Alicia Keyes*
Nas	2000	"Da Bridge 2001" (Alternate Verse)	*QB's Finest Hip Hop*

A political unconscious of Hip-Hop playlist

ARTIST	YEAR	TRACK	ALBUM
Random	2006	Still Ain't Good Enough"	*The Call*
Mod Def	2006	"Dollar Day"	*True Magic*
Jay-Z Ft. Ne-Yo	2006	"Minority Report"	*Kingdom Come*
DJ Drama & Lil Wayne	2006	"Georgia … Bush and Weezy's ambitionz"	*Dedication 2*

The repetition (as a figure) playlist

ARTIST	YEAR	TRACK	ALBUM
The Roots	1999	"Act Won (Things Fall Apart)"	*Things Fall Apart*
Black Moon	1993	"Buck Em Down" (Instrumental)	*Buck Em Down*

ARTIST	YEAR	TRACK	ALBUM
Lauryn Hill	1998	"Lost Ones"	*The Miseducation Of Lauryn Hill*
Immortal Technique	2003	"The Point Of No Return"	*Revolutionary (Vol. 2)*
Jay-Z	2002	"Jay-Z Meet The Parents"	*The Blueprint 2: The Curse*
Jay-Z Ft. Chrisette Michele	2006	"Lost One"	*Kingdom Come*
Pharoahe Monch	2007	"Welcome To The Terrordome"	*Desire*
Ghostface Killah	1996	"Motherless Child"	*Ironman*
Jay-Z Feat. Ne-Yo	2006	"Minority Report"	*Kingdom Come*
Lauryn Hill	1998	"Miseducation Of Lauryn Hill"	*The Miseducation Of Lauryn Hill*

The suicide dayz playlist

ARTIST	YEAR	TRACK	ALBUM
Scarface	2007	"The Suicide Note"	*Made*
Nas	2004	"Suicide Bounce"	*Street's Disciple*
Lupe Fiasco Ft. MDMA	2011	"Beautiful Lasers (2 Ways)"	*Lasers*
Gravediggaz	1997	"1-800 Suicide"	*6 Feet Deep*
The Notorious B.I.G.	1994	"Suicidal Thoughts"	*Ready To Die [Bonus Tracks]*
Redman	2007	"Suicide"	*Red Gone Wild Thee Album*

The most likely to be sampled playlist

ARTIST	YEAR	TRACK	ALBUM
Incredible Bongo Band	1973	"Apache"	*Bongo Rock*
George Clinton	1982	"Atomic Dog"	*Computer Games*
Sly & The Family Stone	1969	"Sing A Simple Song"	*Stand!*
Lyn Collins	1998	"Think (About It)"	*James Brown's Original Funky Divas*
James Brown	1973	"The Payback"	*The Payback*

ARTIST	YEAR	TRACK	ALBUM
James Brown	1974	"Funky President (People It's Bad)"	*Reality*
Skull Snaps	2005	"It's a New Day"	*Snapped*
James Brown	1986	"Funky Drummer"	*In The Jungle Groove (Compilation)*
Bob James	1974	"Nautilus"	*One*
Ultimate Breaks & Beats	2008	"Synthetic Substitution"	*Instrumentals*
Kool & The Gang	1971	"N.T."	*Live at PJ's*

Twitter rap narratives

ARTIST	YEAR	TRACK	ALBUM
Big Boi Ft. Vonnegutt	2010	"Follow us"	*Sir Lucious Left Foot… The Son Of Chico Dusty*
-Eric B & Rakim	1988	"Follow the Leader"	*Follow the Leader*
K-os	2002	"Follow Me"	*Exit*
Birdman Ft. Freeway	2010	"Follow My Moves"	*The Stimulus Package*
M.O.P.	2000	"Follow Instructions"	*Warriorz*
Lupe Fiasco	2007	"Put You On Game"	*Lupe Fiasco's The Cool*

Weapon metaphors in Hip Hop

ARTIST	YEAR	TRACK	ALBUM
Public Enemy	1987	"Miuzi Weighs A Ton"	*Yo! Bum Rush The Show*
Nas	1996	"I Gave You Power"	*It Was Written*
Gunshow Blues	DATE?		*Welcome to the Gunshow*
Jay Electronica	2011	"Uzi Weighs A Ton"	*What The F*ck Is A Jay Electronica*
Pharoahe Monch	2007	"When The Gun Draws Featuring Mr. Porter"	*Desire*
2Pac	1996	"Me And My Girlfriend"	*Don Killuminati: The 7 Day Theory*

Notes

Introduction

1 In the summer of 2015, Philadelphia rapper Meek Mill "broke the internet" with assertions that Drake uses ghost writers and is not the sole author of his own lyrics. This claim and the social media fallout from it further underscore the commoditized nature of rap lyrics but also points to the importance of authorship in the Hip-Hop universe.

Chapter 1

1 Alex Haley, *Roots: The Saga of an American Family* (New York: Doubleday, 1976).
2 *Roots*, television miniseries, January 23–30, 1997.
3 The Sugarhill Gang, "Rapper's Delight," in *Sugarhill Gang*, Sugar Hill Records (1979).
4 Chic, "Good Times," in *Risqué*, Atlantic Records (1979).
5 The Fatback Band, "King Tim III (Personality Jock)," in *Fatback XII* (1979).
6 James Brown, "Funky Drummer," in *In the Jungle Groove,* King Records (1970).
7 James Brown, "Funky President (People It's Bad)," in *Reality*, Polydor Records (1974).
8 Explain the entomology of "bling bling."
9 Grandmaster Flash and the Furious Five, "The Message," in *The Message*, Sugar Hill Records (1982).
10 Run–D.M.C, "Proud to be Black," in *Raising Hell*, Profile Records (1986).
11 Boogie Down Productions, "Self-Destruction," in *Stop the Violence Movement*, Jive Records (1989).
12 Boogie Down Productions, "Why Is That?" in *Ghetto Music: The Blueprint of Hip Hop*, Jive Records (1989).
13 KRS-One, "Black Cop," in *Return of the Boom Bap*, Jive Records (1993).
14 Public Enemy, "Can't Truss It," in *Apocalypse 91…The Enemy Strikes Black*, Def Jam Recordings (1991).
15 Public Enemy, "Shut 'Em Down," in *Apocalypse 91…The Enemy Strikes Black*, Def Jam Recordings (1991).
16 Public Enemy, "911 Is a Joke," in *Fear of a Black Planet*, Def Jam Recordings (1990).
17 David Toop, *Rap Attack 3: African Rap to Global Hip Hop* (London: Serpent's Tail, 2000).
18 Including Tricia Rose, *Black Noise: Rap Music and Black Culture in Contemporary America* (Hanover, NH: Wesleyan University Press, 1994); and Houston Baker, *Black Studies, Rap, and the Academy* (Chicago: University of Chicago Press, 1993).

19 Baker, *Black Studies, Rap, and the Academy*.

20 Zora Neal Hurston, "The Characteristics of Negro Exrpession." In *The Norton Anthology of African American Literature*, ed. Henry Louis Gates and Nellie McKay, 2nd edn (New York: W. W. Norton, 2004), 1041–53.

21 Imani Perry, *Prophets from the Hood: Politics and Poetics in Hip Hop* (Durham: Duke University Press, 2004).

22 Rose, *Black Noise: Rap Music and Black Culture in Contemporary America*, 1994.

23 Charlie Aheam, *Wild Style*, directed by Charlie Aheam (1982; New York: Submarine Entertainment, 1983).

24 Alex Ogg and David Upshal, *The Hip Hop Years: A History of Rap* (New York: Fromm International, 2001).

25 In the late stages of the publication of this work, several serious allegations have been made against Afrika Bambaataa. If any of these are true, any claim regarding his embrace of non-violence in the culture must be adjusted accordingly. That said, it is beyond the purview of this essay to judge him based on these allegations at this time.

26 Selwyn Hinds, *Gunshots in My Cook-Up: Bits and Bites from a Hip-hop Caribbean Life* (New York: Atria Books, 2002).

27 Byron Hurt, *Hip-Hop: Beyond Beats & Rhymes* (PBS Indies, 2007).

28 Nelly, "Tip Drill," in *Da Derrty Versions: The Reinvention,* Universal Records (2003).

29 Timothy J. Brown, "Welcome to the Terrordome: Exploring the Contradictions of a Hip-Hop Black Masculinity." In *Progressive Black Masculinities*, ed. A. D. Mutua (New York: Routledge, 2006), 191–213.

30 Todd, Boyd. *The New H. N. I. C.: The Death of Civil Rights and the Reign of Hip Hop.* (New York: New York University Press, 2003), 5.

31 Brown, "Welcome to the Terrordome," 193–4.

32 Ibid., 194.

33 James G. Spady, Samir Meghelli, and H. Samy Alim, *Tha Global Cipha: Hip Hop Culture and Consciousness* (Philadelphia: Black History Museum Press, 2006), 264.

34 Ibid., 264.

35 Linden Lewis and Glyne Griffith, with Elizabeth Crespo-Kebler, *Color, Hair, and Bone: Race in the Twenty-First Century* (Lewisburg: Bucknell University Press, 2008), 47.

36 Jeff Chang, *Can't Stop, Won't Stop: A History of the Hip-Hop Generation* (New York: St Martin's Press, 2005), 70–1.

37 Ogg and Upshal, *The Hip Hop Years*, 23.

38 Lewis et al., *Color, Hair, and Bone: Race in the Twenty-First Century*, 47.

39 Ogg and Upshal, *The Hip Hop Years*, 14.

40 Chang, *Can't Stop, Won't Stop*, 91.

41 Ibid., 93.

42 Dick Hebdige, *Cut 'n' Mix: Culture, Identity and Caribbean Music* (London: Methuen, 1987), 138.

43 Lewis et al., *Color, Hair, and Bone: Race in the Twenty-First Century*, 47.

44 Nelson George, *Hip Hop America* (New York: Viking Penguin, 1998), 16.

45 Steven Hagar, "Afrika Bambaataa's Hip Hop," in Raquel Cepeda (ed.), *And It Don't Stop: The Best American Hip Hop Journalism of the Last 25 Years* (New York: Faber and Faber, Inc., 2004), 13.

46 Ogg and Upshal, *The Hip Hop Years*, 17.
47 George, *Hip Hop America*, 19.
48 Don Simpson and Jerry Bruckheimer, *Flashdance*, directed by Adrian Lyne
    (1983; Hollywood, CA: Paramount Pictures).
49 Charlie Aheam, *Wild Style*, directed by Charlie Aheam (1982; New York:
    Submarine Entertainment, 1983).

Chapter 2

1 The Sugarhill Gang, "Rapper's Delight," in *Sugarhill Gang*, Sugar Hill Records
   (1979).
2 Geneva Smitherman, *Talkin that Talk: Language, Culture, and Education in
   African America* (New York: Routledge, 2001), 150–62.
3 Here is a brief note derived (and paraphrased) from one such discussion. "To
   preface, let me say a couple of things about Wiz Khalifa, because I do a lot of
   work in Pittsburgh, and this community work shapes my evaluation of Wiz,
   because I work with inner city high school kids in Pittsburgh. For those of you
   who are not aware of what inner city Pittsburgh is like, the residential structures
   are eroding, the public school systems are failing, and the residents are faced
   with a lot of social challenges that are exacerbated by the fact that the economic
   stability of Pittsburgh has been waning for a long time. So, Pittsburgh is,
   especially in the kind of neighborhoods that I grew up in, struggling in a lot of
   poignant ways. As per my rubric, I always want to think about these artists and
   where they are from.
       My rating for Wiz Khalifa regarding Lyrical Flow and Content (which ranges
   on a scale from one to ten), is a six. My rating for Wiz regarding the Dual
   Rhythmic Relationship is seven and a half out of ten. Now this number, I hope,
   will go up when I actually hear more. He has been doing a lot of college touring
   and I have been viewing his performances on tape. For his Artistic Persona (his
   artistic and aesthetic presentation), I gave him an eight. My reasoning behind
   this score is really quite simple. First, he is distinctly tatted. In fact, his entire
   upper body is covered with ink. Secondly, Wiz Khalifa is an avid smoker of
   marijuana. Certainly, I am not encouraging or promoting this behavior, but
   there are a couple of things that I am able to appreciate about his approach:
   (1) He embraces it as a part of his artistic identity; and (2) The trends in the ideas
   about smoking marijuana in this country are changing. So, in the most positive
   interpretation of this behavior, I am thinking of him as being on the cusp of that
   change. More importantly, he advocates messages of health in his songs that are
   often overlooked. Unlike his rapping contemporaries—many of whom seem to
   glamorize drug use—Wiz Khalifa urges us to smoke 'papers' instead of blunts.
   In fact, he is actually selling his own brand of papers. Now, you might think that
   his promotion of smoking papers (or anything at all) is equally harmful. That
   criticism may be totally warranted, but the fact remains that smoking papers
   is a slightly safer alternative than smoking blunts—and Wiz recognizes that.

I appreciate those facets of his artistic persona. I am deeply interested in what level of consciousness an artist is trying to cultivate in their audience. For me, it seems like Wiz is investing in this consciousness. His surname for his rap moniker, Khalifa, was given to him by his grandfather. So, his artistic persona is the highest rating I gave him, which earned eight out of ten. For Historical Knowledge and Respect, I gave him seven out of ten. For me, historical knowledge and respect is acknowledging the MCs that influence you. For Wiz, a lot of times, he goes to his crew, which is Taylor Gang, and he goes to Mel. If you guys are unfamiliar with Mel, he is an old school producer from Pittsburgh. Wiz Khalifa has also collaborated with Big Snoop and gestures towards Snoop with the kind of respect that any artist would afford his or her most influential mentors. Wiz has a sense of the immediate history in his environment, but I am not sure if he has a sense of the broader history of the environment and the ways in which other artists reflect him. Finally, for the fifth category, Space and Place, I gave Wiz five out of ten. This is my lowest rating for him and that is because even though 'Black and Yellow' is about the Pittsburgh Steelers, I am still not sure if Wiz has done a good job representing Pittsburgh. For all of my work in Pittsburgh, and all of those young people facing all of those challenges, I am not sure if he has done a good enough job genuinely representing them and their struggle. Now, maybe he consciously chooses not to represent that, but in terms of my rubric for space and place, it is a fundamental element in Hip Hop."

4   I teach a course entitled "Women's Voices in Hip Hop Culture" that attempts to explore these issues directly and more deeply. The syllabus is available in the appendix to this book.

5   T. Denean Sharpley-Whiting, *Pimps Up, Ho's Down: Hip Hop's Hold on Young Black Women* (New York University Press, 2007).

6   Nelly, "Tip Drill," in *Da Derrty Versions: The Reinvention*, Universal Records (2003).

7   Nicki Minaj, "Cuchi Shop," in *Sucka Free*, Dirty Money Records (2008).

8   Snoop Dogg, "Beautiful," in *Paid tha Cost to Be da Boss*, Doggystyle Records (2003).

9   Finally, for Space and Place, Nicki Minaj earned a six mostly because she chooses not to represent New York City in her songs and only occasionally references her Trinidadian roots. Nicki may have severed her New York roots in order to achieve international stardom through a label (Cash Money Records) that established itself based upon the rise of New Orleans rappers and producers, most notably, Lil Wayne.

10 In the latter half of 2014, Lil' Kim, released "dis" track directed at Nicki Minaj's collaboration on Beyonce's hit single, "Flawless." She clearly still has great lyrical skills but it is also clear that the positioning of women in the popular spaces afforded to them in Hip Hop is extremely limited. Her issue is on point as well. Her claim is that Nicki Minaj stole her style. And I agree.

11 Morgan, Joan, *When Chickenheads Come Home to Roost: A Hip Hop Feminist Breaks it Down* (New York: Simon and Schuster, 2000).

12 In addition to some of the artists and songs that are frequently mentioned during my classes, I want to briefly share a couple of records and books that

are particularly noteworthy. First is a record by John Legend and The Roots called *Wake Up!* The liner notes are extraordinary. Not only do they divulge the history of each song, but they explain it to you based upon how the song has been sampled and used within Hip Hop. As such, you have an album that is a throwback to socially conscious 1970s music, with liner notes that explicate the ways this music has been reused in Hip-Hop culture. In terms of animated productions, Aaron McGruder's Boondocks is the best satire that Hip Hop has ever produced. In general the banned episodes reveal McGruder in his most acerbic critique of Black culture icons—BET's Debra Lee and MLK and/ or R. Kelly. These episodes are some of the smartest ones—the most socially compelling. And finally Jay-Z's *Decoded*, co-written by activist and journalist dream hampton, *Decoded* is the strongest self-interpretive text produced by a Hip-Hop artist.

13   Evie Shockley, *Renegade Poetics: Black Aesthetics and Formal Innovation in African American Poetry* (Iowa City: University of Iowa Press, 2011), 13.

14   J. A. Cuddon, *The Penguin Dictionary of Literary Terms and Literary Theory* (New York: Penguin Books, 1998), 835.

15   Laurence Perrine and Thomas R. Arp, *Sound and Sense: An Introduction to Poetry* [Eighth Edition] (Orlando, FL: Harcourt & Brace Company, 1991), 375.

16   AAE or more accurately here African American Vernacular English or AAVE is the variety of English spoken by African Americans complete with its own set of rules—a grammar—replete with deep structures and the full set of linguistics that adhere to standard and/or vernacular languages.

17   The "who's your favorite rapper" question can be so limiting, but in response to it I often name four to five artists that I really enjoy—and by enjoy I mean critically engage their lyrics across multiple albums and performances. First, I am a huge fan of Nas. I have major respect for his music—especially his more substantive found on all of his records but *Hip Hop is Dead* and the *Untitled* album have more than a few gems on them. Nas is one of the most prolific and maybe the most influential rapper(s) Hip Hop has ever produced. Second, is Black Thought, who is the lead MC from the Philadelphia-based Hip-Hop group, The Roots. He is an exceptional artist, and on some records, he is more powerful than some of the most popular mainstream of any given era of Hip Hop. Third on my list is Lauryn Hill. She is one of Hip Hop's most brilliant lyricists and her artistic commitment to addressing social justice issues is both intense and consistent over the course of her career. And as I have mentioned before and throughout *Headphones*, Lupe Fiasco, Kendrick Lamar, and Rapsody are all favorites of mine. Honorable mention goes to an artist by the name of Blu. Consumers of mainstream Hip-Hop music might not know Blu, but he is an extraordinary underground artist from Los Angeles. There are two albums I would recommend: *Below the Heavens* (2007) and *Johnson & Johnson* (2008). I am not exaggerating when I say that these are two of the best records produced in the last ten years. Unlike his underground contemporaries, he is not an overtly "conscious" rapper. He does not have a lot of socially conscious material, but his mastery of rap poetics is complete. If forced to choose just one artist, I often turn to Lupe Fiasco. I feel like what Lupe does is extraordinary because he can, as a

lyricist, be in an authentic environment and still maintain his own identity. Very few rappers can do that. Several songs showcase his ability to do this including "Dumb it Down," "Put You on Game," "Two Ways," and "Mural." Listen to how he personifies the evil entities in our society in these songs for proof of his lyrical ingenuity. Lupe Fiasco, like many of the artists mentioned in these pages, has the potential to project what is most important about Hip Hop—which for me involves poetics and social consciousness. Many of the college students I have encountered love Lupe, but Lupe is not a top-selling, mainstream artist and he never will be. The reason why I think he is one of the best artists (especially in the last ten years) is based on his excellence in the craft of rhyming.

Chapter 3

1   Carlton A. Usher, *A Rhyme is a Terrible Thing to Waste: Hip Hop and the Creation of a Political Philosophy* (Trenton, NJ: Africa World Press: 2006), 25.
2   The Notorious B.I.G., "Sky's the Limit," on *Life After Death* [Disc 2], Bad Boy Records (1997).
3   Horatio Alger Myth.
4   The Sugarhill Gang, "Rapper's Delight," in *Sugarhill Gang*, Sugar Hill Records (1979).
5   The turntable was transformed from a machine that played recorded music into an instrument that produced original sounds through scratching. Cardboard boxes were used as stages and/or dance mats for b-girls and b-boys, while brick walls became canvases for Hip-Hop graffiti artists.
6   Being able to purchase a rap record in a store was a privilege in the old school era of Hip Hop. If you wanted to participate in the culture, you had to be a b-boy or b-girl—that is, you had to BE there or you had to borrow a tape from one of your friends or go to a local party where DJs played the music. There was a tangible immediacy to the culture that generated a powerful communal vibe that in turn made the culture infectious to young people. Class consciousness and class distinctions operated in the culture and the music with blurred lines of distinction and a deliberate sense that the class categories of the early-mid twentieth century were inadequate estimations of the economic world inherited by the Hip-Hop generation(s).
7   Around the mid-1980s we are introduced to the members of Run–D.M.C. for the first time. Admittedly, Run–D.M.C. has done more for Hip Hop than any other group within the culture, although that was probably not their intention. Given that the members of Run–D.M.C. were all middle-class guys who went to college, they were not particularly invested in articulating and/or portraying a low or working-class experience. Still, they shaped the culture from a middle-class perspective in profound and unprecedented ways. Consider the brands that they wore—Adidas, most notably—and it becomes clear that they changed the aesthetic of the culture. The fact that Run–D.M.C. revolutionized Hip Hop's fashion sense is another class narrative worth explicating. Without digressing

too much, consider the famous song, "My Adidas" by Run–D.M.C. One thing that Hip Hop is often critiqued for is its exaggerated promotion of consumerism and materialism. The narrative of poor people of color spending beyond their means is one with which the world of Hip Hop is unfortunately familiar. Consider how the kid from a single-parent household who lives in the projects (and is a recipient of welfare) can possibly afford to spend $200 on a new pair of Michael Jordan sneakers. This kind of pejorative narrative is the unfortunate byproduct of a certain responses to Hip-Hop culture. Essentially, artisans of Hip Hop took these ashy items and made them classy. Again, we can attribute that shift in fashion (at least, partially) to Run–D.M.C. and "My Adidas." Eventually, an Adidas executive got word of this and attended a Run–D.M.C. show. Soon after, they offered Run–D.M.C. what happened to be the first endorsement deal in Hip-Hop culture. I mark that as an important shift—a poignant progression from ashy to classy—because essentially, you went from rappers mentioning name brands in songs just because, to getting paid to mention name brands in songs. That is a significant moment in Hip-Hop culture in terms of artistic production that we need to account for.

8   Recent *New York Times* article on the confluence of mass incarceration, homicide rates, police brutality—that is, early death of Black men—produces an aggregate impact on communities like Baltimore, Ferguson, and Charleston.
9   Referring here to the Michael Brown and Eric Garner cases—all officers involved with these murders were not indicted in the grand jury processes—on in New York/Staten Island and the other in Ferguson, Missouri.
10   The debacle at McKinney, Texas, pool party, June 2015.
11   Christopher Holmes Smith, "Bling Was a Bubble," *International Journal of Communication*, vol. 3 (2009), 274–6.
12   Kendrick Lamar, Rebel Diaz, Lupe Fiasco, Rapsody, Rhymefest, and Talib Kweli, among many others.
13   Smith, *International Journal of Communication*, 274–6.
14   Dick Hebdige, *Cut 'N' Mix: Culture, Identity and Caribbean Music* (New York: Routledge: 1987), 136.
15   The Roots, "What They Do," in *Illadelph Halflife*, MCA Records (1996).
16   Ahmir Thompson and Ben Greenman, *Mo' Meta Blues: The World According to Questlove* (New York: Hachette Book Group, 2013), 146.
17   Ibid., 135.
18   Ibid., 146.

Chapter 4

1   Christopher Hooton, "Hip-hop is the most listened to genre in the world, according to Spotify analysis of twenty billion tracks." http://www.independent. co.uk/arts-entertainment/music/news/hiphop-is-the-most-listened-to-genre-in-the-world-according-to-spotify-analysis-of-20-billion-tracks-10388091.html last accessed July 14, 2015.

2   Saadiah Yahya, Erny Arniza Ahmad and Kamarularifin Abd Jalil, "The definition and characteristics of ubiquitous learning: A discussion," *International Journal of Education and Development using Information and Communication Technology (IJEDICT)* 6, no. 1 (2010): 117–27.

3   Vicki Jones and Jun H. Jo, "Ubiquitous learning environment: An adaptive teaching system using ubiquitous technology." In R. Atkinson, C. McBeath, D. Jonas-Dwyer and R. Phillips (eds), *Beyond the comfort zone: Proceedings of the 21st ASCILITE Conference*, 468–74. Perth, December 5–8, 2010. http://www.ascilite.org.au/conferences/perth04/procs/jones.html

4   Consider the popular weekly conversation on Twitter—#HipHopEd. Every Tuesday at 9:00 pm Hip-Hop scholars, artists, activists, and teachers from all levels participated in pointed virtual conversations about the impact and import of Hip Hop as an educational phenomenon.

5   Joseph Schloss, *Making Beats: The Art of Sample-Based Hip-Hop* (Middletown: Wesleyan University Press, 2004).

6   The Roots, "Act Won (Things Fall Apart)," in *Things Fall Apart*, MCA Records (1999).

7   Chinua Achebe, *Things Fall Apart* (London: William Heinemann Ltd., 1958).

8   Wu-Tang Clan, "Motherless Child," in *Ironman*, Epic Records (1996).

9   Jay-Z, "Meet the Parents," in *The Blueprint2:The Gift & The Curse*, Def Jam Recordings (2002).

10 Immortal Technique, "The Point of No Return," in *Revolutionary Vol. 2*, Viper Records (2003).

11 Immortal Technique, "The Point of No Return."

12 Jay-Z, "Minority Report," in *Kingdom Come*, Def Jam Recordings (2006).

13 Public Enemy, "Welcome to the Terrordome," in *Fear of a Black Planet*, Def Jam Recordings (1990).

14 Lauryn Hill, "Lost Ones," in *The Miseducation of Lauryn Hill*, Ruffhouse Records (1998).

15 Jay-Z, "Lost One," in *Kingdom Come*, Def Jam Recordings (2006).

16 Lauryn Hill, *The Miseducation of Lauryn Hill*, Ruffhouse Records (1998).

17 Carter G. Woodson, *The Mis-Education of the Negro* (Trenton, NJ: Africa World Press, 1990).

18 There are different points of pedagogical entry between college classrooms and correctional facilities. For example, I taught at a university located in central Pennsylvania. There are multiple prisons and correctional facilities in the region. I volunteered in several of those systems for the three-plus years that I lived there. In terms of my volunteer time, I typically prefer to deal more with the youth who are in the system. The young males in one correctional facility in which I volunteered were not allowed to rap. There were signs posted around the facility that read, "No rapping in here." But, when I was there, they were able to rap a little bit, and I was often surprised by the level of sophistication with which they understood the music. Usually, what happens is that I have to allow them to teach me about the music that I hate, because the music they listen to is not music that I necessarily like.

    Gradually, I employed this playlist pedagogy within the correctional facility. I said, "Make me a mixed tape. Essentially, make me a playlist of your favorite stuff" and they gave me playlists full of Lil Wayne, Young Jeezy, and T. I. Mind you, most of this music talks about the streets and hustling. So, what I was challenged to do, in turn, was to remove my academic, didactic cap and spend some time unbiasedly engaging these playlists. Upon listening to these tracks with an open, rather than critical ear, I found that there is a lot more depth and substance to their music than I had previously anticipated.

The music on their playlist was not necessarily the same music that we hear on the radio. They had different album cuts and honestly, they all had music that spoke to their individual situations and circumstances. I mean, they are in jail (in some cases for crimes of violence, and/or violence perpetrated against them), and drug trafficking. We have a very aggressive incarceration system, and a lot of the music that I try to steer clear from is the music that so perfectly articulates the experiences of the people who are caught up in that aggressive system. What I had failed to consider, however, was that it was a constructive way of working through, and coming to terms with, their experiences. College classes, on the other hand—the elite majority of white college classrooms—are a little bit different. I have two exercises that I do with them. For example, a couple weeks back, I had to give a talk somewhere, where I had to use Hip-Hop songs that articulated urban experiences. So, I have a public speaking class that has nothing to do with Hip Hop, but I asked them to create a playlist for me. They must have given me a hundred songs, but I think the playlist ultimately was comprised of just five songs. But the excitement and energy around that collaboration was empowering for all of us. Most of the inmates are from Philadelphia, Newark, and Danville. Most of them will have a chance to get out and live freely. Almost all of the men I mentor, if you will, will have a second chance to get it right. Ironically, though, the music that they brought to me for our sessions was not celebratory. It did not reflect or celebrate their impending freedom. It kind of fingered the grain of it. In hindsight, the only thing it may have celebrated was the consumer's aspect of it. There was not much celebration of the violence or the misogyny. It is interesting because the music that we see in the mainstream is not necessarily the music that young people think is the most important.

What I came to realize is that my bias against that glorification is also always affecting younger people more than it should. In the reality, seven- to eight-year-old kids are unfortunately confronted with some horrific circumstances, and sometimes the words of these artists are helping them to wrestle with those situations. In that particular example, they brought me stuff that was substantive, most likely because we had already been having substantive discussions. So, they knew they better come with something that we can seriously talk about; otherwise I would probably be very dismissive. I understand that my dismissive demeanor is off-putting, but what I hope they understand is that I do it because it challenges them to broaden their horizons and recognize the many complex ways that Hip Hop shapes the world. We can certainly have any number of discourses around it, so why not have some constructive ones? But those particular citizens of the correctional facility understood the "game" a bit, and their lived experiences gave us more substance in that talk. In fact, the college students are the ones more inclined to give me the less substantive playlists. More often than not, they select songs that celebrate what is worst about Hip-Hop culture—that is, songs that are full of materialistic and misogynistic sentiments.

Chapter 5

1   Beastie Boys, "Slow and Low," in *Licensed to Ill*, Def Jam Recordings (1986).

2   Run–D.M.C., "King of Rock," in *King of Rock*, Arista Records Inc. (1985).

3   Beastie Boys, "(You Gotta) Fight for Your Right (To Party!)," in *Licensed to Ill*, Def Jam Recordings (1986).

4   Beastie Boys, "Paul Revere," in *Licensed to Ill*, Def Jam Recordings (1986).

5   Beastie Boys, *Licensed to Ill*, Def Jam Recordings (1986).

6   Beastie Boys, *Paul's Boutique*, Capitol Records (1989).

7   Beastie Boys, *Check Your Head*, Capitol Records (1992).

8   Beastie Boys, *Ill Communication*, Capitol Records (1994).

9   Beastie Boys, *Hello Nasty*, Capitol Records (1998).

10 Beastie Boys, *To the 5 Boroughs*, Capitol Records (2007).

11 Beastie Boys, *The Mix-Up*, Capitol Records (2007).

12 Beastie Boys, *Hot Sauce Committee Part Two*, Capitol Records (2011).

13 Damian Jones, "Beasties promise 'strange' record." Published February 23, 2009. http://news.bbc.co.uk/2/hi/entertainment/7906287.stm (Accessed January 30, 2016).

14 Ruth Manuel-Logan, "Black Conspiracy Theories 101: Did Elvis Presley Say 'The Only Thing Negroes Can Do For Me Is Buy My Records, Shine My Shoes'?" http://newsone.com/2067452/black-urban-legends-elvis-presley-racist/ (Acccessed February 1, 2016).

15 Vanilla Ice, *Ice Ice Baby*, in *To the Extreme*, SBK Records (1990).

16 Queen and David Bowie, "Under Pressure," in *Hot Space*, EMI Group Limited (1981).

17 Vanilla Ice, *To the Extreme*, SKB Records (1990).

18 David Kellogg, *Cool as Ice* (Universal Pictures, 1991).

19 Vanilla Ice, *Extremely Live*, SKB Records (1991).

20 3rd Bass, *The Cactus Album*, Def Jam Recordings (1989).

21 3rd Bass, "The Gas Face," in *The Cactus Album*, Def Jam Recordings (1989).

22 Ibid.

23 3rd Bass, *Derelicts of Dialect*, Def Jam Recordings (1991).

24 3rd Bass, "Pop Goes the Weasel," in *Derelicts of Dialect*, Def Jam Recordings (1991).

25 MC Serch, *Return of the Product*, Def Jam Recordings (1992).

26 MC Serch, *Many Young Lives Ago: The 1994 Sessions*, Serchlite (2007).

27 *Ego Trip's The (White) Rapper Show*. VH1, Mike Taylor, dr. MC Serch, host. Produced by Ken Mok/10x10 Entertainment (January 8, 2007 to February 26, 2007).

28 Marshall Mathers and Sacha Jenkins, *The Way I Am* (New York: Plume, 2009), 33.

29 Curtis Hanson, *8 Mile*, directed by Curtis Hanson (2002; Los Angeles, CA: Imagine Entertainment, 2002).

30 Eminem, *The Way I Am* (Boston, MA: Dutton Penguin, 2008).

31 Eminem, *The Marshall Mathers LP*, Interscope Records Inc. (2000).

32 Eminem, "The Way I Am," in *The Marshall Mathers LP*, Interscope Records Inc. (2000).

33 Mathers and Jenkins, *The Way I Am*, 33.

34 Eminem, "Like Toy Soldiers," in *Encore*, Interscope Records Inc. (2005).
35 Michael Eric Dyson, *White Reign: Deploying Whiteness in America*, ed. Joe Kincheloe et al. (New York: Palgrave Macmillan Ltd., 1998), 299–328.
36 Ibid., 37.

Chapter 6

1 Adam Mansbach, *Rage is Back* (New York: Viking Penguin, 2013).
2 Homer, *The Odyssey*, trans. by Robert Fitzgerald, 1963.
3 Mansbach, *Rage is Back*, 1–2.
4 Ibid., 28.

Chapter 7

1 Eithne Quinn, *Nuthin' but a "G" Thang: The Culture and Commerce of Gangsta Rap* (New York: Columbia University Press, 2013).
2 N.W.A., "Fuck tha Police," in *Straight Outta Compton*, Priority Records (1988).
3 Tupac Shakur, "Dear Mama," in *Me Against the World*, Interscope Records Inc. (1995).
4 Quinn, *Nuthin' but a "G" Thang*, 15.
5 Ibid.
6 John Singleton, *Boys n the Hood*, directed by John Singleton (1991; Los Angeles, CA: Columbia Pictures Industries, Inc., 1991).
7 Quinn, *Nuthin' but a "G" Thang*, 7.
8 Ibid., 17.
9 John Roberts, *From Trickster to Badman: The Black Folk Hero in Slavery and Freedom* (Philadelphia: UPENN Press, 1989), 174.

Chapter 8

1 Michael Rapaport, *Beats, Rhymes & Life: The Travels of A Tribe Called Quest* (New York City, NY: Sony Pictures Classics, 2011).
2 A Tribe Called Quest, *Beats, Rhymes & Life*, Jive Records (1996).
3 A Tribe Called Quest, *The Love Movement*, Jive Records (1998).

Chapter 9

1 Janks Morton, "What Black Men Think," (Iyago Entertainment Group, 2007).
2 In the interest of full disclosure here, I must say that I appear on Fox News regularly. However, I am not paid to do so, and I am ALWAYS debating one (or all) of the hosts and/or conservative pundits on their "news" programs.

Chapter 10

1   Tim Wise, *Colorblind: The Rise of Post-Racial Politics and the Retreat from Racial Equity* (San Francisco: City Lights Books, 2010).
2   In *African American Viewers and the Black Situation Comedy: Situating Racial Humor* (2000), Robin R. Means Coleman discusses hyperracial humor as a way of thinking about the way race is depicted in Black situation comedies. Although the focus of book is the Black situation comedy, it introduces the concept of hyperracial in a meaningful and useful way for scholars invested in debunking the myth of popular culture being postracial.
3   Although many scholars discuss Hip Hop as masculine music, Imani Perry's *Prophets of the Hood: Politics and Poetics in Hip Hop* (Durham, NC: Duke University Press, 2004) presents one of the most compelling arguments for this gendered framing of Hip-Hop music.
4   For further discussion of the iconicity theory, please see Nicole Fleetwood's study *Troubling Vision: Performance, Visuality, and Blackness* (Chicago: University Chicago Press, 2011).
5   White female rappers, Kreayshawn and V-Nasty, encountered significant backlash for their usage of "nigga/nigger" in their lyrics. White female rapper, Iggy Azalea referred to herself a "runaway slave master," in the song "D.R.U.G.S." She later clarified and then apologized to anyone offended by her identifying herself as a slave-master.
6   Treva Lindsey, "Black No More: Skin Bleaching and the Emergence of New Negro Womanhood," *The Journal of Pan African Studies* 4, no. 4 (2011): 96–115. Special Issue; Global White Supremacy and Skin Bleaching *in Africa and Her Diaspora*, June 2011.
7   Margaret Hunter, "The Persistent Problem of Colorism: Skin Tone, Status, and Inequality," *Sociology Compass* 1, no. 1 (2007): 237–54.
8   The collection, *Inequity in the Technopolis: Race, Class, Gender, and the Digital Divide in Austin* (Austin, TX: University of Texas Press, 2012), edited by Joseph Straubhaar, Jeremiah Spence, Zeynep Tufecki, and Roberta G. Lentz critically explores these digital divides in the specific location of Austin, Texas. Although this collection does not speak specifically to the effects of digital divides on popular culture production, it provides a point of departure for further scholarship on these issues to emerge.

Chapter 11

1   Turntablism refers to the whole art of mastering, manipulating and instrumentalizing the turntable—an art form that emerges in the mid-1970s as a direct result of the ingenuity of Hip Hop's earliest artisans like DJ Kool Herc, Grand Wizard Theodore, and Grand Master Flash.
2   Somewhat clumsily articulated (repeatedly) in his apology on the Al Sharpton Radio Show. *New York Times*, nytimes.com. Transcript. "Don Imus on Al Sharpton's Radio Show," April 9, 2007.

3   *Beyond Beats and Rhymes* is an award-winning documentary that premiered on
     PBS mere weeks before the Don Imus scandal exploded on cable news networks.
4   Claude Chastagner, "The Parents' Music Resource Center: From Information
     to Censorship." *Popular Music* 18 (May 1999): 179–92. The PMRC, consisting
     mostly of Washington Wives, that is, the wives of senators and congressmen, was
     initially created to address concerns about the effects of Heavy Metal music on
     the moral constitution of young (white) people in the United States.
5   Chastagner, "The Parents' Music Resource Center: From Information to
     Censorship," 189.
6   Ibid., 181.
7   Amy Binder, "Constructing Racial Rhetoric: Media Depictions of Harm in
     Heavy Metal and Rap Music," *American Sociological Review* 58 (December 1993):
     753–67.
8   Baker, *Black Studies, Rap, and the Academy*, 1993; Binder, "Constructing Racial
     Rhetoric," 1993; and Crenshaw, "Beyond Racism and Misogyny: Black Feminism
     and 2 Live Crew," *Boston Review: A Political and Literary Forum*, 1992.
9   Bakari Kitwana, *The Hip Hop Generation: Young Blacks and the Crisis in African
     American Culture* (New York: Basic Books, 2002).
10 Baker, *Black Studies, Rap, and the Academy*, 1993.
11 Author's name. "Bach, Beethoven ad the (Home)Boys: Censoring Violent Rap
     Music in America." *USC Law Review*, 1993 (Part I, C). Public Enemy certainly
     comes to mind here as does Dead Prez and Immortal Technique.
12 Salikoko S. Mufweme, John R. Rickford, Guy Bailey and John Baugh (eds), *African
     American English: Structure, History, and Use* (London: Routledge, 1998), 230.
13 Supra (Bach, Beethoven and Homeboys).
14 Amy Adler, *What's Left?: Hate Speech, Pornography, and the Problem for Artistic
     Expression*, 84 California L. Rev. 1541, 1499–1572 (1996).
15 T. Denean Sharpley-Whiting, *Pimps Up, Ho's Down: Hip Hop's Hold on Young
     Black Women* (New York University Press, 2007).
16 MSNBC, *MSNBC Live*, April 14, 2007.
17 Propeller, *Snoop Dog: Talking About Ho's that's in the 'Hood*, AOL News/Sports
     Web Site, http://sports.propeller.com/story/2007/04/12
18 Snoop's appearance at an awards show with two women wearing dog collars while
     he held their leashes certainly underscores his unrelenting misogyny, but again,
     people from within the Hip-Hop community were outraged by this and they
     expressed their outrage, on-line, in the media, and judging from Snoop's sluggish
     album sales on this side of 2000, some of us are even speaking with our wallets.
19 CNN LARRY KING LIVE. "Snoop Dogg On Reality, 'Fatherhood', Politics &
     More!" Aired February 1, 2008—21:00 ET.
20 The Black Eyed Peas, "My Humps," in *Monkey Business,* A&M Records (2005).
21 See MSNBC, *supra* n. 5.
22 This important program was also framed in part by the firing of Don Imus and
     the comments that led to his firing.
23 Hip Hop vs. America
24 Nelly, "Tip Drill," in *Da Derrty Versions: The Reinvention,* Universal Records (2003).
25 Andrea Dworkin and Catherine MacKinnon, *Pornography and Civil Rights:
     A New Day for Women's Equality* (1988).

26 Clifton Crais and Pamela Scully, *Sara Baartman and the Hottentot Venus: A Ghost Story and a Biography* (Princeton: Princeton University Press, 2010).
27 Toni Morrison, *Beloved* (London: Penguin Books, 1987).
28 BET, *Hip Hop vs. America*, Episode I, September (2007).
29 See Amy Adler, *supra* n. 13, at 1519.
30 Ibid.
31 DW Griffith—The Birth of a Nation
32 Touré, *I Live in the Hiphop Nation* in *Never Drank the Kool-Aid: Essays*, 333–8, Picador (2006)
33 Michael Eric Dyson defines "femiphobia" as the fear of women expressed in the culture of Hip Hop usually in misogynistic lyrics. He coined the phrase in *Holler if You Hear Me: Searching for Tupac Shakur*, Basic Civitas 2001.
34 See Amy Adler, *supra* n. 13 at 1542.
35 CNN, *Anderson Cooper 360*, July 11, 2007.
36 AP—"Ban on Hip Hop Epithets Endorsed"
37 *The Oprah Winfrey Show*, Town Hall, http:www2.oprah.com/tows/pastshows/200704/tows_past_20070417
38 S. Craig Watkins, *Hip Hop Matters: Politics, Pop Culture, and the Struggle for the Soul of a Movement*, 153 (Beacon Press, 2005).
39 Lupe Fiasco, Lupe Fiasco's The Cool (New York: Atlantic Records, 2007).
40 Lupe Fiasco and Snoop Dogg, "Hi-Definition" in *The Cool*, Atlantic Records (2007).
41 Jay-Z, "Ignorant Shit," in *American Gangster,* Dej Jam Recordings (2007).
42 Jay-Z, American Gangster (New York: Def Jam Records, 2008).
43 *Scarface* (film).
44 CNN, *Anderson Cooper 360*, July 11, 2007.
45 In his groundbreaking Yale Law Journal article entitled: "The Freedom of Imagination: Copyright's Constitutionality," Jed Rubenfeld teases out these problems.
46 The Last Poets, "Niggers Are Scared of Revolution," in *The Last Poets*, East Wind Associates (1970).
47 Chris Rock, *Bring the Pain*. HBO (cable television). Dir., Keith Truesdell. June 1, 1996.
48 The image is in dialogue with an infamous quote from Malcolm X when he queries: "What do you call a Black man with a Ph.D. - a nigger."
49 Jeffrey O. G. Ogbar, *Slouching toward Bork: The Culture Wars and Self-Criticism in Hip-Hop Music*, 30 *Journal of Black Studies*, 181 (November 1999), 164–83.
50 Jeffrey O. G. Ogbar, "Slouching toward Bork: The Culture Wars and Self-Criticism in Hip-Hop Music," *Journal of Black Studies* 30 (November 1999): 164–83.
51 Queen Latifah, "U.N.I.T.Y.," in *Black Reign*, Motown Records (1994).
52 Queen Latifah, "U.N.I.T.Y." Black Reign (1994).
53 Michael Eric Dyson has occasionally referred to himself as a P.I.M.P.—a public intellectual with moral principles.
54 Stanley Crouch, *Hip Hop Takes a Hit*, New York Daily News (January 23, 2005).
55 Three 6 Mafia, "It's Hard Out Here for a Pimp," in *Hustle & Flow Soundtrack*, Atlantic Records (2005).

Chapter 12

1   Houston Baker, *Blues, Ideology, and Afro-American Literature: A Vernacular Theory* (Chicago: University of Chicago Press, 1983).

2   *The Wire* (TV show).

3   Common and The Last Poets, "The Corner," in *Be*, Geffen Records (2005).

4   Michael Eric Dyson coined the term "juvenacracy" in his brilliant collection of essays entitled *Race Rules*. It refers to urban communities that are dominated by youth who are emboldened and empowered by their status in various and nefarious underground economies.

5   Davis, 292.

6   "We got our thing, but it's just part of the big thing" (4.08).

7   Elijah Anderson, *Code of the Street: Decency, Violence, and the Moral Life of the Inner City* (New York: W. W. Norton, 1999).

8   At various points in the season the corner-boy students are referred to as "corner kids," especially notable when Bunny Colvin theorizes that corner kids distinguish themselves from stoop kids based upon their domestic situation and how that situation (drug-addicted parents, neglect, etc.) translates for them in the school system. More often than not though this group of students is referred to as corner boys.

9   Davis, 298.

10 James E. Davis, a professor and researcher in the Department of Educational Leadership and Policy Studies at Temple University.

11 Ibid., 296.

12 Alcyee J. Jane states that "Intersectionality calls into question the construction of monolithic identities and forces one to consider how one is positioned by the intersecting and multiple hegemonies that structure American culture" (Jane, 325).

13 "Game is rigged" quote.

14 Ofc. Mcnulty talks him (Bodie) into informing on Marlo, but Marlo has him killed before he can do any damage.

15 Mark Anthony Neal, *New Black Man* (New York: Routledge, 2005), 29.

16 Ibid.

17 Craig Watkins, Moynihan Report, 218–19.

18 David Simon et al., *The Wire*, Season 4 Episode 13 (New York: HBO Video, 2008).

19 Ibid.

20 Ibid.

21 Simon et al., *The Wire*, Season 4 Episode 1 (New York: HBO Video, 2008).

22 Simon et al., *The Wire*, Season 4 Episode 9 (New York: HBO Video, 2008).

23 Simon et al., *The Wire*, Season 4 Episode 10 (New York: HBO Video, 2008).

24 Simon et al., *The Wire*, Season 3 Episode 12 (New York: HBO Video, 2008).

25 Mark Anthony Neal refers to as "black meta-identities," various and varied identities that exist beneath the surface of the American public sphere.

26 "Omar is coming! Omar is coming!" quote.

Chapter 13

1 Geneva Smitherman, "The chain remains the same: Communicative practice in the Hip Hop Nation," *Journal of Black Studies* 28, no. 1 (1997): 3–25.

2 Emery Petchauer, *Hip Hop culture in college students' lives: Elements, embodiment, and higher edutainment* (New York: Routledge, 2011).

3 Jay-Z, "Minority Report," in *Kingdom Come*, Def Jam Recordings (2006).

4 Lil Wayne, "Georgia Bush," in *Dedication 2* (2006).

5 Yasiin Bey, "Dollar Day," in *True Magic*, Geffen Records (2006).

6 Reef The Lost Cauze, "The Prey (For Trayvon & My Son)." *Self-Released*, March 20, 2012.

7 James Peterson, "The Elements and Eras of Hip Hop Culture" (Westport, CT: Greenwood Press, 2006).

8 Murray Forman, *The 'Hood Comes First: Race, Space, and Place in Rap and Hip Hop* (Middleton, CT: Wesleyan University Press, 2002).

9 Aaron McGruder's, *The Boondocks*. Adult Swim/Cartoon Network. Animated Sitcom. 2005–14.

10 Patrick Neate, *Where You're At: Notes from the Frontline of a Hip Hop Planet* (New York: Riverhead Books, 2003), 58.

11 Joseph Schloss, *Making Beats: The Art of Sample-Based Hip-Hop* (Middletown: Wesleyan University Press, 2004).

12 Jay-Z, "Hard Knock Life (Ghetto Anthem)," in *Vol. 2 ... Hard Knock Life*, Def Jam Recordings (1998).

13 KRS-One, *Ruminations* (New York: Welcome Rain Publishers, 2003), 211.

14 Imani Johnson, *Dark matter in b-boying cyphers: Race and global connection in hip hop* (University of Southern California, 2009).

15 Lawrence Lessig, *Remix: Making Art and Commerce Thrive in the Hybrid Economy* (New York: Penguin Press, 2008).

16 Joseph Harris, *Rewriting: How To Do Things with Texts* (Utah: Utah State University Press, 2006).

17 Lessig, *Remix*, 76.

18 Harris, *Rewriting*, 2.

19 John Austin, *How to Do Things with Words* (Oxford: Oxford University Press, 1965).

20 Harris, *Rewriting*, 6.

21 Bakari Kitwana, *The Hip Hop Generation: Young Blacks and the Crisis in African American Culture* (New York: Basic Civitas, 2002).

22 Kermit Campbell, *Getting Our Groove On; Rhetoric, Language and Literacy for the Hip Hop Generation* (Detroit: Wayne State University Press, 2005), 329.

23 Ibid.

24 James Snead, "Repetition as a Figure of Black Culture" (New York: Routledge, 1984), 69.

25 Ibid.

26 James Brown, "The Payback," in *The Payback - Part II*, Polydor Records (1974).

27 EMPD, "I'm Mad," in *Business as Usual*, Def Jam Recordings (1990).

28 EMPD, "The Big Payback," in *Unfinished Business*, Priority Records (1989).

Chapter 14

1   Kurtis Blow, "The Breaks," in *Kurtis Blow*, Mercury Records (1980).
2   "… that they must represent the experiences of b-boys and b-girls", Tazk, Blog post on www.bboy.com (Last Accessed February 2005).
3   Ibid.
4   Adam Mansbach, "The Hip Hop Intellectual." June 2003 from Decapo's *Best Music Writing of 2004.*
5   Ibid.
6   Harold Cruse, *The Crisis of the Negro Intellectual: A Historical Analysis of the Failure of Black Leadership* (New York Review Books Classics) (New York: NYRB Classics, 2005).
7   Ibid.
8   David Toop, *The Rap Attack: African Jive to New York Hip Hop,* 1st edition (London: South End Press, 1984).
9   Houston Baker, *Black Studies, Rap, and the Academy* (Chicago: University of Chicago Press, 1993).
10 Tricia Rose, *Black Noise: Rap Music and Black Culture in Contemporary America* (Hanover, NH: Wesleyan University Press, 1994).
11 Cruse, *The Crisis of the Negro Intellectual*, 2005.
12 Mark Harris, "The Rise and Fall of Hip Hop's Intelligentsia Part 1," April 1, 2005, http://www.popmatters.com/feature/050401-edutainment/ (Last Accessed February 1, 2016).
13 Yvonne Bynoe, *Stand and Deliver: Political Activism, Leadership, and Hip Hop Culture* (Brooklyn, NY: Soft Skull Press, 2004).
14 Ibid., 14.
15 Nasir Jones, "Sly Fox," in *Untitled*, Def Jam Recordings (2008).
16 Flobots, "Handlebars," in *Fight with Tools*, Universal Republic Records (2008).
17 Flobots, *Fight with Tools*, in Universal Republic Records (2008).

Conclusion

1   Copeland, Evelyn, Sharon Floyd, and Douglass Hesse (eds), "Good Writing Instruction Is What's Needed: NCTE Task Force on SAT and ACT Writing Releases Report" (2005), 3.
2   Campbell, *Getting Our Groove On*, 328.

Appendices

1   This course was originally designed (and titled) by Professor Georgia M. Roberts at the University of Washington, Seattle.

Bibliography

A Tribe Called Quest. *Beats, Rhymes, & Life.* Jive Records, 1996.

A Tribe Called Quest. *The Love Movement.* Jive Records, 1998.

Achebe, Chinua. *Things Fall Apart.* London: William Heinemann Ltd., 1958.

Adler, Amy. *What's Left?: Hate Speech, Pornography, and the Problem for Artistic Expression.* California Law Review 1541. 1996.

Aheam, Charlie. *Wild Style.* Directed by Charlie Aheam in 1982. New York: Submarine Entertainment, 1983.

Baker, Houston. *Black Studies, Rap, and the Academy.* Chicago: University of Chicago Press, 1993.

Baker, Houston. *Blues Ideology, and Afro-American Literature: A Vernacular Theory.* Chicago: University of Chicago Press, 1983.

Banjoko, Adisa. *Lyrical Swords: Hip Hop and Politics in the Mix.* San Jose, CA: YinSumi Press, 2004.

Beastie Boys. *Check Your Head.* Capitol Records, 1992.

Beastie Boys. *Hello Nasty.* Capitol Records, 1998.

Beastie Boys. *Hot Sauce Committee Part Two.* Capitol Records, 2011.

Beastie Boys. *Ill Communication.* Capitol Records, 1994.

Beastie Boys. *Licensed to Ill.* Def Jam Recordings, 1986.

Beastie Boys. *The Mix-Up.* Capitol Records, 2007.

Beastie Boys. *Paul's Boutique.* Capitol Records, 1989.

Beastie Boys. "Paul Revere." In *Licensed to Ill.* Def Jam Recordings, 1986.

Beastie Boys. "Slow and Low." In *Licensed to Ill.* Def Jam Recordings, 1986.

Beastie Boys. *To the 5 Boroughs.* Capitol Records, 2004.

Beastie Boys. "(You Gotta) Fight for Your Right (To Party!)." In *Licensed to Ill.* Def Jam Recordings, 1986.

BET. *Hip Hop vs. America.* Episode 1. September 2007.

Binder, Amy. "Constructing Racial Rhetoric: Media Depictions of Harm in Heavy Metal and Rap Music." American Sociological Review, December 1993.

Blow, Kurtis. "The Breaks." In *Kurtis Blow.* Mercury Records, 1980.

Boogie Down Productions. "Self-Destruction." In *Stop the Violence Movement.* Jive Records, 1989.

Boogie Down Productions. "Why Is That?" In *Ghetto Music: The Blueprint of Hip Hop.* Jive Records, 1989.

Brown, James. "Funky Drummer." In *In the Jungle Groove.* King Records, 1970.

Brown, James. "Funky President (People It's Bad)." In *Reality.* Polydor Records, 1974.

Brown, James. "The Payback." In *The Payback – Part II.* Polydor Records, 1974.

Brown, Timothy J. "Welcome to the Terrordome: Exploring the Contradictions of a Hip-Hop Black Masculinity." In *Progressive Black Masculinities.* New York: Routledge, 2006.

Bynoe, Yvonne. *Stand and Deliver: Political Activism, Leadership, and Hip Hop Culture.* Brooklyn, NY: Soft Skull Press, 2004.

Campbell, Kermit. *Getting Our Groove On: Rhetoric, Language and Literacy for the Hip Hop Generation.* Detroit: Wayne State University Press, 2005.

Chang, Jeff. *Can't Stop, Won't Stop: A History of the Hip-Hop Generation.* New York: St. Martin's Press, 2005.

Chang, Jeff. *Total Chaos: The Art and Aesthetics of Hip-Hop.* New York: Basic Books, 2006.

Chastagner, Claude. "The Parents' Music Resource Center: From Information to Censorship." 18 Popular Music, May 1999.

Chic. "Good Times." In *Risqué.* Atlantic Records, 1979.

CNN. *Anderson Cooper 360.* July 11, 2007.

Common. *Be.* Geffen Records, 2005.

Common and The Last Poets. "The Corner." In *Be.* Geffen Records, 2005.

Copeland, Evelyn, Sharon Floyd, and Douglass Hesse (eds). "Good Writing Instruction Is What's Needed: NCTE Task Force on SAT and ACT Writing Releases Report." *The Council Chronicle: The National Council of Teachers of English* 15, no. 1 (2005).

Crouch, Stanley. *Hip Hop Takes a Hit.* New York Daily News. January 23, 2005.

Douglass, Frederick. *Narrative of the Life of Frederick Douglass, an American Slave.* New York: Dover Publications, Inc., 1845.

Du Bois, W.E.B. *The Souls of Black Folk.* Chicago: AC McClurg & Co., 1903.

Dworkin, Andrea and Catherine MacKinnon. *Pornography and Civil Rights: A New Day for Women's Equality.* Minneapolis, MN: Organizing Against Pornography (Resource Center for Education and Action), 1988.

Dyson, Michael Eric. *Holler If You Hear Me: Searching for Tupac Shakur.* New York: Basic Civitas Books, 2001.

Ellison, Ralph. *Invisible Man.* New York: Vintage International, 1995.

Eminem. "Like Toy Soldiers." In *Encore.* Interscope Records, 2005.

Eminem. *The Marshall Mathers LP.* Interscope Records Inc., 2000.

Eminem. "The Way I Am." In *The Marshall Mathers LP*. Interscope Records, 2000.

Eminem. *The Way I Am*. Boston: MA: Dutton Penguin, 2008.

EMPD. "I'm Mad." In *Business as Usual*. Def Jam Recordings, 1990.

EMPD. "The Big Payback." In *Unfinished Business*. Priority Records, 1989.

Fiasco, Lupe and Snoop Dogg. "Hi-Definition." In *The Cool*. Atlantic Records, 2007.

Fiasco, Lupe. "Put You On Game." In *The Cool*. Atlantic Records, 2007.

Flobots. *Fight with Tools*. Universal Republic Records, 2008.

Flobots. "Handlebars." In *Fight with Tools*. Universal Republic Records, 2008.

Forman, Murray. *The Hood Comes First: Race, Space, and Place in Rap and Hip Hop*. Middleton, CT: Wesleyan University Press, 2002.

Forman, Murray and Mark Anthony Neal (eds). *That's the Joint! The Hip-Hop Studies Reader*. New York: Routledge, 2004.

Foucault, Michel. *Power/Knowledge: Selected Interviews and Other Writings, 1972-1977*. Brighton: Harvester publishing, 1980.

George, Nelson. *Hip Hop America*. New York: Viking Penguin, 1998.

Grandmaster Flash and the Furious Five. "The Message." In *The Message*. Sugar Hill Records, 1982.

Haley, Alex. *Roots: The Saga of an American Family*. New York: Doubleday, 1976.

Hanson, Curtis. *8 Mile*. Directed by Curtis Hanson in 2002. Los Angeles, CA: Imagine Entertainment, 2002.

Harris, Joseph. *Rewriting: How To Do Things with Texts*. Utah: Utah State University Press, 2006.

Hill, Lauryn. *The Miseducation of Lauryn Hill*. Ruffhouse Records, 2006.

Hinds, Selwyn. *Gunshots in My Cook-Up: Bits and Bites from a Hip-hop Caribbean Life*. New York: Atria Books, 2002.

Holiday, Billie. "Strange Fruit." In *Lady Sings the Blues*. Commodore Records, 1939.

Holiday, Bllie and William Dufty. *Lady Sings the Blues*. New York: Penguin Books, 1956.

Homer. *The Odyssey*. Trans. by Robert Fitzgerald, 1963.

Hurt, Byron. "Hip-Hop: Beyond Beats & Rhymes". In *Independent Lens*. PBS Indies, February 27, 2007.

Immortal Technique. "Dance With the Devil." In *Revolutionary Vol 1*. Viper Records, 2001.

Immortal Technique. "The Point of No Return." In *Revolutionary Vol. 2*. Viper Records, 2003.

Jay-Z. *Decoded*. New York: Random House Publisher, 2010.

Jay-Z. "Hard Knock Life (Ghetto Album)." In *Vol. 2 … Hard Knock* Life. Def Jam Recordings, 1998.

Jay-Z. "Ignorant Shit." In *American Gangster*. Def Jam Recordings, 2007.

Jay-Z. "Lost One." In *Kingdom Come*. Def Jam Recordings, 2006.

Jay-Z. "Meet the Parents." In *The Blueprint²: The Gift & The Curse*. Def Jam Recordings, 2002.

Jay-Z. "Minority Report." In *Kingdom Come*. Def Jam Recordings, 2006.

John Legend and The Roots. *Wake Up!* Columbia Records, 2010.

Johnson, Imani K. *Dark matter in b-boying cyphers: Race and global connection in hip hop*. Unpublished doctoral dissertation. University of Southern California, 2009.

Jones, Nasir. "I Can." In *God's Son*. Columbia Records, 2003.

Jones, Nasir. "Sly Fox." In *Untitled*. Def Jam Recordings, 2008.

Kahan, Jeffrey B. "Bach, Beethoven, and the (Home) Boys: Censoring Violent Rap Music in America." *USC Law Review*, 1993.

Kellogg, David. *Cool as Ice*. Universal Pictures, 1991.

Kitwana, Bakari. *The Hip Hop Generation: Young Blacks and the Crisis in African American Culture*. New York: Basic Civitas, 2002.

Kitwana, Bakari. *Why White Kids Love Hip Hop: Wankstas, Wiggers, Wannabes, and the New Reality of Race*. New York: Basic Books, 2002.

KRS-One. "Black Cop." In *Return of the Boom Bap*. Jive Records, 1993.

KRS-One. *Ruminations*. New York: Welcome Rain Publishers, 2003.

Langshaw, Austin J. *How to do Things with Words*. Oxford: Oxford University Press, 1965.

Lessig, Lawrence. *Remix: Making Art and Commerce Thrive in the Hybrid Economy*. New York: Penguin Press, 2008.

Lopez, Jennifer. "Jenny from the Block." In *This is Me … Then*. Epic Records, 2002.

Mansbach, Adam. *Rage is Back*. New York: Viking Penguin, 2013.

MC Serch. *Many Young Lives Ago: The 1994 Sessions*. Serchlite, 2007.

MC Serch. *Return of the Product*. Def Jam Recordings, 1992.

Morrison, Toni. *Beloved*. London: Penguin Books, 1987.

Morton, Janks. "What Black Men Think." Iyago Entertainment Group, 2007.

Minaj, Nicki. "Cuchi Shop." In *Sucka Free*. Dirty Money Records, 2008. Mixtape.

Miyakawa, Felicia M. *Five Percenter Rap: God Hop's Music, Message, and Black Muslim Mission*. Bloomington: Indiana University Press, 2005.

MSNBC. *MSNBC Live*. April 14, 2007.

Mufweme, Salikoko, John Rickford, Guy Bailey, and John Baugh (eds). *African American English: Structure, History, and Use*. London: Routledge, 1998.

Murray, Albert. *Stomping the Blues*. Boston: Da Cap Press, 1976.

Neate, Patrick. *Where You're At: Notes from the Frontline of a Hip Hop Planet*. New York: Riverhead Books, 2003.

Neal, Mark Anthony. *New Black Man.* New York: Routledge, 2005.

Nelly. "Tip Drill." In *Da Derrty Versions: The Reinvention.* Universal Records, 2003.

N.W.A. "Fuck tha Police." In *Straight Outta Compton.* Priority Records, 1988.

N.W.A. *Straight Outta Compton.* Ruthless Records, 1988.

Ogbar, Jeffrey. *Hip-Hop Revolution: The Culture and Politics of Rap.* Lawrence, KS: University Press of Kansas, 2007.

Ogbar, Jeffrey. *Slouching toward Bork: The Culture Wars and Self-Criticism in Hip Hop Music.* 30 *Journal of Black Studies* 181, November 1999.

Ogg, Alex and David Upshal. *The Hip Hop Years: A History of Rap.* New York: Fromm International, 2001.

Ogren, Katherine. *The Jazz Revolution.* Oxford: Oxford University Press, 1992.

Perry, Imani. *Prophets from the Hood: Politics and Poetics in Hip Hop.* Durham: Duke University Press, 2004.

Petchauer, Emery. *Hip hop culture in college students' lives: Elements, embodiment, and higher edutainment.* New York: Routledge, 2011.

Peterson, James. "The Elements and Eras of Hip Hop Culture." In S. Steinberg, P. Parmar, and B. Richard (eds), *Contemporary Youth Culture.* Westport, CT: Greenwood Press, 2006, pp. 357–65.

Public Enemy. "Can't Truss It." In *Apocalypse 91 … The Enemy Strikes Back.* Def Jam Recordings, 1991.

Public Enemy. "Shut 'Em Down." In *Apocalypse 91 … The Enemy Strikes Back.* Def Jam Recordings, 1991.

Public Enemy. "Welcome to the Terrordome." In *Fear of a Black Planet.* Def Jam Recordings, 1990.

Public Enemy, "911 Is a Joke." In *Fear of a Black Planet.* Def Jam Recordings, 1990.

Queen and David Bowie. "Under Pressure." In *Hot Space.* EMI Group Limited, 1981.

Queen Latifah. "U.N.I.T.Y." In *Black Reign.* Motown Records, 1994.

Quinn, Eithne. *Nuthin' but a "G" Thang: The Culture and Commerce of Gangsta Rap.* New York: Columbia University Press, 2013.

Rapaport, Michael. *Beats, Rhymes & Life: The Travels of A Tribe Called Quest.* New York: Sony Pictures Classics, 2011.

Rose, Tricia. *Black Noise: Rap Music and Black Culture in Contemporary America.* Hanover, NH: Wesleyan University Press, 1994.

Rubenfeld, Jed. "The Freedom of Imagination: Copyright's Constitutionality." *Yale Law Journal* 112 (2002): 30–47.

Run–D.M.C. "King of Rock." In *King of Rock.* Arista Records Inc., 1985.

Run–D.M.C. "My Adidas." In *Raising Hell.* Profile Records, 1986.

Run–D.M.C. "Proud to be Black." In *Raising Hell.* Profile Records, 1986.

Schloss, Joseph. *Making Beats: The Art of Sample-Based Hip-Hop.* Middletown: Wesleyan University Press, 2004.

Shakur, Tupac. "Dear Mama." In *Me Against the World.* Interscope Records Inc., 1995.

Simon, David. *The Wire.* June 2, 2002 – March 9, 2008. Premiered on HBO.

Simpson, Don and Jerry Bruckheimer. *Flashdance.* Directed by Adrian Lyne. Hollywood, CA: Paramount Pictures, 1983.

Singleton, John. *Boys n the Hood.* Directed by John Singleton in 1991. Los Angeles, CA: Columbia Pictures Industries, Inc., 1991.

Smitherman, Geneva. "The chain remains the same: Communicative practices in the Hip Hop Nation." *Journal of Black Studies* 28, no. 1 (1997): 3–25.

Snead, James A. "Repetition as a Figure of Black Culture." In H. L. Gates (ed.), Henry Louis *Black Literature and Literary Theory.* New York: Routledge, 1984.

Snoop Dogg. "Beautiful." In *Paid tha Cost to Be da Boss.* Doggystyle Records, 2003.

Swan, Jim. "Touching Words: Helen Keller, Plagiarism, Authorship." In P. Jaszi and M. Woodmansee (eds), *The Construction of Authorship: Textual Appropriation in Literature and Law.* Durham, NC: Duke University Press, 1994, pp. 57–100.

The Black Eyed Peas. "My Humps." In *Monkey Business.* A&M Records, 2005.

The Fatback Band. "King Tim III (Personality Jock)." In *Fatback XII,* 1979.

The Last Poets. "Niggers Are Scared of Revolution." In *The Last Poets.* East Wind Associates, 1970.

The Notorious B.I.G. "Sky's the Limit." In *Life After Death.* Bad Boy Records, 1997.

The Roots. "Act Won (Things Fall Apart)." In *Things Fall Apart.* MCA Records, 1999.

The Roots. *Things Fall Apart.* MCA Records, 1999.

The Sugarhill Gang. "Rapper's Delight." In *Sugarhill Gang.* Sugar Hill Records, 1979.

Three 6 Mafia. "It's Hard Out Here for a Pimp." In *Hustle & Flow Soundtrack.* Atlantic Records, 2005.

Toop, David. *Rap Attack 3: African Rap to Global Hip Hop.* London: Serpent's Tail, 2000.

Touré. "I Live in the Hip Hop Nation." In *Never Drank the Kool-Aid: Essays.* New York: Macmillan, 2006.

Vanilla Ice. *Extremely Live.* SKB Records, 1991.

Vanilla Ice. "Ice Ice Baby." In *To the Extreme.* SKB Records, 1990.

Vanilla Ice. *To the Extreme.* SKB Records, 1990.

Wang, Oliver. *Classic Material: The Hip Hop Album Guide.* Toronto: ECW Press, 2003.

Watkins, Craig S. *Hip Hop Matters: Politics, Pop Culture, and the Struggle for the Soul of a Movement.* Beacon Press, 2005.

Whiting-Sharpley, Denean T. *Pimps Up, Ho's Down: Hip Hop's Hold on Young Black Women.* New York University Press, 2007.

Woodson, Carter G. *The Mis-Education of the Negro.* Trenton, NJ: Africa World Press, 1990.

Wright, Richard. "The Man Who Lived Underground." In *Norton Anthology of African American Literature.* New York: W.W. Norton, 1997.

Wu-Tang Clan. "Motherless Child." In *Ironman.* Epic Records, 1996.

Yasiin Bey, "Dollar Day." In *True Magic,* Geffen Records, 2006.

3rd Bass. *The Cactus Album.* Def Jam Recordings, 1989.

3rd Bass. *Derelicts of Dialect.* Def Jam Recordings, 1991.

3rd Bass. "Pop Goes the Weasel." In *Derelicts of Dialect.* Def Jam Recordings, 1991.

3rd Bass. "The Gas Face." In *The Cactus Album.* Def Jam Recordings, 1989.

Index